EAT
PROFESSIONAL POKER PLAYERS
ALIVE

The Ultimate Guide to today's Texas Hold'em Razz, Stud and Omaha for all skill levels...

FRANK WIESE

Edited by Katie E. Waller

For information contact:
Frank Wiese
Email: frank@eatprofessionalpokerplayersalive.com

Book Websites:
www.eatprofessionalpokerplayersalive.com
www.facebook.com/people/Frank-Wiese/1602773521
www.eatprofessionalpokerplayersalive.blogspot.com
www.myspace.com/burnspanky

ACKNOWLEDGEMENTS

Giving Much Deserved Credit to the success of this book for their hard work and countless days of constant revision and promoting:

Cherie Wiese, for being the complete motivation in finishing this book
Glenn Franco, for co-authoring numerous chapters, and adding insights
Jerry Yang, 2007 World Series of Poker Main Event Champion
Katie E.Waller, completed final editing
Casey Wiesel and Nathan Hess, Design Gurus, for creative input and long hours
Richard Drennan, Business Manager
Danielle Adams-Benham, for co-authoring some chapters
Jack McAdoo, Pokerpodradio.com
Alfred Markarian, *Australian Poker Weekly*
Ken Callis, Drcheckraise.com
Lee Childs, Acumenpoker.net
Matthew Parvis, *Bluff Magazine*
Eric Morris, *Bluff Magazine*
John "Johnny Quads" Wenzel, *Poker Pro Magazine*
Stan Seiff, Bay 101 Casino
John Helander, Promoting
Evert Caldwell, *Rounder Magazine*
Mike Sexton, Host for the (WPT) World Poker Tour
Scott Long, *Ante Up Magazine*
Christopher Cosenza, *Ante Up Magazine*
Greg Lang, Founder of the (HPT) Heartland Poker Tour
Scott Dedoes, *Card Player Magazine*
Steven Ohno, Promoting

CONTENTS

FOREWORD

BY JERRY YANG

Frank Wiese just might be one of pokers best kept secrets. He is an accomplished cash game and tournament player from the Chicago area. Amazingly enough what Frank reveals in this book may cause shock and fearfulness. By purchasing this book, you have just taken a very important step in expanding your poker skills.

This book will show you a completely new, uniquely developed type of poker. Wiese coined the brilliant concepts outlined in this book "medium ball." They are designed for today's No Limit Texas Hold'em. Inside there you'll find valuable information inside covering a range of topics from some of the finest poker rooms in the United States to table image.

Table image appears to be the least covered of all topics in most poker books, yet Wiese feels it to be one of the most important. A great player must have the perfect facade (basically an image of deception). You want to be thought of as pathetic and weak, when you're actually brilliantly strong. In addition, when you're pilfering blinds and taking stabs at small pots, you want the other players to think you're strong and fold their winning hand.

This book will teach you how to make the sharks of the poker world look at you and see a tiny little bait fish, only to realize their mistake too late. Dozens of various poker books claim to be the ultimate guide to refining your poker skills but many are incomplete. This misleads many amateurs down a dismal path of disaster. This book has done a great job at filling in the gaps that others left out.

Poker is not a game of luck! It is actually the ultimate game of skill. This book is for players of all skill levels; written by an accomplished poker player and strategist who will help you to see the game through the eyes of a hunter. The lessons discussed inside will significantly improve your poker game and prepare you to contend with professional poker players on their level.

If you apply the techniques discussed in this book towards your current poker game, rest assured you will begin to "Eat Professional Poker Players Alive!" This drastic refinement will turn you into a shark's worst nightmare, something I like to refer to as "a fisherman!" Please continue reading for further clarification.

INTRODUCTION

I would like to thank the following professional poker players: *Phil Hellmuth, Daniel Negreanu, Erick Lindgren, Doyle Brunson, Joe Hachem, David Sklansky, Collin Moshman, Hevad Khan and Jerry Yang*

Without having these players to watch for strategies or their poker books to read, I would not be the poker player I am today. In this book, these nine players are revered with utmost respect. Someday, I hope to take all of them "Head's up." Having to decipher each of these players' ideas and strategies was a complex and time-consuming mission of mine. The end result has improved my game in 5 years, what would take most players over 20 years to pull off.

By using the methods in this book, you will limit your risk and encourage an aggressive play style and increase your wins at all forms of Hold'em. Smart, aggressive play has been proven successful since the discovery of NL Texas Hold'em. This type of play allows you to build your chip stack, which will help make you the "person in charge" and wins tournaments time and time again.

Once you have mastered the Fish: Beginner strategy, you will become a serious threat to most of the players you meet and play against today. These ideas come from the fact that many beginners use an aggressive pre-flop strategy similar to what they see on TV watching the WSOP and WPT tournaments in early rounds. By going "all-in" the majority of time, their success is short term. They have no idea how to play poker after the flop. The Fish: Beginner strategy works well against these types of players. You should achieve greater success in tournaments by applying it.

After you've mastered the Fish, (or have gotten bored with it) you're ready to take on the challenge of the Barracuda: Intermediate strategy. This will give you great insight on what it takes to make it to the final table and be "in the money" (ITM) consistently. Obviously, this book will not be read and digested quickly. It may take several readings to grasp and follow the dynamic formulas that are exposed here. Many years of thought and effort went into crafting this book. Leaks in your poker game will not have a chance after following these simple ideas and formulas.

Once you get to the Shark: Advanced strategy, I am positive you will be amazed by all the advanced insights that are shown here. Hopefully it will lead you along the path to becoming a poker world champion.

Before jumping to the more advanced Shark strategy, I strongly recommend that you read about the Fish and Barracuda strategies. If not, you risk drowning in this ocean of poker knowledge and you may get lost at sea. So start slowly and let me teach you how to swim. Soon, my young and sometimes older fishermen, you will be "Eating Professional Poker Players Alive!"

PART ONE

NO LIMIT
Texas Hold'em Concepts

CHAPTER ONE:

HOW TO PLAY

No Limit Texas Hold'em is one of the most ubiquitous types of poker in the world. It seems that everywhere you turn there is another show, website, or article dedicated to the subject. But how do you play the game? And what is a Flop, anyway? This chapter will walk you through a NL Texas Hold'em game from start to finish. You will learn the rules and by the end you will be ready to hear the tournament director say "Shuffle Up and Deal!"

A NL Texas Hold'em table typically has nine or ten players. If there are any less, perhaps six players, the game would be a "six-pack" (my favorite), or it may also be referred to as short handed. In order to determine who begins the game a single card is dealt face-up to each player. The highest ranked card marks the starting dealer position and is tracked by a white plastic chip placed in front of the player. This is sometimes referred to as "being on the button." Following each round of play, or hand, the dealer button rotates to the clockwise, ensuring that everyone gets to play in this and all other positions. The purpose of being on the button is to stagger the betting rotation.

Pre-flop:

Before any cards are dealt, the forced bets must be paid. These are labeled the big blind and small blind. The small blind is always half the big blind. A bet is when money is put into the pot for the first time in a round. The amount of the bets and blinds are predetermined each round or on a set time frame. The small blind position is always the seat to the left of the dealer button and the big blind follows to the left of the small blind.

The dealer then deals two cards (referred to as hole cards) face down to each player. They come one at a time, starting with the player to the left. Once the cards are dealt, each player may look at their cards. On their turn, each player must then decide between three courses of action. They may call the current bet (the big blind the highest possible bet at this point). This means they will match it. They may fold the hand without betting, or raise the bet by putting in more money. The initial action is on the player to the left of the big blind. If a player raises the bet, each subsequent player must now call the new amount to remain in the hand; including those who have already acted. Only on their turn player may re-raise, meaning that they raise the bet again. If no player raises, the big blind may check, meaning they do not want to raise. It is important to note that if a player raises, he may not raise again unless his bet is re-raised. The round of betting concludes when all the players have either folded or called the final raise.

Flop:

To begin the next round the dealer burns a card, which means they deal it to one side and it is not used in play, and then deals three cards face down. These cards are then turned face up simultaneously; this is called the Flop. These are the first of five community cards that all players can use, along with their hole cards, to build the best possible hand. The common poker hands and ranks are explained later in this book. The player in the small blind position (once again, the first seat to the left of the dealer) is now UTG, or (under the gun), meaning they are first to act now and on every subsequent round of betting. They must make one of the decisions listed in pre-flop play, with one change: they may choose to check if they don't want to bet or to fold. To check basically means to say check or tap your hand on the table and decline to make an open bet. You can do this to gather information on what the other players want to do after you. In most cases, they will either check after you or put in a bet. Then it will be on you to either fold or re-raise them. The betting round ends only when all players have folded or called the last bet or raise.

Turn:

The dealer burns another card and then deals a fourth community card, called the Turn, face up next to the flop. There is another round of betting, exactly as after the flop. The first player to the left of the dealer who has not previously folded is now UTG (under the gun).

River:

After one final burn card, the dealer turns over the fifth and last community card, called the River. There is one final round of betting. At this point, (or before) if all but one player folds, that final player wins the pot. If this is the case, the winner may muck his hand, which means to toss it into the discard pile next to the dealer without showing anyone what it was.

Showdown:

A showdown takes place after the river, when a player is called and could involve any amount of players. All players still in the hand show their cards, starting with the last person to bet. At any point after the first hand is revealed, the other players in the showdown may muck their hand or concede the pot. Mucking should be thought of as folding. This action admits defeat without showing the hole cards. This strategy (mucking) helps keep the other players from learning your play and betting styles.

The best five-card poker hand wins.

These are key points of Texas Hold'em, but there are a number of other important aspects to understand.

Position:

Your position at a NL Texas Hold'em table is an imperative factor in how you play. The dealer position is considered the most powerful spot in any given round, as being on the button means you act last in every post-flop round. This enables you the act with the most information, which is essential to making the right decision, whether it is to bet, raise, check, call, or fold. The game of poker is all about making the right decisions.

Being in early position means you are one of the first to act in a round of betting, and are considered weak due to the lack of information about the other players. Middle position is slightly stronger and falls between the early and the late position. The late position is the strongest. Such as the button and the player to his right, who can be referred to also as the cutoff. The cutoff could take the choice away from the dealer with a big raise and bumping him out, thus becoming the last player in the hand. The last player to act always holds the strongest position.

Winning a hand:

With the exception of all the others folding, the only way to win a hand is in a showdown. The best five cards are chosen out of any combination of the five community cards and the player's hole cards. This allows the possibility for some interesting situations to arise. For example, if the board, or community cards, is

wrong

If no players have better than a pair of eights in their hand, the board is the best possible hand, and all players in the showdown will chop the pot. Chopping is the division of the pot evenly among the players. The same holds true if two players tie a hand. In the event of both players holding a flush or straight, the player holding the highest card in the series wins. If the board has the five highest, the pot is chopped.

Types of Texas Hold'em can be played as Limit, No Limit, and Pot Limit

Limit Hold'em means that bets and raises are limited to a predetermined amount, typically equal to the big blind. Raises are typically limited to four or five "bets" total, meaning the big blind, the first raise, and then three or four more raises. Pot Limit Hold'em means your raise can equal the amount currently in the pot, but no more. NL Texas Hold'em is the most dramatic of the three, where any player (when it's their turn), can declare "all-in" and bet their entire stack. A player calling an "all-in" move with a lesser amount of chips creates a side pot, which they cannot win and is separate from the main pot.

Here are the 10 best starting hands in NL Texas Hold'em

1. **A-A**   **Ace-Ace**, known as "pocket rockets," or "American Airlines."

2. **K-K**   **King-King**, known as "cowboys," or "King Kong."

3. **Q-Q**   **Queen-Queen**, known as "ladies," or "Hilton sisters."

4. **J-J**   **Jack-Jack**, known as "fish hooks," or "Johnny's."

5. **A-K**   **(same suit) Ace-King suited,** known as "Big Slick," or "Suited Slick."

6. **10-10** **Ten-Ten** a pair of tens, known as "dimes."

7. **A-K**   **(off-suit) Ace-King off-suit**, known as "Big Slick."

8. **A-Q**   **(same suit or off-suit) Ace-Queen**, known as "Big Chick."

9. **K-Q**   **(same suit) King Queen suited**, known as "Royal Couple."

10. **A-J**   **(same suit) Ace-Jack suited**, known as "Blackjack," or "Ajax."

Poker Etiquette:

If you want to be invited back to play Poker with a group of people, follow these five simple tips to be sure you're a welcomed player. Some of these rules aren't followed during friendly games, however it's a great starting point if you're playing with any new players or especially in casinos.

Act in Turn:

What "act in turn" usually means is this: don't fold your cards early. It you look at your cards and know that you're going to fold, wait until it's your turn to do so. It is unfair to the other players if someone gets to know that you're going to fold out of turn. The same holds true for calling and raising, but it's much less common for players to try to call or raise out of turn.

Remain Quiet During a Hand:

Don't ruminate about the possibilities, "Oh, a third spade just turned up! I wonder if anyone has a flush." This is important whether or not you're still in a hand. Sit quietly and let the hand end before you offer any commentary, no matter how brilliant you believe it to be.

Don't Splash the Pot:

In other words, keep your chips in a tidy pile in front of you until it's time to move everyone's chips into the middle. Also note that the action of gathering the pot together is the dealer's job. With a lot of players, this really helps keep track of where things stand and it can help avoid some truly malicious arguments. Throwing your chips into the pot is always a terrible idea.

One Player to a Hand:

You don't get to receive advice during a hand nor should you give it. Play your own hand and let everyone else play theirs.

Pay Attention:

This rule is self-explanatory: Few things are more aggravating than a player who says, "Whose turn is it?" when it's been their turn for several minutes.

Poker Terms:

Poker has its own terminology, and reviewing the glossary provided will help you understand the chapters and lessons in this book.

You should also familiarize yourself with these Texas Hold'em Poker Terms:

Aces Up: A hand that contains two pairs, one of which is Aces. If you hold A-7, and the board is A-7-4, you have Aces up.

All-In: That moment when all your chips are in the middle and your fate is resting with the poker gods.

Bad Beat: This refers to losing a hand when you had strong odds to the favored to win. An example of a bad beat would be holding pocket Aces against a player holding pocket 9's, and the other player ends up beating you by hitting another 9 on the river.

Behind: A player at the poker table, whose turn, follows yours. "I had three players acting behind me."

Belly-Buster: This is an old-school term for an inside straight draw or gut shot draw.

Blinds: NL Texas Hold'em Poker uses what's called a "blind" structure, meaning that two people on the table must post a bet prior to seeing any cards. Since they are forced to bet without seeing their cards, they are playing "blind", thus the name. There are two blinds, the big blind and the small blind. The small blind position must post half the minimum bet and sits immediately to the left of the dealer. The big blind must post the full minimum bet, and sits immediately to the left of the small blind, two seats to the left of the dealer. As the dealer button rotates around the table, each player takes turns posting the small blind and the big blind bets. This blind structure forces the action on the table since there will always be a pot to win. For example, if you are seated at a $5/$10 NL limit Hold'em table, the small blind must post $5 and the big blind must post $10 bet. As play rotates around the table, each player may choose to call the $10 bet, raise, or fold. When it's the small blinds turn, that player only needs to call $5 to play the hand or fold. When they announce that they are folding their hand, their cards should be pushed forward and face down. This is done so that they are not revealed.

Board: The board refers to the community cards that are dealt face up on the table: the flop, turn, and river. In NL Texas Hold'em, there will ultimately be five community cards on the "board." The board does NOT include the two private card dealt to each player. So, if someone were to say, "the board plays," the player means that the five community cards make his best poker hand and he is not using either of his two hole cards.

Button: Also called the "Dealer Button", this is a white plastic puck (usually with the word "Dealer" imprinted on it), that signifies the dealer's position on the table. The dealer's position is significant because he is the last player to act for that hand. The Dealer Button rotates around the table, so each player takes turns being "on the button."

Check-raise: The act of checking a hand, in hopes of luring the other player to bet, so that you may then raise over him and build a bigger pot to win.

Connectors: A starting hand of two cards in sequence, such as Q-J, 7-6, or 9-10.

Donkey: Someone who is a poor poker player.

Final Table: This is the last table of a large multi-table tournament. Ahhh… The Promised Land!

Flop: The first three of the five community cards that are dealt at together on the board. The fourth card is called the "turn," and the final, fifth card is known as the "river."

Pot Odds: The odds offered to you by the money in the pot. If the pot is $400 and you must call a $100 bet, you pot odds are 4 to 1. You must include other players' bets and calls as part of the pot.

A complete is list is available in the Glossary.

CHAPTER TWO:

TYPES OF PLAYERS

There are four main categories that most poker players fall into. As you gain experience you will be able to recognize theses types and adjust your play style in your favor. Listed below are the detailed definitions of these different types of poker players. At every table you play, you should as attempt to glean as much information about the players as possible in order to accurately place them into a category. Every poker player will have their own unique playing and decision making style. However, they will still fall into these categories. Each style has rewards and downfalls, and each of these styles can be profitable in certain situations. Your goals as a poker player make adjustments to your current playing style to adjust so as not to be fitted into one of these groups but to the other players at the table.

However, remember that the boundaries that define these groups are not always definite and may fluctuate. The best pokers players can change their style of play very quickly to mislead the rest of the table.

Each style is based on two main evaluations:

- **Is the player is tight (plays very few hands) or loose (plays a lot of hands)?**
- **Is the player is aggressive (raises and bluffs) or passive (calls other players bets)?**

Loose-Aggressive (Maniac):

Some of the most famous poker players are loose aggressive. These players have no qualms going "all-in" often. The best loose-aggressive players will mix up their aggressive and passive play, making it difficult to read their hands.

They go all-in with

or just a simple

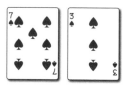

In the poker scene, this seems to be the weakest category. These players are always raising pre and post the flop. This strategy often works against new players and will win a lot of small pots, because it tends to scare off most timid players. These fish will go broke very quickly. I can tell you from experience that Loose-Aggressive players attract sharks. The sharks are fine with letting these fish have ten small pots because they are after the three large pots. This will eventually break the Loose-Aggressive player.

The "Donkey" is exactly that, an ass. He will talk and taunt and loves to push people out of pots by over-betting. He is annoying. He tends to remain in pots with mediocre hands and you won't know whether he's just pushing it. There's no knowing unless you've picked up some kind of read on him. The best thing you can do against the donkey is to watch him. Pick up on the signs he gives when bluffing or when he actually has a decent hand. It is difficult because his bets are so hard that players rarely call him. When you have a strong hand, don't be afraid to fire right back at him. That action puts him on the defensive. Be wary that he still may not back down because then others will mimic you, killing his plays. The donkey then has two options; he can stubbornly stick it out, or back down. Either way, odds are some trash talk will be involved. Whatever you do, DON'T play into the donkey's game. Don't let him affect you emotionally; he would love nothing better than to goad you into betting on a mediocre hand while he's holding something strong.

Maniac Loose-Aggressive:

These guys will buy a fair share of pots. However, they will often get themselves trapped, and will lose their stacks quickly. What separates the manic loose-aggressive from good loose-aggressive is their lack of discipline. They love the action of NL Texas Hold'em so much that they allow themselves to be trapped easily. These types of players are rarely seen…for long.

Strong Loose-Aggressive:

These guys seem like they are horrible maniacs, but in reality, they are a very dangerous players. They will lose a lot of money in pots, but will also buy small pots and win huge ones. The way these players win is mainly by obtaining a good read on the other player, and then betting well.

A trick I bring into play against this player is taking them down in one large pot. Another word of caution, only play in games that the stakes are not too high to your bankroll. You should not let these players scare you financially when they make a large bet or raise. You need to be able to play back at (re-raise) these guys or call them down. Since they will play a lot of hands, especially shorthanded, they'll often play hands that lend themselves to being the second-best hand. Once I catch them in this situation, I just have to make sure I don't let them go easily.

These players only do well when people have large stacks. If the loose-aggressive player has a small stack, you are at an advantage because their ability to bluff is limited.

Loose-Passive (New Player):

In the NL Texas Hold'em scene, this seems to be another ineffective category. These players only make money in a game with a large number of wild players, and generally depend on luck to be successful. Typically, they will simply call the bets of the other players, disregarding the pot odds or strength of their hand. These players will lose very slowly. Often they are able to stay in against the other players, but unable to beat the house rake. I was this type of player as a beginner. I thought that any two cards could win, so why not play them? This type of play is profitable against Loose-Aggressive players who will typically try to bluff at a terrible flop without knowing that it is likely the Loose-Passive player got lucky with two bad cards in the hole. There really is no strategy this type of player can use to win in the long run, since they are never in control of the betting or players. Loose passive players are also known as "calling stations." They call any bet you place. It's best to avoid bluffing these players because they'll seldom fold once they've seen the flop.

Loose passive players can be a lot of fun, as long as you're getting decent cards. They call everything all the way to the river, regardless of what they are holding. The best way to play the loose passive players is simply let them do their thing. You can play more hands against them because they will play weak hands. Bet at a higher than normal levels only when it's you verse them since you understand their play style.

"WARNING: Whatever you do, DO NOT try to stone-cold bluff the loose passive players. They are liable to call anything even with poor hand."

Tight-Passive (Tight)

A tight-passive player is one that won't raise or call unless they have a very strong hand. This type of player is normally best suited for Limit Texas Hold'em poker and will very seldom take a risk on their hand. If a tight passive player calls your raise you'd better have the courage and the hand to back up your bet.

These players will win money simply because there are so many fish in the sea of poker games and tournaments. One of the biggest downfalls of a Tight-Passive player's strategy is that they are very easy to spot. You never have to be concerned about a bluff from them. If this type of player has a decent hand or a lot of outs, he will call your bet or the raise. If not, they will fold. This player can win money against any loose player as long as the loose player does not notice how many hands the Tight-Passive is staying in. I turn into this type of player when I am on the verge of going on tilt (when a player is emotionally upset and starts making poor decisions), but I do so on purpose to regain my mindset and focus.

The tight-passive player can be a very frustrating player. He'll sit at the table for hours and only play one or two hands. If you're at a table with too many tight-passive players, request a table change, unless you enjoy activities comparable to trying to squeeze tequila from a cactus.

Fortunately when in tournaments, they'll eventually just blind or ante themselves to death. When you do find yourself playing against a tight-passive player, be wary, they rarely bluff. They are, however, very protective of their chips. They can be pushed out of a pot by over-betting them. However, they are so selective that many times when they're in a pot they already have the nuts so be careful.

Tight-Aggressive (Solid)

This style can be very successful for general poker play. This style works for me most of the time. These players will only see a flop with a decent hand and will then make a bet. In general, these players are hard for passive players to beat. This "medium-ball" style is vulnerable to a Loose-Aggressive poker style. It seems to be difficult enough to bluff a loose player without having any idea what cards he holds. A bad flop can result in a huge loss. These players should be careful not to let other players label them as bluffers. Typically, an average poker player will notice the amount of hands that are being played by other players instead of how often a player takes a stab at the pot. Once the other players notice the constant bluffing, they will usually stay in the pot.

I hope you can see after reading these definitions how important it is to change your style to fit the other poker players' styles at the table. For instance, if a player in the pot is a Tight-Passive player, you should bluff to see if they fold. If another player in the pot with you is Loose-Aggressive, you can slow-play a good hand and let them do the betting for you. The ability to use a combination of styles to fit the situation is what separates the good players from the bad. Get to know your opponents and fire bets accordingly.

Most of the truly great poker players are Tight-Aggressive. The Tight-Aggressive player is one sneaky bastard. Sometimes they'll be hiding in the shadows waiting to pounce, and other times they'll be out in the open flaunting their stuff. They can usually pretend to be any type of player they want and then turn on a dime. They'll throw away money on a weak hand to make you think they're loose so the next time you will call them in a huge pot they'll have the absolute nuts.

You'll have to watch the Tight-Aggressive player closely during every hand and try to pick up a read on their hands. To beat the Tight-Aggressive players; you have to play truly exceptional poker. You must be able to change gears and represent various types of players just like they do. They only bluff occasionally. They play good hands and once they've got that it they'll bet aggressively. Beware when this player raises, because he could end up taking a huge chunk out of your chip stack.

If you are like me, occasionally you will come to the tables and be stuck in a style that differs from your usual style. When this happens it is hard to change and I usually just walk away from the poker room. Emotions often govern your playing style and it is difficult to control them. It is better not to play than to play poorly.

You need to begin by placing yourself in one of these categories. Then, try it out at a casino. Watch to see if you can spot the different types of players and adjust your strategy accordingly. The only way this loose-aggressive strategy works, is for the player to change tables roughly every 50 hands. Otherwise, they will be recognized and eventually lose all their chips.

Showdown Percentage

This is a critical concept in NL Hold'em. Since NL often leads to bluffing, one can make a lot of money simply by stealing pots if your opponents are very tight. However, this strategy obviously fails if everyone participates in a showdown on the river.

Generally, before I join a game, I pay attention to the number of hands ending in showdowns. This is really easy to do in a poker room, because you don't pay to watch the game. By being able to see more showdowns, this will reveal what cards are played by the other players so, the more showdowns the better. While it is impossible to bluff if everyone calls, you stand to make a lot more money if people call you with tenuous holdings. The best way to make money at NL Texas Hold'em games is to simply sell your hand when you have it. If people call down often, you will be able to extract a lot of money from pot-sized (or larger) bets when you hit a premium hand, such as a flush or set.

" Why do the pushin' when the donkey will do the pullin'? "

—*Layne Flack, winner of six W.S.O.P. Bracelets and a WPT Title.*

CHAPTER THREE:

POKER HAND RANKING

ROYAL FLUSH

The best possible hand, a royal flush, is a straight flush involving the Ten, Jack, Queen, King and Ace of the same suit.

STRAIGHT FLUSH

Five cards of the same suit in sequential order.

FOUR OF A KIND
Four cards of the same rank, for example four Queens.

FULL HOUSE
Is a hand that has a combination of any pair and any three of a kind.

FLUSH
Five cards of the same suit, like five diamonds. If two players have the same hand, the winner is the player holding the highest valued cards.

STRAIGHT
Five cards of any suit in ascending order. The ace can be either high or low and the high straight wins the tie.

THREE OF A KIND
Also called trips or a set, this is where you have three cards
of the same rank, for example three queens.

TWO PAIR
A hand that contains two sets of pairs. The player holding the highest pair
takes the pot in the event that more than one player is holding two pairs.

ONE PAIR
A hand that contains any two cards of the same rank, for example here is a
pair of twos. The strongest pair is a pair of Aces and the weakest is a pair of twos.

HIGH CARD
Highest card takes all in the event there is a complete absence of the above hands.

❝Your best chance to get a Royal Flush in a casino is in the bathroom. **❞**

—*V.P. Pappy, he was a renowned Las Vegas gambler.*

CHAPTER FOUR:

POKER ODDS AND PROBABILITIES

Whenever you sit down at a poker table, your prospects of winning are determined by a combination of chance and your own expertise and proficiency. By improving your knowledge and skill, you can reduce your reliance on chance and dramatically increase your winnings. The relative values of poker hands were not just made up by some rule maker or arbitrarily assigned by the first poker players. They were discovered through the use of permutation and combination formulas. The exact number of possible five-card poker hands in a 52-card deck is 2,598,960.

These hands were separated into groups (ranks) of: no pair, pair, three of a kind, straight, flush, full house, four of a kind, straight flush and royal flush. The ranks were then arranged in relative value according to the frequency of their occurrence. The hands which are expected to appear most often have the lower rank; those which appear least have the highest rank.

A competent poker player must have a fair idea of poker odds and probabilities. Without such knowledge, he has no good way of deciding on his course of action in the various situations which arise. That is, he has no way of making a mathematical analysis on which to base a decision. The tables that follow provide the information that will help a poker player make these analyses.

Interesting Facts About Texas Hold'em:
- Whenever a player is dealt their hole cards, they receive one of 1,326 possible starting hands.
- If they don't fold, they'll see one of the 19,600 different probable flops.
- Following the flop, there are 1,081 possible two-card combinations on the turn and river.
- By the showdown, the winning hand will be one of the 2,598,960 possible five-card hands.

Assuming Your Chances
If you've ever questioned why you've never hit a Royal Flush, here's why. Of the 2,598,960 possible hands you could get in a game of poker, only four are Royal Flushes (spades, clubs, hearts and diamonds). The math means that to reasonably expect to hit a royal you'd have to play for eight hours a day, seven days a week for seven years. If you get one, take pleasure in the moment.

The likelihood of hitting hands in Texas Hold'em with all five cards on the board

| ROYAL FLUSH | Possible Hands = 4 | Odds of hitting in play = 649,739 to 1 |

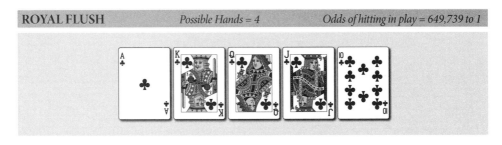

| STRAIGHT FLUSH | Possible Hands = 36 | Odds of hitting in play= 64,973 to 1 |

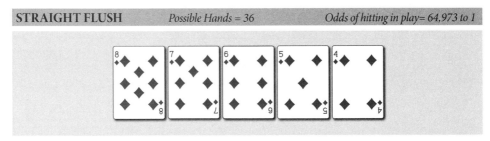

| FOUR OF A KIND | Possible Hands = 624 | Odds of hitting in play = 3,913 to 1 |

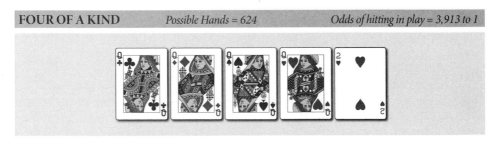

No

FULL HOUSE   *Possible Hands = 3,744*   *Odds of hitting in play = 589 to 1*

FLUSH   *Possible Hands = 5,108*   *Odds of hitting in play = 272 to 1*

STRAIGHT   *Possible Hands = 10,200*   *Odds of hitting in play = 131 to 1*

THREE OF A KIND   *Possible Hands = 54,912*   *Odds of hitting in play = 34 to 1*

TWO PAIR   *Possible Hands = 123,552*   *Odds of hitting in play= 12 to 1*

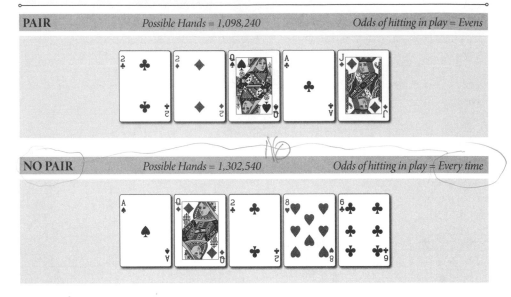

After the Deal...

With hole cards that are an off suited pair, the odds of flopping the following are...

- **Pair** = *2.5 to 1*
- **Two pairs** = *49 to 1*
- **Three of a kind** = *73 to 1*
- **Full House** = *1,087 to 1*
- **Four of a kind** = *9,799 to 1*

A player's chances of flopping *at least* one of the above is 2.1 to 1. So in other words, two thirds of the time, your hand is not going to improve. This fact indicates that you should fold aggressively, until you make a hand worth attempting to double up on.

Pocket Pairs

With hole cards that contain a pair, the odds of flopping the following are...

- **Three of a kind** = *8.3 to 1*
- **Full House** = *136 to 1*
- **Four of a kind** = *407 to 1*

The most revealing stat above, in terms of calculating pot odds, are the odds of flopping at least three of a kind or better. (7.5 to 1).

Some Other Useful Odds to Remember

A player with four cards of the same suit after the flop is 1.85 to 1 to make a flush by the river.

A player with an open ended straight draw is 2.2 to 1 to make at least a straight by the river.

A player holding an open-ended straight flush draw after the flop is .67 to 1 to make at least a straight by the river. That is, the player is more likely to improve the hand than not improve it.

? Turn odds?

A player drawing to an inside straight is around 11 to 1 to make it on the next two cards combined.

How to Calculate Your Current Outs

The cards left in the deck that can make your hand are called outs. So, the total number of cards left unseen that could make your hand is your total number of outs. Let's say you're holding a drawing hand after the flop. You already know one important thing: you're behind anyone who has hit a pair. Calculate your outs and you'll know another, even more important thing, your chances of beating that pair. Do this by dividing the number of outs that haven't been seen with the number of cards that haven't been seen, those are your chances of filling in your hand. Here's an illustration of this concept.

You're holding

against the other player who is holding

The flop comes:

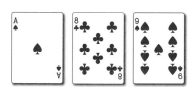

Even if the other player has made top pair, you can win with any spade, queen or seven giving you a total of 15 outs (the seven remaining spades, four remaining queens and four remaining sevens). Your hand is statistically favored to win if all five cars are dealt, even thought your behind before the turn.

Number of outs	Two cards to come	On the turn	On the river
20	0.48 – 1 (68%)	1.3 – 1 (43%)	1.3 – 1 (43%)
19	0.54 – 1 (65%)	1.5 – 1 (40%)	1.4 – 1 (42%)
18	0.6 – 1 (63%)	1.6 – 1 (38%)	1.6 – 1 (38%)
17	0.67 – 1 (60%)	1.8 – 1 (36%)	1.7 – 1 (37%)
16	0.75 – 1 (57%)	1.9 – 1 (34%)	1.9 – 1 (34%)
15	0.85 – 1 (54%)	2.1 – 1 (32%)	2.1 – 1 (32%)
14	0.95 – 1 (51%)	2.4 – 1 (29%)	2.3 – 1 (30%)
13	1.1 – 1 (48%)	2.6 – 1 (28%)	2.5 – 1 (29%)
12	1.2 – 1 (45%)	2.9 – 1 (26%)	2.8 – 1 (26%)
11	1.4 – 1 (42%)	3.3 – 1 (23%)	3.2 – 1 (24%)
10	1.6 – 1 (38%)	3.7 – 1 (21%)	3.6 – 1 (22%)
9	1.9 – 1 (34%)	4.2 – 1 (19%)	4.1 – 1 (20%)
8	2.2 – 1 (31%)	4.9 – 1 (17%)	4.8 – 1 (17%)
7	2.6 – 1 (28%)	5.7 – 1 (15%)	5.7 – 1 (15%)
6	3.1 – 1 (24%)	6.8 – 1 (13%)	6.7 – 1 (13%)
5	3.9 – 1 (20%)	8.4 – 1 (11%)	8.2 – 1 (11%)
4	5.1 – 1 (16%)	11 – 1 (8%)	11 – 1 (8%)
3	7 – 1 (13%)	15 – 1 (6%)	14 – 1 (7%)
2	10.9 – 1 (8%)	23 – 1 (4%)	22 – 1 (4%)
1	22.4 – 1 (4%)	46 – 1 (2%)	45 – 1 (2%)

Take notice that all odds provided are odds against you making your winning hand. Following this chart, anytime where the first digit is below zero means that you are the favorite to win. Anything above 1 to 1 means that you are the underdog.

~~⌒ PART TWO ⌒~~

FISH
Beginner Strategy

CHAPTER FIVE:

PATIENCE, EVEN MORE FOCUS

The Fish: Beginner Strategy for NL Texas Hold'em: As a beginner, this will be an entirely new strategy for you but trust me. With discipline and patience you will master this technique. First, forget any ideas you might have about poker. Try this method for the next couple of weeks only.

Only Play these Starting Hands Before the Flop:

A-A	9-9	4-4
K-K	8-8	A-K
Q-Q	7-7	A-Q
J-J	6-6	
10-10	5-5	

Fold Everything Else!

These starting hands come often enough and when you flop a "set" you have an excellent chance of increasing your chip stack, depending on how many suckers you are trapping in a hand. This method may seem very boring, but trust me. I have won both money and tournaments using this very simple method. Where is there fun in playing almost every hand and losing? Playing in a limited amount of hands does four main things:

- You will last longer in a tournament or cash game.
- It allows for time to pick up tells on the other players when the cards hit the air.
- By only playing these hands, the other players will respect your bets and fear you.
- After knocking out several players, your odds of making bluffs are more successful.

Another thing I want to mention is if your hands are A-A, K-K, Q-Q, OR A-K, don't be discouraged from going all in, regardless of position. Also these four hands give you an opportunity to set traps, but we will address that later in the book. Now, the good stuff, or the main reason you bought this book.

You Must Keep the Other Players Guessing in the Dark

From the moment you join a poker table, the other players will be sizing you up. They will watch your moves, dissect your bets, and look for your poker tells. If you want to become a successful poker player and mimic pros, (dine on them, actually) you must learn how to avoid giving off these signals. Period!

In order to do this, you must disguise your movements and hide your activities. You must also learn how to force other weaker players to fold, even when they "know" they have the best hand. Make other players "out-think" themselves by staying extremely unpredictable. These are some ideas I recommend that you must employ at the poker table every time you play. These methods have been used and perfected over my poker career, and if used properly, you will become virtually unreadable.

Recommendation I: *Vary the Size of Your Bets*

I cannot believe the multitude of players that I see using the same bets over and over again. If you want to be unpredictable, you must change your betting and raising patterns as much as possible. Imagine that you are sitting at a table where a beginner player gets stuck in the same betting patterns. Now, let's say that he is dealt an A-A or K-K. He leads out with a large bet, exactly as he did in the past with a similar hand. Now you have a great read on him. This can easily prevent you from losing a big chunk of your chip stack. It can also keep you from getting any callers on your premium hands, or get too many on poor hands.

Recommendation II: *Keep the Players Out of Your Hands*

The real sign of a great poker player is the ability to win countless small pots with aggressive play. Forcing others out of small pots allows your opponents to see fewer hole cards. Every time the other players see your cards, a little bit more of your style is revealed. It is crucial that you play aggressively to keep yourself veiled in mystery.

Recommendation III: *Shift Styles Completely Back and Forth*

If you watch poker games on TV such as W.S.O.P. or WPT closely, the successful players will always be the ones who fluctuate from aggressive to tight throughout the match. When you are at the table, it is paramount that you mix up your betting patterns with any given hand…and then hit the switch button. Switch your overall playing style between loose and tight.

Recommendation IV: *Never Show Your Cards*
There are so many players I see who like to reveal their cards when they pull off a good bluff. It is usually an "Ass-like" gesture from the player to show off their own ego. If you're playing Texas NL Hold'em to feel better about yourself, then be my guest and reveal your cards. If you're like me and play Texas NL Hold'em because you love this game and love to win, **DON'T** show your cards. It doesn't matter if you're Daniel Negreanu, Erik Lindgren, Phil Hellmuth or someone who has just begun; these habits are hard to break. These four recommendations will give you a competitive edge in disguising your bad habits.

Finding Your Game
The first big decision you'll have to make when starting out in poker isn't which hand to play, it's which table to play it on. Choosing the right table is critical for reasons that you will continue to apply throughout your poker career.

Choosing a Tournament
Tournaments are less complicated to budget for because possible losses are capped by the entry fee: you can only lose as much money as you've paid to buy-in (unless it's a re-buy tournament). The upside is pretty good too. Take down a multi-table tournament with 100 entrants and you should expect to see a 50-fold return on your investment. When choosing a multi-table tournament, keep in mind that it will take time to complete (depending on how you fair). Make sure you've got enough time to see it through. If you're struggling for time, but still like the idea of a tournament, a single-table tournament or a sit and go may be the answer. A ten-seat sit and go will usually take about an hour to play, while a "six-pack" should be wrapped-up in about 45 minutes.

Cash Tables
First, you'll want to find a game that matches your style. Limit Hold'em tables, where betting is capped, are popular with beginners because there is less chance you'll lose your stack on one hand. The next factor to consider is the table stakes. The majority of poker rooms have cash poker tables with blinds that range from pennies and to $30/$50. I don't want to sound like your mother, but it's important that you always select a game that suits your budget. Most poker rooms require you to sit down with a minimum buy-in of 10-times the lower stake level (so, to sit in a $2/$4 game you'll need to bring at least $20 to the table). Showing up with the bare minimum will leave you short stacked and open to attack from aggressive players. It's best to choose a blind level where you can afford a healthy buy-in.

Once you've determined your stakes you could just dive into the first game that matches your criteria. But you'll give yourself a gigantic edge if you look before you leap. Check out the average pot size on the tables of interest. Those with larger pot size averages tell you that the play has been very aggressive on that table. Smaller averages indicate a more calculating (or just cautious) table. The latter might reward aggressive play, while the former is more suited to a conservative style.

Common Mistakes I see "Beginning Poker Players Make"

If you play poker, this will be the most important tip that I can give you PLEASE MEMORIZE!! Take this advice seriously and you could quickly and consistently win more pots. There are several major (yet easily correctable) mistakes that both "fish" and "shark" players make when playing poker. Learn to prevent these mistakes and you will dominate others. The reason that I am pointing these out right now is because throughout my poker career I have made every single mistake on this list at some point...

Mistake 1: *Reaction to Cards: Hole Cards/Flop/Turn/River*

While players react to situations differently, the only tell in a game is the amount of time a player takes before acting on his hand. When the other players look at their cards, they are usually not on guard at this point since they don't think they're being scrutinized. It is not beneficial to look at your cards while the other players are looking at theirs. Your cards will still be there, and if you look at them now, you'll miss some of the most valuable tells in poker. See if the other players quickly glance toward their chips after seeing their next cards. This reaction usually means they liked what they saw and are planning to bet.

This is especially true if they glance at their chips and then stare conspicuously away as if uninterested. Remember, players staring away from their chip stack usually represents that they have strong hands. The longer they look, the more likely it is that the hands are weak and they're pretending to show interest. Conversely, if the other player looks and recognizes a big hand, he will usually cover it quickly and then pretend to show no interest in pursuing the pot.

On the other hand, your opponent may not bother to look away. It's the quick glance at the chips just after the flop that's an especially powerful tell in Hold'em. Watch how the other players watch the flop. You don't need to see it yourself just yet. It won't go away.

The Commonly Accepted Formula is this:

- **A delayed check = Weakness**
- **Immediate call = Strength**
- **Immediate check = Weakness**
- **Quick bet/raise on turn or river = Strength**

The only reason that this formula is so widely accepted is that it is surprisingly accurate. The first tell is simply an understanding of poker psychology and theory. The others are proven with experience. Think about it. If you have a weak hand and immediately check, you are saying that you have a weak hand.

Yet, by pausing a moment, people are forced to ponder "Are they slow playing it? Is this a trap? Will I be check-raised? How has he played in the past?"

Mistake 2: *Distractions, Becoming distracted*

Poker is a game of skill, not luck. It takes concentration and attention to detail. When you are distracted, you lose your abilities which can be a bad situation in a game where serious money is involved. Turn off that iPod and don't ruin your chances at winning the game. When players are distracted they make costly mistakes that often get them eliminated. Watch players for the "sucker" at the table. If it takes more than 30 minutes for them to be revealed, the sucker may be you.

Mistake 3: *Talking Way Too Much*

Many believe that talking in poker is a good thing; that it isn't a dead give away. This will give others a look into your personality and you're true playing style. Don't waste time and energy taunting or talking to other players. Excessive talking also leads into the next poker mistake.

Mistake 4: *Don't Make Enemies*

Making enemies in poker is never ever a good idea. If you take down a big pot, quickly and quietly move the chips to your pile. If you lose a pot to someone who sucks out; don't whine. The reason that you don't want enemies is very simple: they will be "gunning" for you. This is when players who want you out of a game call you down and make chances of winning more difficult. This causes a power shift because they are now playing against you instead of the table.

> **The unexamined life is not a life worth living.**

~Socrates (469 BC-399 BC), Plato.

With that said, let's give some consideration to how we as poker players process information and respond to the pressures of decision-making. This is an important idea to consider as we strive to gain more success in poker and life in general.

Neuro Linguistic Programming or NLP is a controversial study of body language and human communication. NLP is an interesting and extremely valuable area of study to understand. Initially it was co-created by Richard Bandler and linguist John Grinder in the 1970's. That the most important lesson NLP shows is the effectiveness of creating a mirror image of another person who has already achieved your goal. By doing this one can drastically speed up their own ability to learn and master the same skills. If we act, move, sit, walk, talk, and learn to adopt the exact thinking styles of a professional poker player we can leap ahead in learning. A professional player may have spent 20 or so years learning the secrets of the game but, by making a mirror image of their behavior and thought process, we can learn to emulate and beat a poker pro in a shorter period of time.

Now you're probably thinking this whole approach is just filler for this chapter and I don't blame you. It sounds ridiculous. As students, we're taught that you need to study, study, study for years and slowly work your way towards expertise. However, if you have seen any examples of NLP at work, as I have in my poker career, you would have a completely new understanding of how to increase your abilities to a whole new level in a matter of days. There are many books on NLP and I don't have time to cover all the facts here. Instead let's take a quick look at how most great poker players think, and try to grasp how to become more like them.

Professional poker players ease into the poker game with utter confidence. They have accumulated playing experience that allows for prompt tough betting decisions. Phil Hellmuth is such a great example of this behavior. This means that they always give the odds proper consideration and then make their play.

To Outplay a Shark You Need to Act the Part

Even when playing online, be professional. Keep a clean area around your computer desk and stay organized. Determine the time of day that allows for the best focus. Be prepared! Have a notepad handy and plan your poker games on a schedule. Watch other players carefully and take notes. Note taking on players is a very profitable past time. Manage your playing time by remembering, you're a shark, so keep the pace. As you forage through the ocean, keep your eyes alert. When the time is right and the fish are unprepared, strike aggressively and purposefully. Raise and re-raise with purpose and push out the weaker players. You gain respect from all of the players at the table because they know only a few things about you:

- You have a huge stack of chips in front of you.
- You seem to know everyone's hole-cards before they are exposed.
- Small losses mean nothing in the big picture to you, and small bad breaks have no consequence for you.
- You play to win the long haul.

Keep track of your play and what you learn. This is one of your best secret weapons. You should keep a detailed list of financial records of both wins and losses. Be very precise. If you won $315.25, then make that your answer if someone asks. Let's say maybe you lost $15.50. Get in the habit of being exact. That's the key to tight play. A good business cannot be successful without detailed finances and neither can you. When my poker career started many years ago, I enjoyed participating in exciting poker games with groups of family and friends each week. I have always enjoyed playing poker. The groups I played were great, the food was excellent and it was a great entertainment for the price. Sometimes I lost, sometimes I won. And when I lost, I always justified the money as part of the entertainment cost. I was a typical recreational weekend poker player. But then I watched some poker on T.V., bought a few poker books, and soon realized that I only remembered and talked about my winnings. However, I rarely focused on, or discussed when I lost. You might ask yourself why that is?

It's called selective reasoning. Your brain is always focusing on positive events and I like winning. Instead remember your losses and learn from them. This is a very reasonable approach to real learning. Experts say people, who keep track, stay on track. Businessmen and players in general who track their expenses in detail will spend less and save more money. How successful do you want to be at poker? If you want to make real money in this game, you need to start tracking your efforts, your wins, and your losses.

Professional poker players know exactly how much they won at any given table. They also know exactly how much they lost. Professionals play the game with intention and focus. They won't become distracted. They talk about the game with clarity. A professional poker player studies the game, and evaluates mistakes. He knows all the odds and the rules. As Phil Ivey would say, "Poker is a lot like golf. What's the secret to a great golfer? Study, practice, play, evaluate." This holds true in poker. Good poker players coach themselves. We have hundreds of years of proof to make this a proven technique. So coach yourself!

Don't "wish" yourself a great performance. Prepare your body and mind to perform at peak efficiency. And always have a positive outlook. Don't go to a casino with this idea: "I brought $200 to lose and that's when I'll quit." What you need to be thinking is: "I brought $200 and I'm going to win."

If you surrender to the poker gods, and proceed with a loser's mentality, your play style will set you up to fail. If you've prepared your brain to lose, chances are you will. So you must prepare yourself to win at poker. Visualize your success at the poker table. This means more than just winning it all, because sometimes the damn poker cards just won't cooperate. Your game will improve every day. You will get better by the hour, and will win more often. In addition, you will certainly feel more confident at the tables. Positive thinking and a winner's attitude are of the utmost importance if you want to succeed.

So, be smart, keep it to yourself, and let the chips do the talking...

"Sometimes you'll miss a bet, sure, but it's OK to miss a bet. Poker is an art form, of course, but sometimes you have to sacrifice art in favor of making a profit.**"**

—*Mike Caro, professional poker player, pioneer poker theorist, and an author of many poker books.*

CHAPTER SIX:

AVOID COIN FLIPS

Whether or not you determine to get into a coin flip situation in poker really depends upon what type of game you're playing. Basically, a coin flip is when you have two hands against each other, that both have a 50/50 chance of winning at the showdown. A quick example would be:

vs.

Each hands pre-flop has about the same chance of winning by the time the river card comes. I'm far more likely to take on a coin flip when I'm playing in a cash game rather than a typical buy-in tournament. The same holds to for a live game as opposed to playing online.

NL Texas Hold'em tournaments are increasing in popularity. With the recent explosion of televised poker tournaments, new poker players are pouring into multi-table tournaments. One reason there is such an attraction to NL Texas Hold'em tournaments is the chance to make a big win at the WSOP or the WPT. If you can master the correct strategy you will have a good chance of taking down some big tournaments. These types of tournaments involve a significant amount of luck, because in the late stages massive blinds put extreme pressure on the players. Almost every player will end up an all-in pre-flop at some point in the tournament. Often times, it results in a coin flip. It's almost the same as scratching off a lottery ticket, in comparison.

When playing in a cash game, getting into a coin flip situation can occasionally produce better results beyond simply winning the hand. If you win a race, you can often expect the other player to become a worse player almost immediately following the hand. This should give you the opportunity to take even more money from them over the course of the next several hours. Therefore, you should be more willing to get into a coin flip situation with players who have less control over their emotions after losing a big hand this way.

Early Stages

O.K., let's get to the strategy. Tournaments differ significantly from cash tables. You have to avoid bluffing as much because the chip stacks are smaller in relation to the blinds. Plus, if you win a bluff, you win fewer chips than you risk losing, so it is not a valuable play. Now, obviously you can't just fold your way into the money, so in the early stages you need to play very tight. Your main goal in the early stages of a tournament is to maintain your stack and wait for all the fish to be eaten. The goal of tournaments is to win enough pots to stay alive, not necessarily to instantly building a huge stack. At the beginning of the tournament, you should avoid gambling, because the chips that you gain aren't worth the risk.

Now, if you have a hand like:

and someone goes all-in pre-flop, go ahead and call. But, I strongly advise that there are no bluffing or loose calls here.

Furthermore, if the other player wins the hand, they are not going to be rewarded as much since you're not going to play any differently after losing a big hand. While winning is important, it seems most players put too high a premium on winning in the short-term.

"Remember your goal is to win the tournament, not just a pot or two."

Middle Stages

After you ease your way through the early stage, you need to change your playing style periodically during the middle stage. The blinds are increasing, so you need to start making plays at the pots to stay alive. While you are in the middle stage, you should be stealing blinds and small pots with lesser hands, and only calling raises with extremely strong hands. Your main goal, once again, is just to survive. Basically, you want to avoid going head to head with someone. Pick up small pots without being contested, and avoid gambling in huge pots. There is only one exception to this rule. If you have made a monstrous stack, you should take advantage of the players who are just trying to survive. You should increase your bet size often, and force people to commit their entire stack if they want to play you. The reason for this is that they're less likely to want to risk their whole stack, and you're only risking part of yours.

Considering the other players' demeanor, one of the biggest factors in deciding whether or not you should be willing to get in a race is the amount of money you have invested in the hand. If you have already put some money into the pot and you're odds are good, then no matter how much the other player raises don't let them get rid of you. If you fold, then you would be literally throwing away the money that you already put in there, and you shouldn't get in the habit of doing that.

Late Stages

After the middle stage, you need to start taking gambles. It is during the late stage when you will be deciding whether to go all-in pre-flop in coin flip situations. Often, the stakes are so high that players will be moving all-in with marginal hands. You should be looking to move on Ace-high kicker and pocket pairs. If you are really short stacked, use any two face cards. When you have strong hole cards, move all in pre-flop, then to try to make a raise. If you try to play too many flops, you'll end up getting bluffed out when you have the best hand.

Here's an example of a typical coin flip situation after the flop. Let's say you have:

and the flop comes:

Because you have two over-cards and a nut flush draw, this is a great spot to go on the offensive if the other player makes a bet. If the other player has made top pair with a hand like:

It's about a 50-50 situation, but you have plenty of outs to justify your aggression.

If you raise and the other player comes over the top of you, you have to suspect that he has a set and you can no longer depend on a king or an ace as an out. At this point, all you have is a nut flush draw and it's no longer a coin flip situation. Unless you're both deep-stacked you should back off and wait for a better situation. But don't lose your initiative and remember to keep playing smart-aggressively.

Now let's turn it around. The flop is the same, but now you have:

The other player is the one who has two over-cards and a nut flush draw. You bet, and the other player raises. How you proceed really depends upon what sort of player you're up against.

Because of situations like this one, it is better to be in a live game rather than online. You can always make better decisions in live games because of the reads on the other players. This is always beneficial. If someone calls your raise pre-flop see what the turn brings. But if you raised pre-flop and then they re-raised, throw your queens away because they could very well have a bigger pair.

Your justification for this should completely change in a tournament. In the latter stages of a tournament your chips are worth more than they were at the beginning so your first concern is protecting them, which often means avoiding coin flip situations. After the money bubble bursts, players who get knocked out are increasingly rewarded financially. Then the smartest move is to avoid getting into coin flip situations and waiting for an improved situation.

Like many aspects of poker, the decision of whether or not to get into a coin flip situation depends on a variety of factors, the most important of which are the type of game you're playing and the demeanor of the other players.

% of your chips to go into coin flip

"More and more scientific studies are finding a strong link between regular exercise and higher mental function. People who exercise have faster reaction times, better computational speed, more accurate responses, improved memory, and better awareness of their surroundings. What a perfect recipe for better poker!"

—Michael Binger, after receiving his PhD in theoretical physics, he has set a great example on how to outlast so many players. He continually cashes in large events, including 3rd, in the 2006 W.S.O.P. Main Event and countless cashes in the WPT as well.

CHAPTER SEVEN:

A CHIP AND A CHAIR

Jack Straus is responsible for what may be the most popular quote regarding what you need to win in tournament poker, "a chip and a chair." In order to win poker tournaments, you need to be fully focused at all times, self-assurance, and skill.

During the 1982 World Series of Poker main event, Straus was short stacked and determined to push all-in. The "chip and a chair" myth has grown to place Jack Straus at the final table. Straus lost the famous hand. Upon standing up, he discovered he had one chip left under a napkin on the table. Confusion set in, as it was his intention to go all-in. However, he never said "all-in," so the tournament directors agreed that he was still in the tournament. Jack Straus, of course, went on to take that one $500 chip and go on to win the $520,000 first prize. Modern lore claims that this feat occurred at the final table, but the 1983 poker classic The Biggest Game in Town suggests that this occurred on the first day

Jack Straus is also credited with one of the most illustrious bluffs of all time. While playing in a high-stakes NL Texas Hold'em cash game, he had won several large pots in a row and so decided that he would raise the next hand pre-flop with any two cards. When he looked down he found that he had been dealt, the hammer,

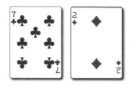

the worst possible starting hand in Texas Hold'em, but, playing a "rush," he raised anyway. He raised and was called by a single player and the flop came:

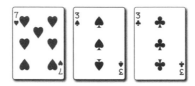

This was a good flop for a 7-2, so Straus bet out. However his tight player made a large raise, indicating a likely over pair to the board. Straus knew he was almost certainly behind, but he decided that he might be able to beat the other player by representing a set of three's, so he called the large raise.

The turn was a

for a board of 7-3-3-2, which was no help to Jack Straus with a better pair already on the board, but he made a huge bet anyway. Since drawing out to win on the river were very slim he was desperate to avoid a call.. After a few minutes, Straus offered the other player a proposition, for $25 he could choose either one of Straus's hole cards to see. The guy considered for a moment, then tossed the $25 chip and chose the deuce.

After another long pause, the other player eventually figured that Jack Straus would only make such an offer if both his hole-cards were deuces, therefore giving him a full house: deuces over threes. He reluctantly folded, and Straus entered poker folklore as one of the most creative bluffers of all time.

Jack Straus' description of poker, particularly involving money and NL Hold'em may be the most truthful quote ever to come out of the game.

"If money is your god, you can forget NL Texas Hold'em poker, because it's going to hurt you too much to turn loose of it. The way I feel about those little pieces of green paper is, you can't take them with you and they may not have much value in five years time, but right now I can trade them in for pleasure or to bring pleasure to other people. If they had wanted you to hold on to money, they'd have made it with handles on."

When Straus fully devoted himself to poker, he definitely didn't leave anything behind. Like his father, who believed in hard work, Jack Straus died while doing what he loved… playing poker. As mentioned, Jack Straus didn't make the public spotlight like the majority of other poker players, but his impact has been equally felt. Straus was inducted to the Poker Hall of Fame posthumously in 1988.

On that day a poker aphorism was born, one that will live on as long as poker does. Commit it to memory just in case you find yourself massively short of chips at the World Series of Poker, remember the Jack Straus story and that all you need is:

"A CHIP AND A CHAIR!"

PART THREE

BARRACUDA
Intermediate Strategy

CHAPTER EIGHT:

PATIENCE, EVEN MORE FOCUS

Patience, Even More Focus! This is the Barracuda: Intermediate Strategy for NL Texas Hold'em. After you have mastered (or gotten bored with) the Fish: Beginner Strategy, it's time to tackle Barracuda: Intermediate Strategy. Trust me, if you have the discipline and patience, you will succeed. As an Intermediate player, forget any other ideas you might have for poker, and try this method for the next couple of weeks.

ONLY and I mean Only Play these Starting Hands Before the Flop:

A-A	9-9	4-4
K-K	8-8	3-3
Q-Q	7-7	2-2
J-J	6-6	A-K
10-10	5-5	A-Q

Now its time to add these starting hands also:

| A-J | K-J | 9-10 |
| K-Q | J-10 | |

QJ?

Same Suit ONLY

These starting hands come often enough, and when you flop a three of a kind, you have an excellent chance of increasing your chip stack ×2, ×3, ×4, depending how many suckers you are trapping in a hand. This method may seem very boring, but TRUST ME I have won lots of money and tournaments using this very simple method. Where is the fun in playing almost every hand and losing? Playing in a limited amount of hands does a bunch of things. Once again, let's point them out:

- **You will last even longer in a tournament or cash game.**
- **It allows for time to pick up tells on the other players when the cards hit the air.**
- **By only playing these hands, the other players will respect your bets and fear you.**
- **After knocking out a few players, your odds of making bluffs are more successful.**

When you have a playable hand, always make a bet that is double the big blind. By doing this, you force out weaker players, therefore giving you a better chance to win. Because large tournaments are a free-for-all, you want to steal as many blinds and antes as possible. If it were possible to do this on every hand, chances are you would win the tournament. Although it would be nice, obviously not every hand is playable. Make sure you take them when they come, especially when you are in optimal position. Once antes are placed, you must begin re-raising players' bets. It is likely they will fold to your re-raise. Set your sights on weak players, and give them a stare that burns right through them.

I need to mention that you should avoid:

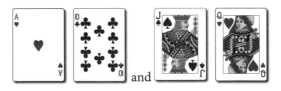 and

I have found over the years that these starting hands do only one thing: get you into trouble and make you lose tournaments. These starting hands should only be used in the later rounds of tournaments to steal blinds; and you should fold them anytime you are re-raised. Other players may disagree with this approach, and they are entitled to that opinion. The fact is that for intermediate players, and in the later rounds, this style wins more than it loses in NL Texas Hold'em..

Suited Connectors

Playing these starting hands is kind of tricky. You either come out looking like an idiot or a complete poker genius. The only suited connectors you should be using at this part of your poker knowledge are as follows:

A-2	K-Q	8-9
J-10	Q-9	
7-8	10-9	

These hands put you in an area of medium-suited connectors, which do very well in low-limit games. You accomplish three things by playing these hands:

- **Set up a monster hand (straights, flushes, and straight flushes).**
- **If you pair these hands, they can turn into sets.**
- **If you miss your straight, you then stand to make a flush. These hands have cracked aces countless times for me.**

There isn't anything more exciting than beating A-A or K-K with your hand of J-10, especially if the other player goes all-in after the flop. This gets even better when you have flopped Broadway and they might have turned their paired hole cards into a set. Sets like those pale in comparison to your straight or flush.

According to famous poker player and fellow poker book author Doyle Brunson, NL Texas Hold'em is the Cadillac of all poker games. The skill involved with no-limit games is tremendous, and even seasoned professionals admit that they still have a lot to learn at NL Texas Hold'em. Don't let this scare you. NL Texas Hold'em, in my opinion, is the most fun of all poker games. It can also be profitable, even for beginners.

After playing NL Texas Hold'em extensively, I've noticed that the keys to winning are one's knowledge of the game and the ability to adapt to the other players' knowledge. You must know what your skills are and what stages of the game you have mastered. Once you realize how superior you are at NL Texas Hold'em, you must then apply this to how others at your table play poorly.

For the sake of simplicity, I am going to divide the skills of NL Texas Hold'em into several stages. After mastering each of these stages, you can expect your profit potential at NL Texas Hold'em to increase.

Pot Odds

You must understand what odds you have if you call a bet with a draw. Since you can decide the size of the bet (it's not fixed), you should know if you are getting or giving good odds to someone.

For example, calling an un-raised pot pre-flop with:

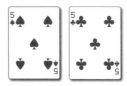

is good odds. If you hit a set, you can expect to make a lot of money (people will not expect it, so they will call with top pair). Let's say you have a flush draw after the turn. The pot is $20 and someone bets $40 all-in. In this situation, you are getting horrible odds. You have roughly a 1 in 5 shot of hitting on the river, and you would be betting $40 to win $60.

As basic as this may be, many NL Texas Hold'em players have not even mastered this stage! So, if you are still insecure about pot odds, don't worry. Just begin to familiarize yourself with this concept.

Knowing the differences between Limit and NL Texas Hold'em

Check-raising for value is far less when playing a NL Texas Hold'em game than a Limited one because you may be giving the other players a lethal free card. In Limit Texas Hold'em poker, if you have the second-best hand, you will lose a couple of chips. In a NL Texas Hold'em, you could lose your entire stack.

Quick Adjustments

Betting is generally preferable to calling in a NL Texas Hold'em game. If you call, you can only win if you have the other player beaten. If you bet, you can win if you have the better hand or if the other player folds. When you bet, you determine the bet size and the pot odds. If you are the caller, you are accepting someone else's odds. Aggressive play is why tight-passive players can win a lot more at Limit Texas Hold'em, rather than in NL Texas Hold'em. You also must adjust to the other players' quality of play. If you are up against weak players, simply giving them bad pot odds and taking money from them bit by bit works well. If you are against better players, you should set some traps.

Aggression

Different types of games require different amounts of aggression. Shorter games require one to be loose and more aggressive. If you're up against many loose opponents, you must tighten up and wait until you have a strong hand. If the game is very loose, tighten up. If the game is very tight, take advantage and steal pots.

Reading Skills

Obtaining an idea of the other players' cards is very important. This takes time and experience. A way to improve your reading skills is to always ask yourself these three questions when someone makes or calls a bet:

- **What does the other player have?**
- **What does the other player think I have?**
- **What does the other player think that I think he has?**

Psychology and Traps

Once you hold the "absolute nuts" and the other player also has a good hand, what's the best way to double-up through him? Learning to get out of and set traps is very difficult; only experience will help in this area of your poker game.

Fundamentally, game psychology and traps are used to manipulate the three questions mentioned earlier. For example, you over-bet the pot with a flush draw and then check when you hold the flush. The other player will either fall for the trap, thinking you had top pair, or he will recognize the trap and check-fold to you on the river. This slow-play is used to manipulate the variable, what does he think I have?

Basically, this sort of game psychology is only used on good players (players that have mastered the previous four topics). Against weaker players, you should just build a good hand and extract money out of them bit by bit. Weaker players just play their hand because they aren't thinking about what you have. These players play cards, not poker. There is such an unequivocal difference in this matter.

❝ I raise… One Million. ❞

—Jerry Yang, a therapist and social worker who entered the main event on a $225 satellite and became the 2007 World Series of Poker Champion.

CHAPTER NINE:

AGGRESSION

Why do you think good players are called sharks? Aggression.

All long term winning poker players share one thing in common: they play an aggressive poker game. Aggression in poker doesn't mean bluffing a lot; it means playing your hands with confidence. An aggressive player doesn't make a lot of checks and calls. He either raises his hands or folds it.

Aggressive players come in with a raise pre-flop, not weak a call. After the flop, aggressive players bet and raise their strong hands while folding the hands that don't pan out. They don't make weak calls and hope to get lucky.

The key to playing an aggressive game is being very selective about which hands you play pre-flop and those you continue after the flop. If you play the best 20% of your hands, you're naturally going to be betting and raising because you're playing great hands.

If you are checking and calling often, you're probably playing poor hands pre-flop and taking your weak hands too far after the flop. You want to either play a hand aggressively or not play it at all. Don't get stuck in that halfway land of mediocre hands that leaves you uncertain of your odds.

Yes, there are times to check and call, but aggressive players keep that kind of play to a minimum. Just save yourself the trouble and drop your marginal hands early.

The philosophy of the aggressive poker strategy is based on the advantages given by aggression:

- **Gets money in the pot with your strong hands.**
- **Makes people more likely to pay off your strong hands.**
- **Charges the other players for draws.**
- **Forces players to play more straightforward poker against you.**
- **Aggression gets money in the pot with your strong hands.**

While this statement may seem obvious, it's commonly overlooked. If you have a strong hand, whether it is a big pair or a full house, you'll probably want to get more money in the pot because, well, isn't that the point.

It's easy to get fixed on trying to be tricky and forget that all we want to do is get more money in the pot while we have the strongest hand. If you wait until the river you'll have a heck of a time convincing someone to put all their money in the middle. Why? After all cards are on the table, all hope is gone. The other players has either made his hand or missed it. If he made his hand, you're just going to lose money. If he missed his hand, he's not going to call anything. You need to charge them early in the hand when they still have hope.

Aggression Makes People More Likely to Pay Off with Chips for Your Strong Hands
An obstinate game gives you an aggressive image. If the people at your table see you making lots of bets and raises, they are naturally going to wonder if you're just full of hot air. Some people even resent your aggressive play and may be rude to you. That's great since these people are just dying to catch you in a bluff, and will pay to see it.

The more forceful your image is, the more likely people are going to be to call you down with weaker hands. All this aggression makes it hard for them to tell if you really do have a strong hand. Your aggressive game doesn't include making weak calls that indicate weak hands. Because of that, it's that much harder to read you.

Aggression Makes It Costly for Players to Draw
By betting and raising with your strong hands, you make it expensive for the other players to stab at luck with their draws. If you don't bet your strong hands you are allowing the other players to draw for free, which could end in a complete disaster. It is your duty to charge the other players for the opportunity of trying to outdraw you.

Occasionally their draws will hit and that's irritating but that's OK. If the other players' draws never hit, they'd never play poker. It's good their draws hit occasionally because its hope that keeps them coming back every day. As an aggressive player, you exploit the hopes of other people.

Aggression Forces the Other Players to Play more Straightforward Poker Against You

When people suspect they're up against a strong hand, they tend to play a straightforward game. They don't really have a choice if you think about it. When up against a strong hand, they obviously don't want to bluff and they don't want to play weak hands. In the end, they fold all of their weak hands and only continue if they have a strong hand. That's oversimplifying it a bit, but the basic idea is sound: aggression makes it harder for others to play sneaky.

So, by playing an aggressive game you give yourself some major rewards over the competition. Not only are you getting more money in with strong hands but you're also charging people to draw and making them more likely to pay off your strong hands. On top of all those advantages, you're making the other players play a more predictable game against you.

Fundamental Tight-Aggressive (FTA) Strategy

Coming within reach of the game of poker can be intimidating for any inexperienced player. Playing poker with sunglasses on takes away a large part of the intimidation factor, but an Intermediate player is still left with the difficult, strategy-based decisions that will determine their own best approach.

Tight-Aggressive is probably one of the most effortless styles to learn in NL Texas Hold'em, simply because you are playing fewer hands. The word "tight," in this case refers to your starting hand requirements. A tight player will rarely open a pot with a very weak starting hand (in contrast most players will loosen their requirements when opening a pot, when they have position).

The word "aggressive," refers to the way you play your hand in relation to the pot size and the other players' actions and reactions. A basic Tight-Aggressive player will mainly be forcing the action pre and post flop by raising or betting, constantly making the other players pay for entering pots with mediocre hands, while putting them to the test after the flop is seen.

Two things a consistent FTA player should always be on the lookout for are kicker strength and the possibility of being dominated by a huge hand post-flop. Most Intermediate players in today's game would be surprised to learn the FTA strategy, on its own, is not enough to be profitable at any game level above micro stakes. If you're going to employ any broad-based strategy, you'll need to learn and adapt to how the other players are playing against your table image.

Tight-Aggressive players, for the most part, enter pots where their starting hand represents an above average showdown value that has a reasonable chance of dominating others' starting hands. In other words, there truly is enormous value in raising with:

on the button, and getting one of the blinds to flat-call with a weaker Ace. More often than not, your continuation bet will double in value, since you're likely to be holding the best hand after the flop comes.

Intermediate FTA players bet their hand strength, and bet it aggressively (at least on the flop), hence the beauty of repeatedly getting the other players to pay for the privilege of seeing flops with inferior starting hands. The other players are repeatedly forced to either donate expectation with their post-flop draws, or muck. This is pretty much the beginning of Tight-Aggressive play.

However, FTA strategy is highly exploitable, and simply cannot survive on its own, especially versus competent players. Non-expert FTA players are constantly caught off-guard by players who trap with their own premium hands. Perhaps the most common, and least profitable, trait of playing this type of strategy is becoming stubborn. Once you enter a pot or bet a relatively strong hand after the flop, it requires an enormous amount of discipline to rethink your betting lines once the other player plays back at you. It can be argued that one of the main reasons people are willing to flat-call pre-flop raises with mediocre hands is because stubborn FTA players blindly bet their starting hand strength in spite of unfavorable community cards.

In order to play any of these strategies successfully, a player must put in the necessary work and make accurate decisions in situations where "style" gives way to "what's best right now." Successful FTA players know how to value their strong starting hands...but perhaps more importantly, they know (more often than not) when they are up against a superior holding. If you are consistently stacking off with hands like Top Pair, Top Kicker in a deep-stacked blind structure, it won't be long until you're pegged by players who take notice.

Especially in cash games, there are plenty of players who simply lie in wait for predictable (FTA) players. Every now and then, it is common to find a player who gives away tons of information without comprehending it. More than anything, you do not want to become predictable in deep-stacked blind structures.

So what's the answer to turning a profit as a Tight-Aggressive player? Well, you must recognize both the pros and cons of such a style. Take note of why exploiting edges is so necessary, but also work to discover how another player will attempt to chip away at your edge, and react/adapt appropriately. FTA is a style, and an awfully common one at that. It's highly profitable against the other players who have a strong disregard for patience but it is also highly exploitable against the other players who know exactly what you're doing.

Drawing hands should be played aggressively by betting out or even raising instead of checking and calling. This may seem to contradict the strategy of trying to make our hands as cheaply as possible, but it does have some very big advantages which can lead to us making more money from our drawing hands. The FTA approach is more suited to advanced players, who are able to read their the other players and situations well, as putting money into a pot without a made hand can become very costly if you are unsure of what you are doing. If you feel that you would like to experiment with the aggressive approach, stick to the drawing hands that will give you the nuts on completion, such as an Ace-high flush or top straight draw.

As with many poker situations, there are two ways to win a hand. You can win by having the best hand, or by making the other players fold. The FTA style of play lends itself well as it leaves the doorway open to win pots when you do not have the best hand. Betting with a draw works well as a semi-bluff, because it is possible to take the pot without even needing to complete a hand. However, if the other player calls, we still have the opportunity to catch the right card to make a draw for the pot.

To promote this point, the benefit of betting out with a draw is that it disguises your hand. By making bets or raises, the other player is more likely to believe that you have already made a hand and will find it harder to put you on a draw.

An additional advantage of betting with a draw is that it builds the pot, and can force the other players into giving you the correct odds to call their raises if they try to take control of the hand. As the size of the pot increases, you are more likely to be given the correct odds to call if the other player decides to bet and raise with a strong but vulnerable holding.

For example, we are in a hand with

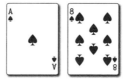

against one player, who is holding

The flop comes:

giving you the nut flush draw and the other player top pair with ten kicker. You are first to act and decide to bet $50 into the $100 pot. The other player with top pair decides to raise, but because they are a little inexperienced and want to protect their hand, they bump it *wrong*

$50 more. There is now $200 in the pot and you have to call a further $50 to win $200, giving us pot odds of 4:1. The odds of completing your flush by the next two cards are 4:1

This is an ideal situation that has arisen from a simple aggressive bet on the flop. Even though the semi-bluff did not work, you are still priced in to continue with the hand. If you did not bet on the flop and checked, your opponent may have come out betting around $50 or more into the pot himself, which would have given you the wrong pot odds (3:1). Although this looks like a wonderful situation, it happens frequently enough where you can influence the amount your opponent will bet to keep the pot odds in your favor.

Even in the above example, if you went on to check the turn and didn't make the flush, the other player may well still be scared about the strength of your hand and bet a small amount into the pot. This would still gain the correct pot odds to warrant a call. Because the pot is much larger, the other player will be making a much bigger mistake by giving you the correct odds, and thus you will be profiting from their bad play.

As always, the determining factor of probability is you. Learn how to play as a FTA. Practice it, embrace it, and make the best use of it. When the other players figure out what you're doing, discard it in favor of a more-profitable "style" that will earn you the probability a situational decision-maker deserves. Use your best judgment when deciding to try this strategy as I have many different approaches to try throughout this book.

CHAPTER TEN:

STEALING BLINDS AND SMALL POTS

Blind stealing is a term used in NL Texas Hold'em for when a player in late position raises pre-flop in a challenge to win the uncontested blinds. This play is often successful because the players in the blinds will have any two hit and miss cards, meaning there is a small chance that they will have a hand worth calling a raise with, permitting you to take their blinds. The first to act will be the players in the blinds and in order to call they need better than a mediocre hand to pay to see a flop.

There are two different positions to take when stealing blinds. You will have the opportunity to steal blinds from late position, and you will have players attempting to steal your blinds. So how should you play in both of these situations? The suggested plays are determined by whether you are playing in a tournament or a cash game.

When should I steal blinds?

Tournaments
Blind stealing is most effective in tournaments like Sit-n-Go's and Multi-Table Tournaments. If you are in need of chips, sometimes you simply cannot afford to wait for a premium hand.

As with all varieties of poker, I don't advocate instantly putting up $10,000 to enter a large buy-in event. Even though the strategies in this book are designed with these events in mind, it is still better to start in lower limits and work your way up gradually and thus building your skills. However, after you have successfully applied the strategies from the previous chapters and win a few low cost satellites that put you in one of these events, I certainly have no problem with that.

Blinds, Antes, and Tournament Structure

When you break down the science of tournament poker to its foundation, it's a battle for the blinds and antes. Usually, the current size of blinds and antes dictates how many hands you should play and also how much you should put into a hand. Let's do an unlikely example to get a full understanding this means. ⌐ of what

You are in a small casino tournament, playing NL Texas Hold'em that has no blinds or antes at all. In this present scenario, why would you want to play any hand unless it was A-A or K-K? You could fold every hand until you get premium hands and hope another player plays ball. If the other players have any common sense at all, they will be doing the same thing turning the game into a complete marathon lasting for weeks or even months. This is because the only cause for a flop, turn, and the river is multiple players holding A-A or K-K in the same hand. Odds say this rarely happens. Talk about one very long boring tournament!

Now let's look at a complete opposite from the previous scenario. This time you are playing in NL Texas Hold'em tournament that a single table. There are ten players and every player gets $5,000 in chips. The blinds are $2,000/$4,000 with $500 ante. Crazy as this example is, what hands could you rationalize folding in this present situation? Half of your stack goes toward the blinds and a good chunk to the ante, so if you fold you'll be all-in shortly. Chances are if you fold, everyone else will play mediocre hands. This extreme example would eliminate players rapidly and end the tournament rather quickly.

Neither of those extreme blind and ante structures make for an exciting poker game. Most televised tournaments will start you out with $10,000-$20,000 in poker chips and the blinds begin small, usually $25/$50 with no ante. Antes usually don't start until the fourth round. Here is a common basic blind and ante structure used:

Small Blind/Big Blind	Ante	Small Blind/Big Blind	Ante
$25/$50	None	$1,500/$3,000	$500
$50/$100	None	$2,000/$4,000	$500
$100/$200	None	$3,000/$6,000	$1,000
$100/$200	$25	$4,000/$8,000	$1,000
$150/$300	$25	$5,000/$10,000	$1,000
$200/$400	$50	$6,000/$12,000	$2,000
$300/$600	$75	$8,000/$16,000	$2,000
$400/$800	$100	$10,000/$20,000	$3,000
$500/$1,000	$100	$12,000/$24,000	$3,000
$600/$1,200	$200	$15,000/$30,000	$4,000
$1,000/$2,000	$300	$20,000/$40,000	$5,000
$1,200/$2,400	$400	$25,000/$50,000	$5,000

As you can see, the blinds and antes keep increasing until there is only one player left who has accumulated all of the chips. These levels last for varying time frames depending on which casino is running the tournament. Smaller tournaments will have levels moving quickly. Large buy-in tournaments can last for days; the W.S.O.P. main event has lasted nearly two weeks at times.

To hang onto your starting chip stack, you must win at least one set of blinds and antes per round. The blinds and antes keep increasing throughout the tournament, so folding often isn't going to cut it. Your starting chip stack will be in jeopardy, unless you fight to win more than your fair share of blinds and small pots.

Those premium hands are few and far between when large pots are at stake. In today's poker tournaments, the winner usually wins by staying aggressive, stealing blinds, and going after smaller pots. Practice and experience is the key for doing without becoming reckless. Hopefully, if you have read this far, you will have come to the conclusion of what it will take to become a consistent tournament winner.

Therefore, blind stealing offers a great opportunity for you to accumulate chips. However, at the start of these tournaments when the blinds are very low in relation to your stack, blind stealing becomes less beneficial. This is because the blinds are too small to be worth fighting over and the other players are more likely to call raises because of the blinds size in relation to their chip stack.

Cash Games

In cash games, the blinds are usually very diminutive in relation to your chip stack. This means that from a purely money making point of view, blind stealing is not going to be very profitable. In general, you want to stick to playing good hands and avoid gambling money with weaker ones.

Poker is a game that requires skill and a great deal of deception in order to win. By playing smart-aggressive, you can get far ahead of the other players in chip stack size and despite the fact of losing a few rounds here and there; you can still come out on top. However, blind stealing in cash games should be based on whether or not you feel you can easily out-play your opponents when they call. But be sure not to use this play on every orbit because the players in the blinds will become wary of your game. You may notice the size of pots in a cash game tend to be small. This is because only a few players are playing, which is also referred to as "tight poker."

Tight poker is not a game. It just means that whoever wins that night won't be bringing that much money home. Should we as poker players still play when this happens? The answer is yes. No matter how small the pot is, there is still money in it, and other players will still fight for it.

During such games, there will be a lot of checking. This is done in the hopes of catching a free card, when you have a drawing hand. Putting in a bet will certainly make the other players go on the offensive.

In some poker rooms, several different games will be played simultaneously. The player will not know what kind of game is being played until they are seated. If for some reason, you do not like the table you're at, a request can be made to be moved. This is allowed in land-based casinos. If these players are much more skilled than you, then transferring to a different table is a good idea. There is no reason to compete at higher levels if you are not prepared for it. I don't want you to be discouraged when you're at the casino because there is money to be made, but you want to make the money when it's suited to your advantages. However, should the players you find at a certain table be at a lower level of skill, then it is best to take advantage of the situation and get rich. And when playing online, you can just leave the table and find another one. On certain sites I recommend not jumping into the first table you find, you should watch a round played first, notice the average pot size and then determine if it suits your needs.

If as a poker player you are not able to win at a loose table, chances of wining against players who play for higher stakes are slim. It is best to start out playing low-limit first, to learn the basics and develop them before proceeding any further in higher stakes

The goal of any form of poker is still to win money. By finding the niche in the several different types of poker out there, playing as much poker as you possibly can and gaining experience, in time you should establish a name, just like those who are in the big leagues. Every single poker book will tell you to not play, or at the very least, to just play against poor players, when you are not feeling your best. In all honesty, this can't be argued with. Unfortunately, the reality is that for a lot of people who play poker, the only chance they may get is to play is for an hour or two in the evening. Other times, they are completely worn out from working all day and enjoy playing poker to unwind.

How should I play against people stealing my blinds?

As a general rule, you should not actively attempt to protect your blinds on every round. You must remember that you are going to be first to act against anyone who tries to steal your blind, so if you call and don't hit the flop the way you hoped for, what are you going to do? If you check, are you going to re-raise his continuation bet (which is very likely) in a challenge to re-steal the pot? Or, are you going to bluff at the pot when first to act?

During the game, you will have no idea what the other player has and you are risking a decent amount trying to take down a small pot. Information is vital and without knowing anything about the other players' hands, protecting your blinds isn't going to be profitable in the long run. Bear in mind that after you have posted your blind, they are no longer your chips. The chips now belong to the pot and not to you. This is the reason why many players lose chips to raises when in the blinds since they believe it still belongs to them, and they have to defend it.

In certain situations however, you can effectively frighten the other player out of pilfering your blinds on future betting rounds. If you sense a player is betting in late position in an attempt to steal, a decent re-raise on your part will make them think twice about trying to steal on future rounds. Even if the other player does call your re-raise, the fact that you made that play shows that you have the capability to those who steal blinds. This play is most valuable when the blinds are small in relation to your stack, as you are not risking much and there is no forced commitment to the pot.

There are many ways of mixing up and improving your NL Texas Hold'em game. Here is one play I added to my game a long time ago and it has really improved my game. It's "Stealing Small Pots."

I began with only betting the flop when I had top pair. I wasn't betting without top pair, no matter what the conditions.

If there were 1 or 2 limpers and I was holding:

and the flop:

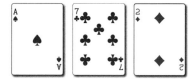

I was absolutely happy to just check. I had nothing. Why would I want to bet that flop? I bet that flop now because I want to steal that small pot. Stealing a lot of these small pots that nobody else wants will significantly increase your game.

Of course, there is a time and place for everything and this is no exception. There are certain criteria that I look for before making this play. Normally, I like there to be 3-4 people in the pot with one Broadway (face) card and no obvious draws. If I get called, I don't want to be tempted to bet again at the turn because I think the other player may be on a draw. I'll give you some examples of when this is a brilliant play.

Examples:

If you have:

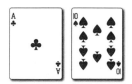

on the button, and limp after another player limps and both blinds play.

The flop is

with no flush or straight draw. If it gets checked to you, bet. When I say I bet, I'm suggesting that you bet the pot. If the pot is $20, then bet $20. It's doubtful that anyone has a king or they would have bet. If you get called, in most cases, you're done with the hand.

In middle position you limp in with

The button limps and the Big Blind checks.

The flop comes:

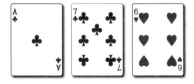

If the Big Blind checks, you bet the pot most times here. If the button doesn't have an ace, he's not going to call and you steal another small pot with nothing.

There are tons of other assortments of hands and flops where the same play will work. Remember that you have to bet the pot here. If you bet $40 into a $300 pot, you're just looking to get check-raised by someone who probably has nothing themselves. Believe me, if you pick the right times to make this play, the bet that is the size of the pot will be successful 75% of the time or more.

This play will also work in reverse. If you are the Big Blind make a pot sized bet and take it down.

Here's another example. You are the Big Blind with:

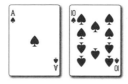

The flop is:

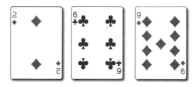

If there are only two other limpers in the pot, I will fire out a pot-sized bet. You would be surprised how often this bet takes down the pot. Of course, if someone calls, most of the time you will have to surrender unless a ten or ace hits the turn.

If you want to give this a try, here is what I suggest. Keep a little tally sheet beside your computer and keep track of all these bets for a few months.

I tracked how many times I made a "steal bet," how often it worked, and the total results of these bets. If I bet $10 and took down the $18.60 pot then I got credited with +$18.60. If I bet $5 and ended up folding, I marked -$5.00.

Remember that only hands where you would normally check it around count for these calculations. If you bet with nothing, but then pick up something at the turn that makes you continue with the hand, that doesn't count. If you bet a flush draw or a gut-shot draw, that doesn't count. You only get to count hands where you are truly betting with nothing.

I stopped tracking this after 3 months when I was satisfied with my results. I was successful approximately 76% of the time and the total amount of money I won with these hands accounted for about 18% of my total winnings. This was pure profit with hands that I used to just check until someone else bet in which case I folded. At the present time, I steal these pots that nobody else wants; you should do the same.

When you get really good at identifying these opportunities, you can start limping in when you are in last position with all kinds of hands for the sole purpose of stealing the pot if nobody bets. You'll get check-raised once in a while when you bet so much, but since you are never showing your cards, other players don't know you are betting with nothing. Most NL Texas Hold'em players will not check-raise you without a real hand, so you can fold to the check-raise and just move on to the next hand.

❝Acting is Hollywood. It's an American dream. If you asked just about anybody and said, 'Would you become an actor if given the opportunity?' Everyone would say yes. Why not? It would be an ideal. It would be an interesting opportunity. But I have other interests as well. ❞

—*Chris Moneymaker, 2003 W.S.O.P. Champion, his victory is credited for being one of the main catalysts for today's poker boom.*

CHAPTER ELEVEN:

BLUFFING

In NL Texas Hold'em, to bluff is to bet or raise with a mediocre hand. This is a useful tool for any poker player, because it can cause other players to believe the bluffing player has a premium hand, causing them to fold. The bluffing player then steals the pot. By extension, the terms are often used outside the context of poker to describe the acts of pretending to have knowledge one does not have, or making threats one cannot execute.

Bluffing is an art form in high-stake games. The higher you go into the poker hierarchy, the harder it is bluff. Bluffing is a skill that is difficult to master and is something you plan at the beginning of a hand, adjusting your play from the start. You don't bluff a hand on the River or the Turn. Good players will realize something is wrong with the betting patterns, and most will take advantage of this. Proper bluffing technique is an attitude you apply as you start the hand. In your mind, you say, "If I miss this flop, I will attempt to steal the pot." Now this may sound easy, but it is not. Most players do not have the ability to realize when this type of bluffing can be utilized.

Obviously, just because you say you will bluff the pot, does not mean you will always succeed. Realizing or learning when the opportunity is right will help you to be more successful at bluffing. People do not realize how important bluffing is at the higher stakes. The number one prerequisite to become a great bluffer is to become a great value bettor.

This can also sound easy, but it is not. Great bluffers and great value bettors are also great readers of hands.

Value betting is what makes great bluffers. Having people call with sub-par hands means the person betting is dictating the game. Eventually, the other players get tired of calling with second pair or bottom pair, or even Ace high. This is why the best players are also the best bluffers and the best hand readers. This is why betting is preferred to calling. This also shows why position plays such a great part in the play.

Bluffing is not as important an issue in low-limit games, because there are too many people in the pot and less chance a bluff succeeding. Smaller stake games are more of a made hand showdowns. In games like this, you tend to adapt a style that eliminates bluffing. Seldom does an opportunity in low-limit present itself for a pot to be bluffed, but the opportunities do occasionally arise. Most players do not mind losing $25 or even $50 to take a shot at a large pot because these are not significant amounts. Simple examples of obvious bluffing can be found in many of the Pot Limit and NL tournaments.

When having this starting hand:

The flop comes:

With several players in the pot and a person from an opening position leads out for a small percentage of the pot, this is likely an indication of a weak hand. Many times in these scenarios, you will notice four or five way action. There may be five people in the pot for $20, making the pot $100. All of a sudden, the person in front leads out with a $20 bet. What kind of bet is this? You should get into the habit of asking yourself, "What kind of a hand would you have to hold to make a bet like this?" Does it make sense in regards to the types of cards on the board and the type of player making the bet? We have gone down in the rank a little ways, actually a long ways, to show you an illustration of a bluff. When a player bets $20 like this, most of the players will call, unless one makes a play at the pot.

Obviously, the possibility is present that some player might be slow-playing, but the other possibility is also that this player is giving away a cheap card. No, you do not have to have position in this hand as you can steal from the front or the back. Just call and see what the next card brings. A card that would not seem to help could be a very advantageous card. Have you ever seen a player come out betting $20 again, and getting several callers again? This is a great opportunity to make a move on the pot, whether you are in the front, (where you checked and now raised), or the back (where you now raise).

You do not even have to raise that much; a pot size bet should do the trick. Even if you are called, it is odds-on for the person is on the right of you, thus you will know the safe cards that will allow you to follow through on your bluff. Watch how many times players make bets like this at the poker tables. Truthfully speaking, these bets do not exist. They are just pointless because if you are sitting with anything why give any indication? Moreover, if you have anything and wish to protect it, you would obviously bet the pot. Now betting the pot in a position like this really does not give much away. The hard thing or shall we say the stupid thing, is to be stone bluffing the pot from the front position. This situation will seldom if ever occur, so you might as well forget the possibility.

Many people having a pair, without much experience, attempt a maneuver to slow down the action and get a cheap card. This maneuver is doomed to fail if anyone in the game can play at all. This is one of the most obvious bluffs in these low-limit games. The higher skilled bluffing will occur in a different manner. A player may sense weakness from a limper or several limpers and raise a pot size bet, knowing he is attempting to steal the pot if he misses the flop. Now bluffing is not for everyone. Many players can attempt a bluff but the real bluffers will follow through.

A better card reader will realize this attempt has been made and will have the nerve or the confidence in his ability to realize this. He or she will follow through and proceed to re-raise or go all in, with nothing but his gut feeling telling him he is making the correct play. Have any of you given much thought when a sizable bet is made pre-flop and you hold:

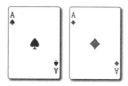

Is it correct to go all-in at this time? If you are guaranteed a call, this is always acceptable. If you will not get a call then why raise? Allow the to have the lead and bluff the money off, thinking he is betting the best hand. Players are always far more eager to bet their chips off, rather than to call.

The main mistake made by players who bluff in Pot Limit and NL Texas Hold'em games is the amount they bet. Use the following as a normal guideline for bluffing. What if the blinds are $25-$50 and you opened for $150 and received a call. If you miss and intend to bluff, follow through with a bet equal to the pot. Also, use this as a guide for betting when you do flop a big hand. The main emphasis of thought for betting and bluffing is thinking like the player who is facing you. If he bets, think of what you would do with what type of hand, and adjust to the play. Consider how other players see you in this pot. Think of what your image is in the other players' mind. If a pot has been checked around to you on the flop and turn throw out a pot sized bet to claim the money. It is hard for the other players to call that bet with a mediocre hand; they will think that you slow-played a great hand on the flop or completed a draw on the turn. Do not wait until the river if you checked the flop.

Certain Types of Bluffs:
Pure Bluff
A pure bluff, or stone-cold bluff, is a bet or raise with a mediocre hand that has little or no chance of improving. A player making a pure bluff believes he can win the pot only if all the other players fold. The pot odds for a bluff are the ratio of the size of the bluff to the pot. A pure bluff has a positive expectation (will be profitable in the long run) when the probability of being called by the other player is less than the pot odds for the bluff. For example, suppose that after all the cards are on the table, a player is holding a hand that missed the flush. He decides that the only way to win the pot is to make a pure bluff. If the player bets the size of the pot with the expectation with the probability of being called is less than 50%. Note, however, that the other player may also consider the pot odds when making a decision whether to call. In this example, the other player will be facing 2 to 1 pot odds. The other player will have a positive expectation for calling the bluff if the other player believes the chance of the other player is bluffing is at least 33%.

Semi-bluff
In games with several betting rounds, to bluff on one round with an inferior or drawing hand that might improve in a later is referred as a semi-bluff. A player making a semi-bluff can win the pot two different ways: by all the players folding immediately, or by hitting a card to improve his hand. In some cases, a player may be on a draw but with odds strong enough that he is favored to win the hand. In this case, his bet is not classified as a semi-bluff even though his bet may force the other players to fold hands with better current strength.

Examples of Bluffing and Semi-Bluffing
I'm going to try to give you two good examples of using bluffs and semi-bluffs. There are a variety of times when both of these would be acceptable, but these in particular, stand out to me.

Bluff Examples:

A common bluff is that you are on the button and a couple of tight players check to you on the flop. The board has no draws and it is either Ace or King high such as:

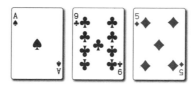

A bet here could win the pot regardless of what you have, since they are unlikely to chase if you already have a pair of Aces.

Another would be if the board comes back with all rags (low cards) and you are one of the blinds. Coming right out with a bet or check-raise in late position player would be a decent bluff example.

Another good example of a bluff would be to raise or check raise someone if the board pairs on the turn card. It will be very unlikely that they will want to call since they assume you already have three of a kind.

Another bluff I like to make, if I have a good read on a player, is that they have missed their flush draw or straight draw. Often I will win by merely betting my broken flush draw against theirs.

Semi-Bluff Examples:

Here is a semi-bluff that I put on another player a few days ago. I had:

and there were a few people in pre-flop. The big blind raised. He was actually a tight, decent player, so I figured he had A-K or better (A-A or K-K, maybe Q-Q). The flop came:

He came out betting and I called. The other players folded. The turn card paired the board:

He came out betting again. I was about to just call, but a little voice in my head was screaming "raise," so I did and he thought for a while and graciously folded. Normally, I would semi-bluff on the flop by raising my flush draw as long as it wouldn't cut off too many players behind me (I want them in the hand). I didn't semi-bluff in this case on the flop, because it was likely he would make it three bets. The turn card brought a perfect opportunity to semi-bluff. The reason was that it clearly shows the ways it can win, by having the other player fold right then or on a later round. My guess was that he would fold, but if he called, I still had the chance to catch my flush. He may have just called with two over cards and then if he missed on the river and I bet, he would most likely fold. Most people semi-bluff when they have an open-ended straight draw or a flush draw. Those are good moves, but don't do it if it cuts off people behind you.

In other cases, you may want to raise in order to cut players off. Here is an example of a semi-bluff I made in another game that same night. I wanted to raise to limit the other players in the hand. I had:

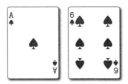

and someone raised from the small blind (another tight player). I was sure he had a big pair (A-A, K-K, and Q-Q).

The flop came:

My turn was after the pre-flop raiser, so when he bet, I raised. I did that because I actually wanted to limit the competition behind me because it might improve my chances of winning if an Ace hit. My six kicker wasn't great, so the fewer players, and the better. As it turned out, I lost that hand because neither the flush nor the Ace hit, but I was correct in that if my Ace did hit, it would have beat his Q-Q. I could also potentially semi-bluff again if the turn card brought:

This makes it seem as if I was holding quad 10's. If he had bet again, I would most certainly have raised again, since it would be very hard for him to call my raise, even with him having pocket queens.

Moderation/Timing is Very Important

Knowing when to bluff and semi-bluff is very important. Winning a pot feels awesome, but stealing one feels a hundred times better, and that feeling is addicting. Don't get too ambitious and bluff all your money away. A few tips are as follows: a bluff works best when you know that the person you are playing against thinks you have a certain hand. Bluffs work best when you are playing a good player instead of a poor one. They also work best on later rounds when the blinds have increased, or if you are only playing one other player. Be careful in trying to bluff really big pots, since most people won't fold under any circumstance in that situation. Both bluffs and semi-bluffs will present themselves by the quality of the game, the other players, your table image, and of course, the cards. When everyone sees you always showing down really strong hands (which they should), you are in the perfect position to bluff them. Remember, once you start bluffing a hand, don't show any weakness. If find yourself bluffing on the turn and get called. You might even prefer betting again on the river instead of checking. If you get called, then it just cost you one bigger bet and you actually get to show that you were bluffing as opposed to checking and giving him a chance to bluff you off a costly hand.

How Often Should You Bluff and Semi-Bluff?

Bluffing shouldn't be a big part of your game in low-limit Texas Hold'em since most of the players are too stubborn to fold. I can go a number of sessions without bluffing at all since the games are usually loose to begin with. Semi-bluffing is totally different and I use it as often as possible, being limited by what cards I get, of course. You should note that if the players are bad, it takes away one way of winning with the semi-bluff: them folding to your bluff. I think that these same moves transfer over into what is called "betting for value" so they are still effective (just for a different reason). I'll explain what that means below. I guess the best answer for how often you should pure bluff is, as often as you can get away with it. That isn't very often in low-limit Texas Hold'em so exercise some caution.

When You Shouldn't Bluff and Semi-Bluff

A bad time to try any bluff, is when the players are really poorly skilled, since it is unlikely you can win by betting them out of a pot. Don't try to bluff into more than a couple of players unless you are feeling lucky. Lastly, I think bluffing into large pots rarely ever works in your favor.

The Opposite of Bluffing (Betting for Value)

Betting for value is when you think you have the best hand and you want to make the other players pay you off. Seems like what you normally do, right? It kind of is, but there is a difference. Sometimes, the cards turn out to be really terrifying, but the player your up against is so bad that you still figure you're have him beat, so you go ahead and bet anyway just to make more money. For example, you bet the whole way into him with:

  and a

comes on the river or, the board pairs. Since he is such a bad player, he could literally have any hand, so I put in another bet instead of checking. In this case, you'll want to be betting more for value and less on pure bluffs. The opposite holds true in tighter high-limit games. You'll make more bluffs, because your good hands will be making you less money, since their skill allows them to dodge more of your bullets.

Benefits of the Semi-Bluff

If you raise on the turn card with a flush or straight draw you had on the flop and then catch it on the river, players will be distressed. This exemplifies semi-bluffing and how it can give your poker game a new and higher level of deception. Deception means cash, so pay attention to that. A semi-bluff can also buy you free cards from apprehensive players. If you raise in late position with a flush or straight draw, it is very likely they will check to you on the turn giving you the chance to also check and take a "free" card to the river. Semi-bluffing takes the initiative away from the other players and gives it to you. You take control of the pot and then they are calling you. That has lots of benefits in and of itself.

A player who bluffs and sometimes uses semi-bluffs wins more than players who don't bluff at all. In your progression as a player, more opportunities will present themselves because your view of the game will be sharper. Until then, I would go easy on the bluffing unless you find a particularly good money making situation. When you do bluff and get picked off (someone calls) don't feel bad. There is value in that move as well. It is called "advertising" and it will most likely get you more action later on your good hands.

Poker players love to catch other players bluffing and it turns them into "calling stations" (a person who calls too much when they shouldn't). Semi-bluffing on the other hand, I would recommend using in your game as much as you feel comfortable doing so. It is a very powerful tool that will turn you from being a tight, book smart player into an ass-kicking poker connoisseur. Knowing how and when not to use these plays will decide whether or not you can fool around with the pros.

CHAPTER TWELVE:

JUST FOLD!

When you're playing poker, one of the most challenging things to do is fold. Almost all poker players think they can draw a winner or they think their pair is always the superior. It becomes even more daunting to fold a good hand. The reason you would fold a good hand is when you know you are beaten.

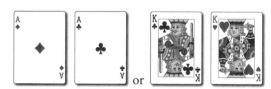

Most players hold onto the above cards regardless of what comes up on the flop. Players hold onto losing hands even though they know they are probably behind in the hand. It is very difficult to fold, but it is something you must be trained to do if you want to be a successful poker player.

When you have the second best hand at the poker table, you are going to lose. Be aware that you need to fold this hand; its one of the devices of a good player. It takes guts to lay down a hand you know is a loser, but sometimes it must be done. What we need to do when playing NL Texas Hold'em poker is to not play those troublesome hands at all.

A starting hand like either of these two is just looking for trouble down the road:

The kickers are just too weak to win a late hand showdown. Avoiding these starting hands is a good way to avoid misfortune and have your chip stack intact. When playing poker, you are not always going to know right away that your hand is weak, but after the flop you should have a better idea. The biggest problem that many players have is getting rid of what was a strong hand, but has turned into a weak one. This is a frustrating situation at times, but knowing how to approach this is the key to having a far greater advantage against most players you come across.

Remember those aces and kings we discussed earlier? If you happen to hit your set on the flop you are in great shape, but on the turn another flush card comes up that makes it four-flushed on the board. How good does that set look now? You are now almost assured that someone has the flush and you have been beaten.

You have to fold your set. Folding hands that should have been winners but now look like losers is one of the tougher things to do when playing poker. Let's say you have those aces again and the flop is:

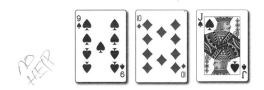

Now there is a straight draw possibility right off the flop, and if the turn card is a 6, 7, 8, Queen, King or Ace, it is almost a given that one of the other players has a straight and your aces are done. You still might be ahead in the hand, but you are sure not going to feel very confident. If someone did hit the straight, you have lost the hand and will be throwing your valuable chips away. If you are fortunate enough to see a king and a queen show up on the turn and the river, you can win the pot with an ace-high straight or possibly split it with another player.

The biggest obstacle almost all poker players face is that they want to be in on the action and play their hand. Poker is a game where patience usually prevails. Most players that you will run into just never get past the fact that by **not playing** the bad hands they are dealt, they are actually giving themselves more chances to win. This is the optimal situation to be in, rather than trying to bluff with bad cards.

Folding every single bad hand and resisting the urge to play mediocre hands in marginal situations is one of the most profitable moves a player has in all types of poker. The greatest impact on a player's bottom line is not folding in less profitable situations. If you want to win money playing poker you must make playing only the profitable hands your number one priority.

It is a wonderful thing if the other players have a great tendency to overplay their cards. When you have the advantage, you are in a profitable situation and can reap immense profits by the other player's misplaying their hands. The more the other players keep playing these bad hands, the more they contribute to the pot, the more profit you can make from them.

Most inexperienced players not only misunderstand the odds of the game they are playing, but also make their situation even worse by having a tendency to enjoy gambling it up until their chips have disappeared. With this mentality, they think that every hand "can" win, but most players just do not understand the mathematics of hand equity. This can also be best described as the overall outcome of playing a given hand in a certain way and its overall addition to their profit or loss while playing.

Since you don't want to be the sucker, but you want the other players to become one, it makes sense that you do not want to continue playing your mediocre hands and contribute to other players' chip stacks. You need to get into your head that the most important thing you should be doing at the table is folding, folding, and yes even more folding. This is particularly pertinent whenever it is not to your advantage to play the cards you're dealt. On average, aside from paying the blinds (or antes) you should only be looking to play about 3 in 20 hands and sometimes you will play fewer. This holds true for certain cash games as well.

Many players will get tired of folding and begin playing mediocre hands, just to be in on the action. I cannot stress enough how important it is not to do this. This is exactly why many good players never make it to the money in tournaments. By doing this, they will have horrible swings at the cash tables and end up watching all the chips disappear from their stack. You must be more disciplined than this, because playing bad hands is just like throwing money and chips away into a garbage disposal.

So finally, you get that good hand that you have been waiting for, possibly pocket Queens or Kings. You will definitely be playing this hand and should raise with it as well. The flop comes:

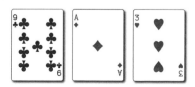

Someone ahead of you bets a decent size bet on the flop. What do you think you should do? You might think, I have been waiting so long for this hand and like hell am I going to just give it away now. You also might be kidding yourself by assuming the other player is trying to bluff you.

In almost every single case, your pair of queens is beaten. You must react with intelligence and toss your queens away. They might have been ahead pre-flop, but after that flop it's just not profitable to keep playing the hand to find out. If you were to call and keep up this behavior of "hoping your hand is still good," you will continue to lose more chips over time.

You would be playing the part of the sucker in this situation. If you held the Aces here, you would love a pair of Queens calling you down. It was a good hand, but the key thing is that it **was** a good hand and is now *not* a good hand.

Separating the top poker players from amateurs is knowing when it's time to lay it down and when to follow through with it. The impatient amateur wants to win the hand so badly that they override their own judgment and play the second-best hand anyway.

Let me further show you this strategy and you decide if it makes sense to you. Folding when you are at a disadvantage will save you at least one bet on average, if not more. Every time you fold in bad situations, tell yourself that you just made a bet. This is actually a true statement, because you will be simply waiting it out until you have the advantage on another player. By doing this, you can now capitalize even more in this situation. This is because you have more chips to use on the other player and have him pay you off, when he misplays their hand. If you take advantage of all the correct opportunities to fold during an hour of play, you give yourself the chance to either save a lot of bets or waste the bets. In my opinion, a bet saved is another bet you could make when it's more advantageous to do so. This results in more money in your bankroll at the end of the day...

I hope you take to heart all that you have read in this chapter and understand what a power play it is to fold bad hands. On a side note, it should be mentioned that my motivation for writing this particular chapter came from watching the 2007 World Series of Poker Final table coverage. A very aggressive player (Jerry Yang, the event's champion) was playing hand after hand and making large bets pre-flop. This in turn caused an unusual set of events to occur. It made many of the other players at the table nervous and off their normal steady game, causing them to become aggressive and loose as well. In this case, it was at their own demise as he eliminated every player from that final table by himself, except for one. Amazingly enough he did this successfully while he was one of the small stacks at the table. This is very impressive for a player with limited experience. He was still able to pull this off against players whom were at the final table with a vast combination of skills and experience.

The reason I bring this up in a chapter about folding is that halfway through the coverage one of the announcers just happened to realize how the eventual runner-up Tuan Lam was playing and exclaimed "Tuan Lam appears to be folding his way up the money list..."

and he was right! Tuan Lam took advantage of Jerry Yang's aggressive play and the effect it was having on the other players. By folding all of his marginal hands and not entering into any of these pots, he actually made hundreds of thousands of dollars before he even played his first final table hand. Can you just take a second and imagine that?

Here are the final money list results:

- Jerry Yang – $8,250,000
- Tuan Lam – $ 4,840,981
- Raymond Rahme – $ 3,048,025
- Alex Kravchenko – $1,852,721
- John Kalmar – $1,255,069
- Hevad Khan – $956,243
- Lee Childs - $705,229
- Lee Watkinson - $585,699
- Phillip Hilm - $525,934

Isn't that just amazing? By tuning in to the temperature and tempo of the players around him, he not only folded his way into greater and greater riches, he ended up winning $4 million dollars more than the players knocked out before he played a hand. Astonishing, but true and it will apply to most poker tournaments out there. Once you have passed that money bubble and are "in the money," folding is even more important and profitable as you take advantage of every single player playing bad hands. Every person out is another step up the money ladder for you. I hope you use this information to improve your play and finish in tournaments.

Folding is not an easy thing to do, but you have to recognize when you are probably holding the second best hand. Professional poker players seem to know this more often than average players. If you want to get to that level of expertise, you always have to be aware of the board, and understand when you should **JUST FOLD**!

PART FOUR

SHARK
Advanced Strategy

CHAPTER THIRTEEN:

MEDIUM BALL PHILOSOPHY

After reading this chapter, you as a poker player will be able to chip away at the other players by slowly gaining chips without anyone noticing. According to Daniel Negreanu, Phil Ivey, Erick Lindgren, Ted Forrest, Phil Hellmuth, and other top pros, this strategy is called "small ball."

They attack amateurs by playing various hands that prey on these new recreational players' lack of expertise in post-flop play. By doing this, they steadily increase their chip stacks without taking much risk at all. Before the other players realize, it's too late. They are simply short-stacked and crippled. Meanwhile, the "small ball" players have large chip stacks and are making it complete hell for all the other players at the table.

Here is my solution. I'm calling it "medium ball." It has various weapons to defend yourself from "small ball" players, and therefore gives you a chance to take professional players down as busting them to the rail is the main objective here. After you apply this strategy, the money you paid for this book will be money well spent; hopefully, the best $ 25.00 you've ever invested.

These professional poker players are playing your hand instead of focusing on theirs. Basically, this creates extra imaginary outs that aren't there. By playing the flop, turn, and the river, they're guessing what cards you don't have and are making large bets to make you fold. More times than not you probably have a better hand than they do. But, for whatever reason, they insist on applying severe pressure in hopes to break you down.

There are several ways to fight this approach. Blinds and antes are of the utmost importance in tournaments. If you won every ante and blind steal, you would win every tournament. So, raising with a large bet pre-flop is a big deterrent to "small ball" players. I'm not saying go all-in every chance you get, but let's make something clear. A nuisance bet of the amount of the blinds is not going to stop a poker pro from taking your chips. You must make a larger than the "normal" pre-flop bet, and this going to help you in the long run.

The other concern we have here is letting small pots go uncontested. Now it's time to stop the small time crooks that win small pots uncontested. These unthinkable acts are going to be the bread and butter for a "medium ball" philosophy. Hopefully, these lessons will stop them in their tracks. Let's get started with "Medium Ball."

How We Should Play Starting Hands using Medium Ball:

Now that you have a loaded gun, let's not be reckless here. Maintaining your chip stack is of the utmost importance, and you will need to steal or win one set of blinds and antes each round. Let's go over the various hands you will come across in playing poker.

A-K: Big Slick and A-Q: Big Sister

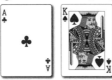

Use caution with these hands, as they are usually over-valued. In a coin flip, they will lose to a

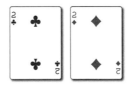

They're great when you flop a pair or let you make Broadway. Other than that, not much excitement comes from these hands. You should think the same about Big Slick's sister:

This is such a bad hand, I've heard Doyle "Texas Dolly" Brunson say "I fold A-Q every time no matter what," on T.V. There is a lot of truth to that comment. If you were to tally up how much money you lost versus how much money you won with this hand, the loss would be greater. I can say from experience that I have lost more than I won. It seems to always come down to this, when holding A-Q and you flop a pair of aces, someone else will usually have A-K, giving them the higher kicker.

Average Pairs

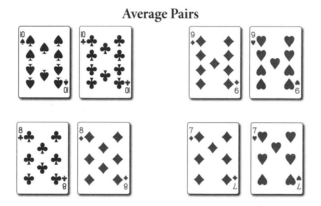

When you are dealt these hands there are many things to consider, so don't overvalue them! Have a little faith in them because of their potential, but not as starting strength. When playing medium pocket pairs, your main goal is to flop a set. These hands are vulnerable because there are many over-cards to dominate your medium pair. Consider pocket tens for example. They seem like a great hand pre-flop, and they are. Unfortunately, all it takes is a single Ace, King, Queen, or Jack to beat your pair of tens on the flop.

Most players play face cards, so it is likely that one of the other players has made a pair higher than yours. A great situation for your pair of tens is when three unsuited rag cards come on the flop, such as 7-2-9. Be sure to bet out because the other player may have a straight draw. You probably have the other players beaten, and they could be willing to put in a sizeable bet if they're holding a hand like 9-A, which is a common hand you'll be up against in Texas Hold'em.

When you do flop a set with your pocket pair, you need to properly assess the flop before you decide how much to bet. Many players will try to slow play this hand or check-raise it. Check-raising is common in low-limit games, but it really shouldn't be a big part of your strategy. It probably won't intimidate the other players as much, and if the other player raised pre-flop, you're probably better off making a bet so he can try to steal it from you. You can then re-raise him and get as much money in the pot as possible. When you have more than a couple of players in the hand with you, you'll usually get a call and sometimes a raise, so you should bet out with your set. Analyze the possibilities of the flop, and if there are two suited or connecting cards, you definitely don't want to give the other player a free card that could complete his draw. You also shouldn't bet a small amount, or you'll be making it statistically correct for the other player to call. At minimum bet the pot and you'll be making him go against the pot odds to draw.

Never go all-in with any average pair; it will take a better hand than one pair to win a big pot worth justifying an all-in. If faced with a large re-raise, FOLD! Wait for a better hand to justify calling a large re-raise.

Ace X Suited

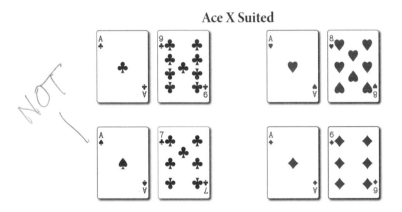

These starting hands are my second favorite to play in this game. "Nut flushes" are the real importance of these hands. There is nothing better than busting someone on a set of Aces or a Broadway straight when your Ace-X suited hand has the "nut flush."

Not only does the Ace kicker help you to win small pots, the rag-end of your Ace-X suited gives you a great chance of a straight flush, which is great for taking down a Full house or Quads.

One last thing to mention is that when you have great position at the table these hands let you see a "free card" when everyone checks before you, making it even easier for you to get a "nut flush."

Baby Pairs

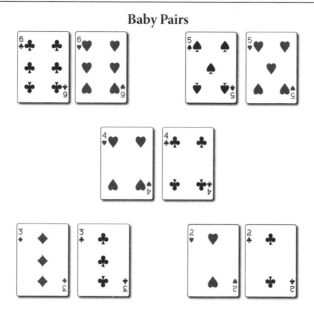

These hands are only good if conditions are optimal, like if you flop a set on the flop, turn, or river. Most of the time, you usually are running into an over pair, and it's not worth losing hard-earned chips over. The best thing about these hands is that in a showdown. They beat:

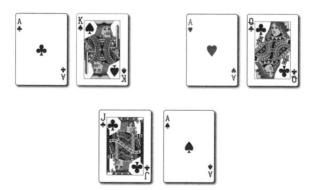

Otherwise I suggest waiting for stronger hands.

Garbage Hands

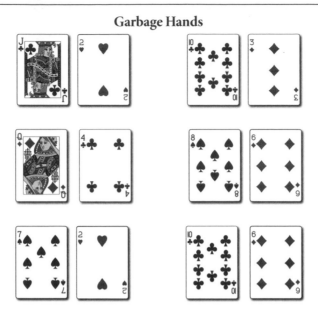

These hands are the worst and folding should be your immediate reaction. The only time not to do so is if everyone folds, the blinds are cheap, and the players are playing extremely tightly. These hands could probably win a blind steal. I advise you not to try to make a living playing these certain hands.

Aces and Face Cards

10 not a face card

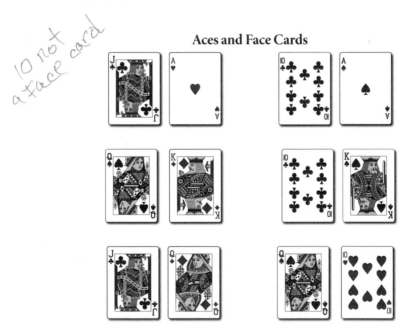

These starting hands have more power than you thought, and thus are my all-time favorite. In a five year span of playing cash and tournaments, these starting hands have earned me the most money and chips. Top pairs are created by these starting hands after the flop, so bet to protect your hand in this situation. Often enough, someone with a smaller pair will pay you off. These hands rarely make flushes or straights. The real importance of these hands is to steal blinds and antes. Also, when you make a pair with a high kicker, you will be in great position to take down small pots. This is how we beat professional poker players: by stealing blinds, antes, and small pots before they do.

Suited Connected Hands

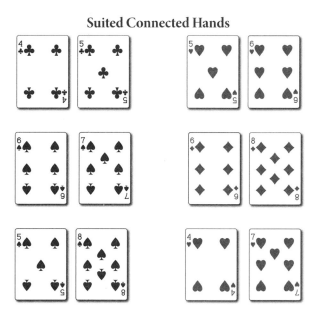

Before you read this book, these are the type of hands that you probably lost to or folded. These hands are easy to fold but when you flop something nice, they turn into a monster quickly. Let's say you have:

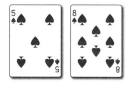

So you limp into the pot. The flop comes:

This is perfect, because some guy will always have an ace, or A-K, A-Q, or A-J. This player can't wait to pay you off. By getting the set of 5's, he just made your day by playing a hand that was cheap to get into, and will increase the size of your chip stack.

King and Queen X Suited

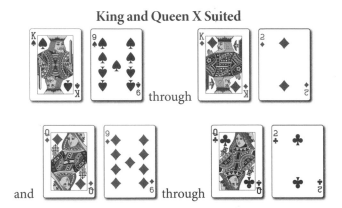

through

and through

These hands are "trouble makers." Never raise with them pre-flop. The best thing about these hands is their potential of flopping two pair. Sometimes they become the nuts when an ace (same suit) shows up on the board. When this happens, it gives you my favorite hand, the "nut flush." The big blind and small blind can play these starting hands, but be ready to fold to a raise on the flop unless two pair or a "nut flush" opportunity presents itself.

Another thing you might want to consider with these hands is that you can limp in with them, because there are multi-way pots to play for. In playing poker, I've had some success doing this. If you don't hit the flop, fold and get out of the hand cheaply. But remember, the most important thing is to never raise pre-flop with these hands.

Premium Pairs

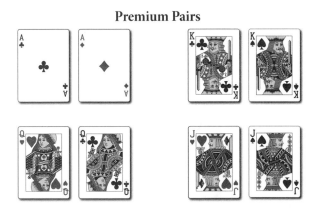

Disguise these hands as much as you can. Slow playing these hands works well. Setting traps is what you need to do with these hands. Get paid off for these hands, as they don't come by often enough.

Pre-Flop Betting Practices Using Medium Ball

Medium ball is a completely different approach to playing NL Texas Hold'em. The hands you're going to play aren't going to be that important. To be successful In NL Texas Hold'em, you must play poker not "cards." To gain confidence as a poker player, these factors play such a role in this strategy. Visualize this thought: Medium ball isn't so much about the hands we choose to play. More important is the amount we choose to bet.

After applying these concepts to your poker game, you will be able to learn how to win more pots by betting less. Most importantly, I'm going to show you how to get away with playing extra hands pre-flop without draining you chip stack.

The hands you decide to get involved with must have a 2× the big blind bet pre-flop. For example, if the blinds are $150/$300, bet $600 pre-flop. Keep the pots small during the pre-flop stage of the hand and minimize the number of players in the hand.

By doing this, you will take down more pots in the long run with minimal risk. Most players will fold and wait for a better hand. By betting 2× the big blind every time you enter the pot, odds will play out in your favor because most of the time players at the table are basically "playing cards." Hopefully, once you've read this far, you have played enough hands to realize the truth in the last statement.

You are going to target weak players first, and you will exploit the others when you are in position. When the dealer button has passed you twice, you have seen enough ways to identify who at the table will be your victim. If a certain player is limping into a lot of hands, this should be a clear indication of what you are looking for. Weak players who are playing way too many hands, will be some of the easiest opportunities to earn chips. It will become more obvious as you watch what they do. Are they playing poker or playing cards?

Is their post-flop play as straight forward as their hole cards? Are they checking and folding when they miss? These are situations we are looking for. You may also hit a real hand often enough to win a really big pot that way as well. Some weaknesses are very subtle, while others are more complex. Identifying and then taking advantage of them is one of the key differences between a real poker player and a card player.

Stopping the small ball player with this approach is the main objective here. If they were to raise 2× the blind, consider making it a re-raise 5× the blind. If they fold, you just made a great steal and won. Do this only enough to cover your blinds and antes for that round. If I lost 3 hands ago on a pre-flop raise, then the next average hand I get, I will usually bet 5× the blinds pre-flop. By doing this you will win your money back. One of the greatest advantages of playing "medium ball" is that you always tend to stay above the blinds each round. As time goes on, you will be the chip leader before you know it. There is one thing to remember is to not get cocky with this approach because it can backfire, particularly when some other player gets lucky.

Making Reads on the Other Players and What to Look For

As you can tell by now, most of your efforts should be figuring out the other players and the physical tells they might be portraying. When you are not in a hand, try to spend some of your energy on playing a "guessing" game. What I mean by this is, try to guess what the other players' cards are. I do this when I am not in a hand, and it is a lot of fun. With practice I have become very good at it and with time so can you.

Watching for physical tells is a strange science because your mind sometimes sees things that aren't there. Pay attention to betting patterns and try to remember what cards the other player lays down on the river. Put that hand with what they bet along the way and in a matter of time you will be able to read them like a stop sign.

As you play and keep playing, your mind will have a huge database of hands. Listening to your subconscious is a great way to pick up on tells. Players call this playing with a gut feeling, but I hope you get the picture here. Reading players is something you develop in time.

Here are some things you might want to try looking for...

Watch for players who start to grab their chips before they realize it. If you know that you are going to be in a hand with this player, take your time and be extremely deliberate about this. Another ten seconds in deciding to call or bet can give the other player time to give you information on whether or not to make that decision. On occasions there will be times when players will "Hollywood" a little bit; they will try to trick you by grabbing their chips to get you to fold, be careful of that as well.

Another thing, I want you to do is pay close attention to is reaction times. How long does it take the other player to bet, call, or raise on the flop, turn, and river. Watch for quick calls and quick raises, a lot of times other players are doing this to discourage you from playing in the hand any further. Basically, each tell they give off has a certain meaning and it is your job to put it with a pattern. At times players will switch gears just to stay away from being too predictable.

This next one is one of my favorites: players who use card protectors. When you are faced against players who use card protectors, you will notice that much of the time you will be able to take advantage of it. The way they use the card protector can give off great information. Are they putting it on their hand the same way they have been, or are they placing the card protector in a way that leads you to believe they have a monster hand?

Playing the Flop Using Medium Ball

An important aspect of medium ball is being able to outplay the other players after the flop. Professional poker players are the best at what they do, because they make good decisions after the flop is revealed. If you want to become better than them, you'll need to improve upon your post-flop tactics.

Playing K-K and A-A using Medium Ball
Here are some examples of how you should play over-pairs in a variety of situations:

Out of Position
During a random hand I played when the blinds were $25/$50, before the flop I made a bet of 5× the small blind ($125) with

The guy on the button called me, and the small blind also called. The flop was:

The small blind checked to me and I bet $300. The guy on the button called me and the small blind folded. The turn:

A strange situation was developing here. I had pocket aces, which is a difficult hand to get away from. I might be in trouble. What does this guy have? He called me pre-flop and he called me after the flop. Before I decided to check or bet on the turn, I had to consider his playing style. I had to ask myself these questions:

- Does he call raises with hands like 8-9 suited?
- Would he call me on the flop with K-10, or would he raise me?
- If he flopped a set, would he smooth call me?
- If I bet the turn and he raises, is this a going to be a bluff?
- If I check the turn, will he value bet or bluff his mediocre hand?

From being at the table for a short period of time, I didn't have much information on this player. So I went ahead and bet $700 on the turn. He called. This had me puzzled for a second. The river card came:

The safe play here was to check. I did as did he. He turned over K-K and I turned over A-A. With a sigh of relief, I won the big pot. This could have gone an entirely different way. By playing it safe in certain situations, you can accomplish these things:

- Keep the pot small when it's convenient for you in a hot and sticky situation.
- When you're beaten, you only lose the minimum amount of cash. Most of the times by doing this you force the worst hand to value-bet against you.

When they have a hand like A-4, you avoid being bluffed. In other words, if the other player has J-J, he may call you on the flop and on the turn. He then thinks he has the better hand, and if the river card isn't frightening, he'll have to pay you off with his J-J. While checking the river may seem weak, there are several advantages to this play, such as keeping the size of the pot manageable and protecting your chip stack.

When You have Position

In the previous section, I discussed playing over-pairs when I was out of position. Here are some hand examples of playing over-pairs when you have position; having position with over-pairs will earn you the most chips and money.

This is a hand I played when the blinds were $500/$1,000. Pre-flop, I was dealt:

So I went ahead and raised $4000. After this aggressive move, everyone at the table folded except the big blind who called. We both had decent chip stacks, I was around $175,000 and the big blind was close to $200,000.

Here came the flop:

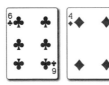

The big blind was first to act so he checked, and because there were no over-cards on the flop, I went ahead and bet twice my pre-flop bet, making it $8,000. He called me. The turn card paired the nine, so now the board looked like this:

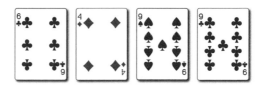

The big blind checked again. The big blind checking again pretty much ruled out that he had a nine in his hand. I have been aggressive throughout this hand because this was a pretty big tournament. I decided to take the safe play here and check. The worst thing that could happen now is for a free card to hit and let the big blind draw against me. On the other hand, checking the turn in this situation brings about these important facts:

- Checking usually protects me from being bluffed at. If I bet the turn here and the big blind puts in a raise, what decision is going to be the correct play here now? Am I supposed to guess in this situation? Guessing usually makes for bad outcomes and this is something I want you to avoid at all costs.

- Checking will sometimes induce a bluff on the river. Since I had checked on the turn, the big blind might bet on the river regardless of whether his hand has improved. By checking on the turn, I am representing weakness (a concept that I want you to portray often in medium ball), and if the big blind misses their draw, most likely they will try to bluff me now at the river.

- Also, it keeps the pot small. Q-Q is a decent hand, but always remember that there are other hands out there that can and will beat you when you least expect it.

Dealing with over-pairs on the turn should be an act of caution rather than excitement, and this is something you must train your poker mind to do. Especially in deep-stacked tournaments, it is extremely rare that an over-pair is in the lead when an all-in pot is played on the turn. As you get further into a tournament, it might happen that your over-pair will be in the lead and take down a nice sized pot. When you are in the early stages of a tournament, you shouldn't get all excited about being all-in with the board looking like this: **7-8-J-Q**. Probably, you will be facing a player with a hidden set or possibly a straight. Unfortunately, the most you can have is two cards in the deck for you to win the pot.

The Importance of "Playing Weak Poker"
After reading so many different poker books by all kinds of different poker players and poker theorists, I have come to the conclusion that they don't want you giving away "free cards." I, however, think there is nothing wrong with checking, and pretending to be "weak."

There are so many great rewards in pretending to be weak, although every once in a while the other player might get their lucky card on the river. But for the most part, it is exciting to set up other players for their demise, when they think you are weak and bluff at you.

Another thing that I have noticed is that theorists talk about the fact that you need to get the most equity for your hand. I strongly disagree. Yes, when you are playing cash games you want to get the most for your strong hands. But in tournaments, your playing style must change completely. Do you really want to risk you entire chip stack with a hand of 9-9? Against an A-K, the risk is simply not worth the reward in a large tournament. Most players have a hard time understanding this, but the most successful tournament players out there are not willing to risk their tournament on one pair. You shouldn't do this either. If you want to win big tournaments, playing "weak" poker is usually the way to go.

Playing Mediocre Hands Using Medium Ball

Thinking aggressively while playing NL Texas Hold'em is preferred, but being passive with mediocre hands in marginal situations is the correct way to play. This especially holds true when there isn't any jeopardy of being outdrawn by the other player. Here is an example. You have:

from middle position and you make a raise pre-flop and the player on the button calls. The rest of the table folds, making this a head's up situation. The flop comes:

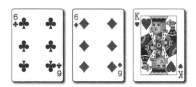

If you don't have the best hand and you think the other player has a King or a six, you have little chance of winning this pot. Getting involved in a big pot is not advisable here.

Essential Tournament theory

In all of the books, blogs, and magazine articles I've read lies a great misconception about tournament poker. There is no simple formula that will create the perfect tournament player in today's style of poker. The poker literature suggests that the most aggressive player will win all of the time. While this holds a modicum of truth, there are other variables that should be considered.

It is caution in marginal situations and well-timed aggression that will separate you from the unfortunate tournament players who dare to compete against you.

Playing the Turn using Medium Ball

Undeniably, the most important and difficult decision you will face in NL Texas Hold'em hand will happen on the turn. There was pre-flop, flop, and now the turn and by this time you must process all the information that you gathered up to this point. This sounds easy, but I can tell you from all the hands that I've played that it is crucial to make the correct decision here on whether or not you want to continue to the end of the hand.

I would like to also point out, that in medium ball, the turn is very important because that is where the size of the pot has gotten larger from all of the pre-flop and post-flop bets.

When You Have position

The greater part of you building a chip stack while playing in a tournament usually comes when you are in position, playing your hands. When you are out of position, it is extremely difficult to get maximum value for your hand unless your winning hand is a monster. This makes it very difficult to carry out bluffs successfully.

The success rate of medium ball is best demonstrated by how you play the turn and river while having position. By doing this correctly, you can keep the pot manageable with your betting, and make it an issue for the other player to take large risks if they decide to get aggressive with you.

Let's go over an example that will point this out to you. The blinds are $300/$600 with $75 ante and you have:

The player under the gun makes it $1,800 to call, and you are on the button and everyone else has folded. You call the $1,800 and are head's up with him with a total of $5,175 in the pot. The flop comes:

He is first to act, and after seeing the flop he bets out $3,600. With a flush and straight draw from the flop, you make the call. The turn comes:

This is nice, you made a flush. This leads to the next conclusion, that the other player can't be too happy about seeing the turn card making the board a flush possibility with the chance of a straight out there. If you were to guess what the other player has for hole cards, I wonder if you would feel confident holding a:

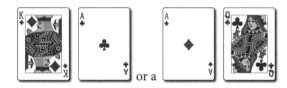

or a

Most players having these hands would probably check in the situation and you should also. You have some options here: if you raise, you run the risk of being re-raised. So if they check, be cautious and do the same. On the river if you make your flush, I recommend betting about ¾ the pot as a value bet. If you missed your flush draw, go ahead and bluff the same amount, and you should be able to take the down the pot either way.

Check-Raising the Turn using Medium Ball
Check-raising on the turn is another tactic that I see being used all of the time. Although I am not very skilled at this, players like Johnny Chan and Ted Forrest demonstrate this play flawlessly. In certain situations, check-raising to gather information can be useful, such as when you are further in a tournament and have chips to spare. In the beginning of a tournament, I strongly recommend that you fold instead of try to pull off this play. The only reason you should ever attempt this play is to accomplish these three things:

- To get help defining the other players hand.
- To protect you from facing a much larger bet on the river.
- To possibly bluff them off a better hand than yours.

Let's do an example to better demonstrate on how to check raise to gather information. You are in the small blind and you have

The blinds are early in the tournament at $50/$100. The woman on the button raises to $150, everyone else folds and you call. The flop comes:

With one over-card out there, you check, and she bets out $200. You call, because she has been aggressive so far in this tournament. The turn comes and is another

You have many choices here. Did she notice that you have been just calling and checking? So again you check the turn, and she bets $700 this time. Now, you could just call and hope the river won't be that expensive or you can check-raise to get a great understanding of what her hand might be. The two sevens on the board should scare her somewhat. There should be only one concern here, if you call what is the river bet going to be?

One way to defend yourself in this situation (since you already checked and she bet $700) is raising to $1,500. I say this because she will not call if she is bluffing you and if she does call, then you can be sure that your pockets eights are beaten. This is a better opportunity than facing a substantial river bet to be bluffed.

The beauty of check-raising here, is that even if she has 10-10, J-J, or even Q-Q, she will probably lay it down with that size of a re-raise.

I hope you see the brilliance of this play. Just like in bluffing, don't get carried away with it and use your best judgment on when to use this controversial play.

Check-Raising when You are on a Drawing Hand

Some of the worst things you can do on the turn is to check-raise, when you are on a drawing hand. This applies for flush draws and straight draws also. Watching the professionals do it on *High Stakes Poker* always makes for a hilarious outcome. One of the reasons why I don't like this play on the turn is that when you check to the other player, are likely to place a bet out there to show strength. Most times when you have check-raised him before, he will likely call you or even put you all-in. This is not a good situation to be in. If he moves all-in on you, is it really worth it to make that call only having a drawing hand? This would force you to gamble and possibly risk your whole tournament on a drawing hand. By check-raising on the turn, you also might waste a bet and never see the river. The best that you could do in this situation is to call the bet, hit your card and make a ton of chips on the river.

There are times when you will be able to pull this off like when you are getting deep into the tournaments and have a huge chip stack. Short-stacked players will be doing all they can do to survive, and check-raising that on the turn can be done only if your chip stack can stand up if they call you or go all-in. Check-raising on the turn will not be a successful play when you are on a drawing hand. To maintain consistency in tournaments, I recommend that to shy away from using this tactic. Every once and awhile you can get that lucky card. But most of the time, this unnecessary play will usually send you to the rail, instead of you having the great feeling of being at the final table.

Check-raising when Making a Complete Bluff

To check-raise as a bluff is something I don't recommend. The reason I say this is if you're new at the table, the information isn't adequate enough to pull this play off effectively. You truly need to have a great read on the other player that you are trying to bluff-raise; it has to look exactly like you have the nuts. After you have been at the table for a while, you should be able to notice who the weak players are and who the timid ones are. It is much easier to make these bluffs and steal pots with absolutely nothing, given that you can make an excellent read on them.

Here is a great example of how I have pulled this of in the past: After a round or two has passed in the tournament, I do nothing but study the other players at the table. This takes a few seconds and is a must. With the blinds at $50/$100, I noticed this really aggressive player stealing blinds right from the start of the tournament. Pre-flop, he was in early position and made a raise of $400, to which everyone else folded. I was the big blind and looked down and saw:

So I called, tired of this guy stealing almost every pot. The flop comes:

Being the big blind and first to act, I checked and he checked as well. The turn came:

I checked again, he fired out $450 now. From watching this guy play the way that he has been, I basically can tell that he doesn't have an ace. If he did he would have most likely bet on the flop to protect his hand. After seeing the turn, there isn't any flush draw or straight draw present. I cannot stress enough how important getting a good read here is. Right now the cards here aren't that important. What matters here is what this guy has in his hand and what he is trying to pull off with another $450 bet. Calculating that there is a bet of $450 to call and about $1,000 in chips in the pot already, I re-raised $1,500 as a stone cold bluff. Believe it or not, he folded and his aggressive ways ended for the next hour.

Now I want to mention that having a great read on the other player made this play possible, as I rarely will check-raise as a bluff. But, if you can pull this off and win half of the time, then that is all you need to make it worth your while. There will be times when you are wrong and the other player will have that ace and has slow-played it. They might even re-raise you in rare occurrences that they have a set and were setting a trap. The reason I wanted to show you this play is that when the hand doesn't cost that much, you can still turn it into a profitable play. If you get caught, you can always use this as advertising and do it again when you have the nuts and really get paid off or even double-up. The next section will illustrate that tactic as well.

Check-Raising When You have the Nuts

Check-raising on the turn when you have the nuts can turn out to be a great play. Most of the other players will notice that you have been check-calling out of position, and check-raising out of position, as well. Some players will get tired of this, and re-raise you just to protect their hand, or try to steal the pot from you with absolutely nothing. When you are faced with this situation, check-raising on the turn with a set, straight, or a flush will have great results.

Another to thing to remember, when pulling the play off, is making sure that your check-raise isn't too large of a bet. You want to keep this player in the hand, and make even more chips on the river because you want him to think that his second-best hand is better than you. This is a great way to "double-up" in tournaments. I have pulled this off many times, and want you to do the same by putting this unique play into your poker style, when you have the nut hand on the turn.

Let's do an example that truly shows the beauty of what I am suggesting:

The blinds early in a tournament are $50/$100, and everyone at the table has around $10,000 in chips. You are in early position and raise to $300 with:

The next player decides to raise you to $800, and everyone else folds. Thinking he might have a decent hand, you go ahead and call. The flop comes:

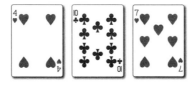

You are first to act so go ahead and check. You have just flopped a set, and the other player bumps it up to $1,200. This hand can be played so many different ways, but I would suggest representing that your hand is on flush draw and just calling here. The turn comes:

which is what you wanted to see. Remember, you are trying to represent that you are on a draw (and if the other player has something like K-K or A-A). So I recommend betting ¼ of the pot size in this situation. That is just enough to keep him interested and won't make him fold. If he has a strong over-pair, and goes all-in, you will be able to call and win a huge pot. This is what this brilliant play can accomplish. You have forced the other player to hang himself by portraying holding a drawing hand.

Calling When You have a Draw on the Turn

When you are playing draws on the turn, this can be problematic. There are some rules and some facts you need to consider when making this play.

Right from the start, you want to consider the pot odds that are being offered. Let's say that there is $1,200 in the pot and the other player bets $300, so your pot odds will be $300 to win $1,500 or 5 to 1. This is a good situation to call $300 to see the river card.

Now that you have determined your pot odds, the next action you need to figure out is the odds of catching the card you need to win this hand on the showdown. Here is an example. You have:

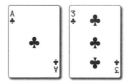

The board looks like this:

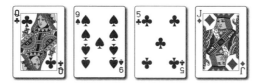

In this situation, you will need to snag one of the nine, last remaining clubs that the dealer has in their hand. You know what your hole cards are and you see the four cards on the board, which now means that there are forty-six cards out there. Now that you know this, there are only nine cards that you would need and thirty seven that won't help you.

Furthermore, your odds of getting your nut flush are roughly 4 to 1 (37 divided by 9 = 4 plus some change).

With this information, this might be a great chance to pay $300 to see the river. Finally, there are a couple of more things to consider. Does the other player have a K-10, giving them a straight? That might end up costing a lot of chips on the river. Does the other player have a set?

If this is a possibility, then the

 and the

will not help you, because it will give them a full house or quads, which leaves you with only seven cards in the deck to give you the winning hand.

Now that you have an understanding of how to figure out your pot odds, and the odds of making your hand, making the decision of drawing a winning hand or second-best hand on the river is going to justify making the call on the turn. There is one final thing to consider, which is figuring out the implied odds. This is not an easy thing to figure out because you never know what the other player is going to do on the river.

head

Planning out the whole hand in your hand is the trick to playing on draws, because you must always think ahead and factor in what you want to achieve on the river. As I have mentioned throughout this book, poker is a game of strategy. When you have the most strategies is when you become successful, because short-term luck will only take you so far.

Playing the River using Medium Ball

As with playing poker in general, your ultimate goal with most of the mediocre hands you'll be playing is simply to make it to the river without using too many of your chips. The exception would be if you have flopped a monster hand, in which case you want as many chips as you can possibly jam into the pot.

By using this strategy as an everyday tactic, your table image will most likely be one that the other players will think is a bluff throughout most hands. More importantly, the river is not the time to prove them correct. While playing medium ball, the amount you should be bluffing should be much lower than most typical styles of Texas Hold'em. The reasoning behind this is simple, the other players will for whatever reasons call you down more often because you are playing more hands than most players.

Throughout my viewing of some of the best NL Texas Hold'em tournament players, I have noticed one obvious thing. The fact is that professional poker players do not bluff on the river, not quite as often as you think. Successful tournament players have the understanding that once you have played a hand to the river, most likely you're going to have a hand and see it to the end at whatever the cost is.

Daniel Negreanu, Gus Hansen, and Phil Ivey are perfect examples of a player who represents a reckless and wild image. But, by studying these players more closely, I have noticed that they will raise with hands:

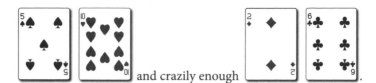 and crazily enough .

Very rarely will they stone cold bluff on the river and waste those valuable chips. Having the unimaginable table image these players have created forces them to have a hand on the river, if they bet. Their image makes the other players give them more action and most of the time it is welcomed. It is no freak of nature why these three players are so successful in tournaments; their amazing approach to the game has so many redeeming qualities.

Furthermore, while this idea of playing the river is still fresh in your mind, be fully aware that the river is not the time to be wild, or to make sophisticated bluffs. You can get away with it only in the ideal situations. The purpose of the river is to get all the chips you possibly can for your monster hands, and to try to avoid losing too many chips when your hands are not as strong. The goal is to beg for a bluff when you have a monster hand but are giving off a weak image.

Bluffing using Medium Ball

More times than not, bluffing should not be a big part of this strategy, and there will be times when the other player pretty much thinks that you play the river in a safe manner. When you are up against new players who don't know your style of playing, I would recommend that you avoid bluffing on the river because they are not paying attention to your method and probably call you.

The optimal time that you should be bluffing on the river is when you're up against smarter players. These players think they have a read on you and have been paying attention. They notice that you play a lot of hands and think that you have the best hand when you place a large bet on the river. When you're up against the other player and you get a great read on them, it makes sense to represent a powerful hand. The key here is to confuse the other players and make them think that you play every hand and exploit them after the fact.

From time to time, you will have to make adjustments and think about when to slow play, to be aggressive, or when to lay down your pair of kings on the river. The decisions are simple for the most part if you stay focused and constantly remain aware of the other players' actions and betting patterns. When you do decide to bluff on the river, you must make it look completely believable and not to do it very often or you will get busted.

Let's do an example to further your understanding of how important it is to bluff and when not to:

I had a starting hand of:

The blinds were getting up there quickly, and at the time of this hand they were $1,500/$3,000. The player under the gun placed a bet of $7,000. He had a huge stack of chips and was playing lots of hands from all kinds of different positions. I had a good sized stack as well, and being on the button, I called. The flop came:

It was just me and him, head's up after the flop, and he bet $9,000. Thinking of how loose this player was being at the table, and my straight draw, I decided to re-raise and put $ 24,000 out there. The other player fumbled for a bit and finally decided to call me. This made me feel like he definitely did not have a king. I put him on a hand like A-Q, or A-10 or possibly a small pair. The turn came:

We both checked here. A bet here would be too risky, especially for a straight draw. Even if I had the king in my hand, I would still check here. The river came:

The other player checked. With my "Hollywood" performance on the turn card, I was trying to represent a hand like K-10. I decided to buy the pot right now, and bet another $24,000. The other player looked like he couldn't beat a king, so my play looked "believable." Making a substantial value bet here was just enough to make him fold. Even though he probably had an Ace high, showing that you rarely ever bluff on the river is the way to go, because it pays off in these certain situations.

Using Medium Ball: Conclusion

It has taken a long time to come up with the idea of this strategy. Watching many poker shows and studying the pros was very challenging and interesting. I would say for the most part, professional poker players stick to a "small ball" way of thinking and most of their success comes from all of their experience playing poker. Most of them have excellent hand reading skills of other players. Over time and practice, you can do the same.

I hope this chapter has given you the added knowledge and helped you understand the importance of building up your chip stack. After you have grasped this concept, getting further in tournaments is actually pretty easy, granted you have a solid system, absolute discipline, and of course, better than average hand-reading skills.

The medium ball mind-set is designed to confuse the other players, professional included, without taking severe risks. It's an approach that will require playing hands more frequently, and making more decisions than you are used too. Basically, you are doing all these things at the same time, plus maintaining the current pot size so that you can avoid making mistakes at times when it isn't worth it.

By reading this chapter, you have learned the correct size of a pre-flop raise and the various hands that will work best for attacking the other players at the table. Finally, you have learned how important position is and when to use it to win pots. Hopefully, I have shown you how to play cautiously post-flop with less than desirable cards, most importantly when you don't have position. These key elements will give you the successful tactics to win most tournaments and cash games. As an added bonus, playing this unique medium ball attack will give extra value when the other players are cocky with your signs of weakness and ignorantly try to bluff you while you are holding the nuts.

Another important aspect I have preached throughout this chapter is maintaining a medium size bet after the flop because it keeps pressure on the other players and in the long run, earns you more chips. You can see more flops than an average bet would allow, thus giving you more chances to hit that monster flop and take down a huge stack of chips.

Finally, I hope that you have learned that bluffing is overrated in today's Texas Hold'em, because players are simply going to call you. There are certain times when bluffing should be done as it is part of the game. It is most effective when done sparingly and is only to be used in appropriate situations. The less reckless and more methodical mind-set that is laid out in this chapter, will without any doubts in my mind build chip stacks in tournaments every chance you play.

"You should always play your best game, no matter what. Just go in, play your strategy, and stick with it. It doesn't matter how long you play, 15 minutes or three hours. The game never ends, and profitable opportunities are always waiting for you."

—Erick Lindgren, 2008 W.S.O.P. player of the year. He has won a W.S.O.P. bracelet and two WPT titles, also a poker book author.

CHAPTER FOURTEEN:

SLOW PLAYING AND SETTING UP TRAPS

Slow playing, also called sandbagging or trapping, is a deceptive play in poker that is roughly the opposite of bluffing. It is betting weakly or passively with a monster hand, rather than betting aggressively with a weak one. The flat call is one such play. The objective of the passive slow play is to entice the other players into a pot who might fold to a raise or to cause them to bet stronger than they would if the player had played aggressively (bet or raised). Slow playing sacrifices protection against hands that may improve and risks losing the pot-building value of a bet if the other player also checks.

There are so many different circumstances in poker; one key to winning is knowing when and how to slow play your hand. What does slow playing actually do for you? It makes the other players think that they have you beaten.

When you've flopped a monster hand, you want to slow play in hopes of the other player getting a hand and doing the betting for you. It also causes the other players to bluff more often. Slow playing is a skill to get the most out of your hand; it can also be a way to have your strong hand taken down by a weaker one if it is not executed correctly.

There are a number of aspects you should keep in mind when slow playing, in terms of when to slow play and when not to.

How many players are in with you at the table? In general, the more people in a hand opposing you, the less likely you want to slow play unless you have the nuts. Sometimes even the safest of flops can cripple you if you aren't careful and playing the hand correctly. You may even think that no card can come to beat you on the turn, but think again. With a lot of players, anything can, and will happen. This point ties in quite well with the next one regarding the strength of your hand and the chance of being outdrawn on the subsequent betting rounds.

What is the strength of your hand? What does the flop, turn, and rivers look like? The point of playing NL Texas Hold'em is to win! You want to take home the money and treat your significant other. Most importantly, you want to make a good number of chips from your good hands. On your unbeatable hands, you can do whatever move you think will make you the most chips. On your weak hands, you'll have an easy choice in mucking. All the ones in the middle are where the real poker game is played.

You want to manage letting other players in with weaker hands to make more money off of them while still winning the pot. Like in the first point, your hand grows vulnerable with more people in the game. In Limit Hold'em, if you slow play, you can usually pull the trigger on the turn card after the other players' bet. In NL Texas Hold'em, you can raise the turn or wait longer if you are sure your hand will hold up. In both cases, your goal is to have the other player commit enough chips to pay you off.

How often I slow play depends upon whether or not I think I'll lose if I keep giving cards away cheaply. For example, if I have

and the flop is:

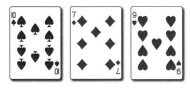

and I'm playing against two other players in NL Texas Hold'em, I'm not going to mess around and slow play. That is just asking for trouble, due to the straight draw on the board.

On the other hand, if I have

and the flop is:

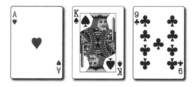

I'll be way more likely to slow play since the amounts of draws that can kill my hand are few. You ask yourself specifically about which hands you should slow play with, and which you shouldn't. I can't answer that for you, because it is very dependent on the situation you are in.

For example, even top pair with a good kicker against one player might be a spot where you slow play and raise on the turn. You wouldn't think of doing that if you were against a number of players. On the other hand, against many players, you might just call on the flop and then raise or check-raise the turn if you flopped two pair, trips, or better.

You should be less likely to slow play against a lot of players if your hand is likely to get outdrawn. Likewise, against a good number of players, your hand will have to go up in strength to make slow playing a good option (like a nut straight or nut flush would be one to slow play if lots of players were in).

With regards to position, Let's say you have

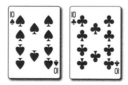

and the flop is:

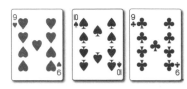

Meanwhile, several of the other players are in, but you have no worries here. How you play the hand will depend on what makes you the most cash. If you are in the front, a check-raise could be the best move.

It would work best if the person to your left would bet. Yet, if you are in last position, you would ideally like the first player to bet and the other players to call. This way you can also call and raise the turn. You may even just call the turn and raise the river so other players could catch up to a no-win situation.

What style are the players you're playing against? The last concern for slow playing is who you are playing against. As you move up into higher limits things change. You'll need to pay more attention to mixing up your game. Slow playing doesn't work as well against good players because they will fold on your raise. This is why in Limit Hold'em games from about $50/$100 on up, the players will do a lot of raising pre-flop and on the flop. They want to get their money in while they can.

First of all, slow playing is a strategy that should be used when facing both advanced and aggressive players. The reason for this is that more advanced players are likely to try and steal pots when they sense weakness and aggressive players like to buy many pots.

The key is to trap the other players, when they bet or raise in hopes of seeing you fold. You do not want to just give them free opportunities to see another card. When you are facing very weak and inexperienced players, it is usually best to bet them out of the hand, as they will often check when they don't have anything.

In NL Texas Hold'em, occasionally you will meet a player who makes large bets on the river regardless of their cards. Others may always commit themselves if they are raised. Against this type of players you should slow play more, so you can exploit them on everything, including the shirt off their back.

You may also run into players who will call you regardless of whether you raise early on or not. Against these players you should never slow play. You should raise to get the money in early and keep betting.

Clearly, slow playing isn't always 100% reliable. But it is a chance you should take. If you never slow play, you won't see as many bad beats and for some players that's what they usually strive for. No one ever wants bad beats, but if you are willing to take a risk you can get paid off dramatically.

The biggest danger of slow playing is that you give the other player a chance to see the next card without having to pay for it. With that "free" card, they could catch a draw or an even stronger hand. If they get a straight or flush draw they may call a pretty large bet from you and of course may eventually hit the wining hand. If you don't want to take the risk, bet strongly so the other players will retreat from playing out their drawing hand. Here are some more examples when you should check all the way to the river.

If you hold

and you flop a full house, slow playing is a good idea. If the flop is

there's only one ace left in the deck, along with two kings. This makes it a long shot that the other player has anything worth playing and will need some runner cards to make an effective bluff. For example, if the other player had

and you bet, he will probably fold. However, you are going to win a substantial pot if you check and the turn is a

Also, if the other player tries to steal at any point because of your checking, you will extort more money from them.

Another situation would be if you had a high pocket pair. You don't want to slow play low pocket pairs even if the flop consists of all under cards because there is a pretty good chance that an over card will come up on the turn or river. If you have a high pocket pair, specifically A-A or K-K, you should slow play them exactly the same way you learned above.

There are so many circumstances when you should slow play and there's no way to talk about them all. But then again, there are plenty of situations where you shouldn't slow play at all. Make sure you think about your odds before you slow play and consider what the other player might have in their hand.

The most important thing to remember is not to slow play when there are several players in the hand, because the chance of one of them catching a stronger hand is much higher. The only exception would be if you catch a monster such as a straight, flush, full house, and so on, but even these never guarantee a win.

In general, it is a great idea to slow play, as long as you pick the right situations, the right players, and only do it occasionally. By following this strategy properly, slow playing will really help you build your chip stack. There is more than one reason to slow play hands. The most obvious is one to make more money. The other reason is to bluff, semi-bluff or mix up your game so you can make more on later hands. A powerful move in Limit Hold'em is to raise in the turn card betting round when you have position, even if you have a mediocre hand. Then, depending on the river, you can either bet or check. Do this to a player and show them a weak hand just once and I'll promise you more action then you could ever hope for in later hands.

Setting up Traps

Setting up traps is a topic that I don't think is addressed nearly enough in many articles or publications. While every professional poker player is usually highlighted by their ability to set, spot, and avoid traps, most amateur poker players rarely know when and where they are about to get pounced on until it's too late.

Trapping Yourself in Poker

Ask any skilled poker player on PokerStars or Full Tilt what they think of the players on the site and they'll all respond with the same answer: "terrible!" This is mainly because the players on these websites are all new to the game. This is a direct result of good advertising. What makes new players so much worse than the good players if poker really is just a mental game as so many players claim?

In short, the biggest answer is starting hand selection. Amateurs tend to have an affinity for poker because anyone can win at the game. But what this really means is that anyone can be dealt a winning hand. The ability to play (or better, to not play) bad cards is what separates the sharks from the fish. It's a lot like the saying goes, that a person's true character is only revealed in hard times, since anyone can act grand during the good times. The reason I illustrated hands like King-X suited, is because this is a very good example of a poker hand that traps itself. For example, suppose this hand plays out, and you hold:

The flop comes:

Now, how are you going to play this flop? You should try aggressiveness. This hand has two things going for it: it's on the second best nut flush draw and it's has top pair. This hand also has two things not going for it: it's on the second best nut flush draw and it's got top pair with a weak kicker. There is the added caveat that if a Queen or Jack drops, it would quite possibly complete another players' straight.

What happens with a hand like this is that many new players will be dragged into over-calling this hand when action starts to develop on the table. They'll take one look at the two spades on the flop and decide that they want a piece of this.

Now, before any skilled players get into a debate, I'm not saying that this hand is unplayable. It is certainly a check and call hand in any full game. In a short-handed game or head's up, this may well be a hand to raise. In a full game, this hand is already half a rope to hang your self with. Here's an idea of why to get out of this hand if action starts up. If the other player was slow playing a Q-J, the only way you would be to beat them is catching the other spade card, preferably the ace.

In conclusion, slow playing and setting traps are some of the best tools you can use to make a great amount of chips. Accessing the correct time and amounts to bet are something you will develop over time. Play as much poker as you can, and sooner or later you will find how remarkable the results are when you pull off these tactics successfully.

" Put yourself in their shoes before you decide on the best way to take their shirts. **"**

—*David Sklansky, is generally considered a top authority on gambling. He has written numerous poker books and has three W.S.O.P. bracelets.*

CHAPTER FIFTEEN:

TABLE IMAGE

One of the most important aspects of any game of poker is how other players see you at the table. Do they see a chump or a champ? Do they see a timid little mouse that plays passively and calls everything, or do they see a tight-aggressive shark ready to pounce and take all the chips? In the beginning, we all began the journey down the poker road playing cards instead of the more advanced and correct method of playing the other players. You must be able to observe and digest ANY information an opposing player is giving you, as well as do your best not to give out ANY information about yourself.

In live play, we have a bounty of information coming at us from all directions. When the dealer is sending out the cards, try to catch tells from the other players. Those hints of a smile, disgust, an eyebrow twitch or anything out of the ordinary can tell you something about the other players' hand. When the flop comes out, try to do the same thing. Put simply, pay attention. Watch as a player bets. Do they always bet the same way every hand? Did they knock over any chips or hurry the bet? Did they seem to hesitate? Were they going to call and then decided last second to raise the bet? All of these things can help you get a read on your competition.

If the flop hits and it is:

and the other player checks to you, it is possible you have already won this hand and can take it down with just a single bet.

So how should you dress for live play success? Honestly, it depends on what your live play consists of. If you're a well known regular at your local casino trying to nab tourist money, don't show up looking like a pro and chatting with the dealer you have known for years because it spooks the other players. In this case, you should show up dressing and acting like a guy who just flew into town and wants to play a little poker. Talk a lot to get to know the other players and the dealer. Everyone loves a friendly guy!

Play a tight-aggressive style, folding any hand you would normally fold and playing premium ones. You will win more than you lose but no one will take you for a pro, and most won't even be upset you took their money. If you dress the part of a pro or card room regular, these tourists may run to other tables they consider easier or leave the casino entirely, which won't do your card playing profit any favors. This is a great opportunity to check out my good friends at badbeatclothing.com, they have all kinds of nice poker shirts and hats that will make you fit into the poker scene nicely.

If you're playing in a major money tournament, dress for comfort and nothing else. If you feel your eyes give you away, wear shades or a hat if you feel the need. If not, just be comfy and ready for hours of poker with few breaks. You also need to be highly aware of your table image in this environment, as others gunning for your chips will be watching your every move on every deal and flop trying to get a read on you, your hand, and any tells you might be giving away! If you find aces in your hand, try your best to keep the same calm facial expression as you would if it was just another toss away hand. Don't raise your eyebrows or show a hint of a smile. If the other player picks up a read on you that's one more player who won't pay you off! Practice placing bets over and over so that whether you're bluffing or have the nuts, you are betting the exact same way.

Don't splash the pot or accidentally knock over chips. Aggressive or nervous behaviors also tip others off that you may have a strong hand or could be bluffing. Give away nothing! Be a rock. If you're in a hand and another player is deciding whether or not to continue, be sure you stare straight ahead and don't talk. Talking or looking at the other player in the hand with you can be telling information you don't want to give away. If you were to talk back with them sounding loose and relaxed, it may cause them to believe you hold the better hand.

On the other hand, if they prod you into talking by being unpleasant and you responded with a short-clipped remark, you could be viewed as being weak or bluffing. It's best to just keep staring silently straight ahead, so they can get zero read, whether you are bluffing or have the nuts.

Appearing to Others as Weak

This has to be one of my favorite things to do while playing poker. Anytime you choose to play what appears to be a weak player, you're probably giving up something. This might be true, but there are so many things you can gain. Let's look at this controversial method of playing poker and get all the facts about doing it.

Here is what you might give up: free cards and some slight chances the other player might be able to win. But how concerned should you be about this? Not much, if the other player has a pocket pair smaller than yours. If you allow them to see the turn and the river, they will win the pot about eight percent of the time. If the other player has a

then they have a total of five outs against you. If they see the turn and the river, they will win the pot about twenty percent of the time. So in reality, this isn't that scary, considering the fact that if they do outdraw your pocket pair, you'll get to see it.

Now only an ace or a jack on the turn would be a scare card to your present hand. The best draw they could get would be A-K. With drawing an A-K, and if they go to the river, they could outdraw you about twenty three percent of the time. Which is a risk, but it wouldn't be the end of the world when you factor in all of the amazing benefits of being cautious while you play "medium ball" poker.

Here is what you can gain: you get to trap the other player with top pair into continuing to bet thinking they have the best hand. By showing weakness, which hopefully they will pick up on, and make the decision to push their hand with

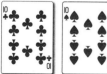, you were pretending to be weak with your

against a flop like:

This will make it extremely difficult to be bluffed off of the best hand by the other player. Throughout the years that I have been in poker, there has been so much emphasis on being aggressive, that the idea of being passive is often seen as weak or even poor play. At times aggressive players will occasionally mock a player who proceeds with caution, not fully understanding that there is a time to be aggressive, and there is a time to be careful and protect those valuable chips in front of you.

As you gain experience, you will notice aggressive players amassing huge stacks of chips by playing wildly and recklessly after the flop. As always, if they continue to be reckless and wild, it's only a matter of time before they will become trapped and not be able to escape, which will usually eliminate them.

Playing medium ball style of poker will keep you involved in quite a few pots, but more importantly, is to win the pots that you are supposed to win without taking any unnecessary risks. Playing medium ball will never put you all-in with pocket queens before the flop, or on the flop with just top pair. In fact, by teaching you this medium ball mentality, I don't want you ever to be all-in at any part of the tournament, unless you have the absolute nuts, of course!

Being a cautious poker player after the flop will help you avoid getting involved in huge pots in those troublesome and frustrating situations. At times, you'll lose some extra chips when the other player outdraws you. You will more than make up for that with the chips you save by avoiding huge pots that you will lose and with the chips you will win by letting the other player bet the hand for you.

Another major factor to understand is that in live tournaments, the action is much slower than it would be online. You're not going to be playing 30-50 hands an hour as you would online when there is an automatic dealer, the chips stack themselves and the deck shuffles itself. Depending on the skill of your dealer and speed of the other players at your live table, you can expect perhaps 10-25 live hands per hour. This is why every hand you misplay can hurt your chances of winning. If you hit a run of cold cards, you might not play a hand during the whole hour. It's very important to wait for playable cards as the urge to play fights against your patience for good cards constantly.

If you give in and start playing marginal hands just to be "in the action," your tournament may be a short and not very sweet venture. You need to have a "long run" mentality as well as patience to make the money.

CHAPTER SIXTEEN:

DESTROYING THE PLAYERS AT THE FINAL TABLE

In a large tournament, being one of the few to make it to the final table is what we play poker for in the first place. It's an experience you'll want to remember when you're telling your grandchildren stories about your life. Play the best poker you possibly can. If you don't win, you'll at least be able to say that you held nothing back. Bring everything out on the felt.

As I have mentioned throughout this book, FOCUS on the task at hand. This is the best advice I can give you as it is one of the things that will get you to the final table more than your fair share of the time. Being focused can put you in a better position to win.

You should play the same way at the final table as you did to get to the final table. Avoiding distractions is the most important concern here. You must focus on poker and what the other players are doing at the table. Surviving is a nice idea, but now that you're at a final table, playing to win is what matters now. The difference between second place and third place is considerable in the amount of money you win.

When the final table gets down to four players, it does sometimes make sense to fold a few hands to ensure your place in the top three. This is an important factor to consider when one or two of the other players have a small stack of chips and the chip leader decides to raise big. When this happens, you should fold your hand and move up the pay scale. If you test the chip leader, you risk finishing fourth if you lose that hand. In this situation, you should have a big hand before ever considering challenging the chip leader. Blinds and antes are going to be enormous; you should only try stealing them when you have position and the risk is minimal.

What I have noticed at final tables, even more so than in other situations, is that whichever player enters the pot first, usually ends up controlling the hand. You can raise opening hands at a final table more than any other time in the tournament but you shouldn't call raises or re-raise yourself, as often as you did earlier on the tournament.

I refer to what Jerry Yang did at the 2007 World Series of Poker Main Event Final table. Regardless of being one of the small stacks, his ambitious and relentless methods made him the champion. Here is how he did it…

Jerry Yang Summarized his Tournament Strategy:
"I study my opponents very carefully, and when I sensed something, when I sensed some weakness, I took a chance. Even if I had nothing, I decided to raise, re-raise, push all-in or make a call…the only way that I could win this tournament was by being aggressive from the very beginning and that's exactly what I did. And thank God I was also able to pick up some good cards at the same time."

At the final table, Yang went from starting eighth in chips to holding a big chip lead that he never relinquished. The process of accumulating the lead involved Yang knocking out seven of the eight other players at the final table.

Let's look at how he actually did it. When the final table started, Jerry was a small stack and Philip Hilm was the chip leader. Strangely enough after two hours at the final table, the implosion Hilm's chip stack sent him to 9th place. Let's take a look how Jerry accomplished this:

Yang showed aggression quickly at the Final Table and never lost the chip lead after the 9th hand. This devout Christian knocked out seven of the eight players at the Final Table, including Tuan Lam heads-up over thirty-six hands.

Jerry Yang raised or re-raised five of the first nine hands, and the ninth one showed who would be the force at the table. Lee Childs raised UTG to $720,000 and with pocket jacks; Jerry Yang made it $2.5 million to go. Lee Childs called, and the flop came:

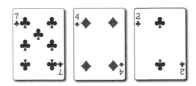

Lee Childs bet $3 million, and Yang immediately moved all-in. Childs was shaken, confronted immediately with his place at the Final Table. He finally folded two queens face up, and the $11.6 million pot went to Jerry Yang. He went to work again on 14th Hand. Yang raised ten times the big blind to $2.5 million from the cutoff, and Philip Hilm called in the big blind. He went to work again on Hand #14. Jerry Yang raised ten times the big blind to $2.5 million from the cutoff, and Philip Hilm called in the big blind.

Philip Hilm checked the:

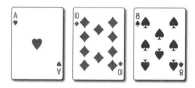

and Jerry Yang bet $3 million. Hilm called again. The turn came:

Hilm checked, so Yang moved all-in. Hilm folded, and Yang moved into the chip lead.

On the next hand, Yang again raised this time to $1 million which Hilm called from the small blind, and the flop came:

Hilm checked, and Yang bet $2 million. Hilm called. The turn came:

Hilm checked, Yang bet $4 million, Hilm moved all-in. After some thought Yang called with:

and Hilm had outs with:

 The river came:

knocking out Hilm in 9th place ($525,934).

One of the favorites many picked to win the Main Event was Lee Watkinson. In a battle of the blinds, Jerry Yang raised to 1 million, and Lee Watkinson moved all-in for $9.715 million from the big blind. After asking for the chip count, Yang called with

Watkinson was dominated, having only

 The flop came:

this showed that the kickers would play, and the turn was:

 The river was

The day was ended for Lee Watkinson in 8th place ($585,699).

Another orbit brought another knockout punch from Yang. Lee Childs raised to $720,000 from the small blind, and Yang moved all-in from the big blind. Childs had $4.98 million in chips, and he called with his in chips, and he called with his

It was a great call for Childs, as Yang was dominated pre-flop and showed

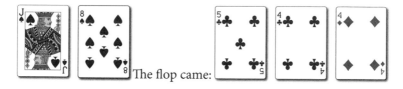The flop came:

and brought some confidence for Childs. The turn came:

Everyone in the room was stunned. The river came, putting Childs out in 7th place ($705,229):

Something Wrong KJ Best Hand

Several hands later in the tournament, Yang made it $1.5 million pre-flop with his pocket jacks, and Hevad Khan raised to $6 million from the small blind. Raymond Rahme folded, and then Yang finally called after several minutes. When Khan heard that, he then mentioned that he was "all-in the dark" before the flop.

The flop came: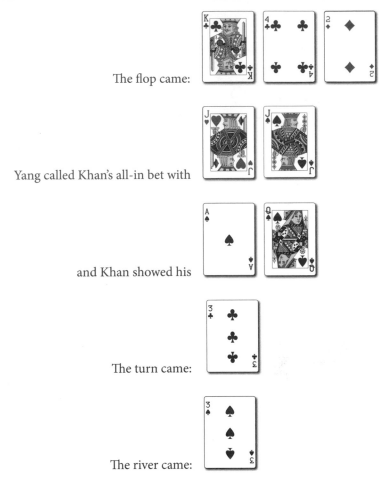

Yang called Khan's all-in bet with

and Khan showed his

The turn came:

The river came:

and Hevad Khan finished in 6th place ($956,243).

On Hand #60, Raymond Rahme made it $2.7 million to go. Jon Kalmar moved all-in for a total of $13.245 million.

Raymond Rahme called with

and Kalmar had

The flop came: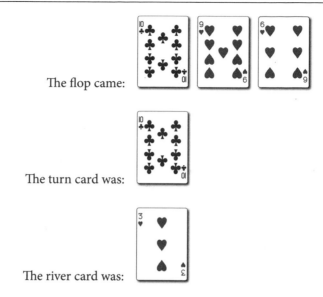

The turn card was:

The river card was:

and Kalmar finished in 5th place ($1,255,069). Rahme moved up to $30.01 million for second place, with Tuan Lam ($17.46 million) and Alex Kravchenko ($8.71 million) chasing Jerry Yang's $71.31 million.

There was a quick run of five dozen hands that sent five players out, but these four played together for a total of 107 hands. Jerry Yang kept the chip lead throughout, but the other three exchanged their stacks back and forth. Alex Kravchenko doubled through Jerry Yang early when he moved all-in with pocket three's then spiked a three on the flop against

Tuan Lam then doubled through Yang with

on the flop :

vs. Yang's

He spiked a queen on the river to move up to $23 million. Alex Kravchenko then finally brought Yang below $50 million for the first time when his pocket kings held up against Yang's

Tuan Lam slipped down to $11.65 million, as he tried to get something going. He came over the top of Yang's $2.5 million raise with

He made a stand, but Raymond Rahme had:

and moved all-in for $28.75 million. Jerry Yang thought long and hard with the chance to take out two players, but he folded. Tuan Lam flopped an ace and rivered a full house to move safely from the short stack. Raymond Rahme moved all-in three times in a row, clearly shaken by the hand.

At this spot in the tournament, the blinds were $300,000/$600,000 with a $75,000 ante.

In Hand #149, Alex Kravchenko was first to act and raised to $1.75 million. Yang made it $6.25 million from the button, and Raymond Rahme moved all-in from the big blind for $17.125 million. Alex Kravchenko got out of the way

Yang was delighted to see that his

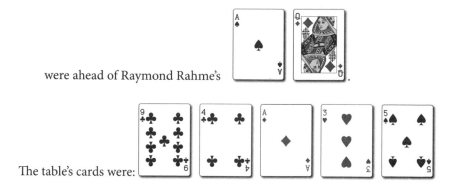

were ahead of Raymond Rahme's.

The table's cards were:

Raymond Rahme's pair of aces brought him up to $36.6 million and Jerry Yang down to $41.63 million.

In Hand #167, Alex Kravchenko raised to $2.1 million from the small blind. Jerry Yang moved all-in from the big blind,.

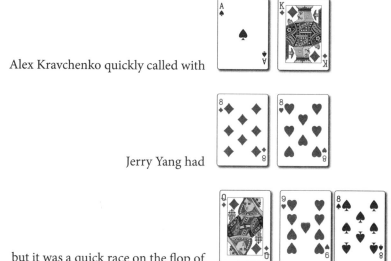

Alex Kravchenko quickly called with

Jerry Yang had

but it was a quick race on the flop of

The set held up, and Kravchenko left with only one WSOP bracelet from this year's summer, out in 4th ($1,852,721).

Two hands later, Yang made it $2.6 million from the button, and Rahme raised to $8.6 million from the big blind. Yang took some time then called, and the flop came:

Rahme checked, and Yang bet $10 million. Rahme moved all-in for another $17.35 million, and Yang started thinking and observing. They sat for several minutes, the 62 year-old South African leaned forward on his knees and said "Make your decision," revealing the weakness Yang was looking for.

He called and showed his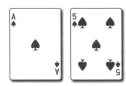

which turned out to be a great call.

Rahme showed his

The turn and river were no help to Rahme and he went out in 3rd ($3,048,025).

Now, the final table turned into a head's up work of art. Yang, with $102.15 million in chips, dominated Tuan Lam's $25.325 million early in head's up play, Yang rolled over the experienced Lam and diminished his stack down to $10.05 million. After the break, the blinds moved up to $400,000/$800,000 with a $100,000 ante and a new Lam emerged. He made a stand with

and spiked a four to breathe new life into him. He fought hard and looked like he might be able to pull the lead.

On the 36th head's up hand, Yang made it $2.3 million to go pre-flop. Lam moved all-in, and Yang called for $22.2 million. Both men anxiuosly awaited each other's cards:

Yang had

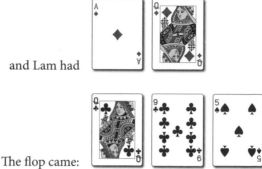

and Lam had

The flop came:

and brought excitement throughout the Amazon Room as it looked like this would keep going for awhile more.

The turn came:

This was a perfect drama card as Yang picked up eight more outs for the straight.

The river came:

which was inconceivable, sending the massive pot and the WSOP Main Event title to Jerry Yang.

Tuan Lam took home $4,840,981 for 2nd place, and his story of how he made it to the Main Event was incredible. "I was at the airport for a flight to Vietnam, and my luggage was on the plane. For some reason, I just felt like I needed to play in the Main Event, and so I decided to head to Las Vegas instead." Changing his mind was well worth it, as he joins the recent ranks of Paul Wasicka, Steve Danneman, David Williams, and Sammy Farha as those being runner up in the WSOP Main Event.

Jerry Yang brought home $8,250,000, and will be one of the most unusual Main Event Champions in the history of poker. He is a devout Methodist and is very open about his faith. He's pledged 10% of his winnings to three charities (Ronald McDonald House, The Make a Wish Foundation, and Feed the Children) and is easily seen as a humble man of conviction. When asked which was more important, the bracelet or the money, he said, "No question, it is the money. I can do so much good work for the community and even overseas in missionary work."

His goal won't be to change poker, but you can guarantee that he will change many lives along the way. He has definitely changed mine in many ways...

CHAPTER SEVENTEEN:

ULTIMATE HEAD'S UP STRATEGY

Ultimate Head's Up Strategy: If you plan to win any poker tournaments, you have to be able to beat the final player in a match of head's up. Most players refer this final session as a "crapshoot," as the often outrageous blinds forces you and the other player to fight it out with mediocre hands. The first thing to mention, and everyone knows this, is that starting hands change in value tremendously when you are only facing one other player. Sometimes you get lucky and hit a big hand, but there are going to be times when luck determines much of your success in head's up. Aggression and skill will take up the difference.

As Doyle Brunson advises, "when luck shuts the door on you... just come in through the window..." Basically, skill will have to prevail; this is because luck can only take you so far. The reason head's up skill is so important to your poker game is the difference in the amount of money you win. Let's say for example, you're at the final table of a W.S.O.P. Main event. 1st place gets $9.1 million and 2nd place gets $5.8 million. The payoff for winning the bracelet is much more important, because of the status associated with the bracelet. Becoming a skillful head's up player should be an essential component to your repertoire.

You must always play your hands aggressively, but your precise strategy will depend on the other player and you must change it accordingly. If they are passive, you should call and bet more often, especially when you are on the button with optimal position. You don't always need a great hand to pull this off. Having position and slipping in a well-timed bluff every now and then will give you chips when you are getting terrible cards. Continuing to fold when they make a raise, which usually means they have a hand, is a great play. This also can be very frustrating to them. If you do miss the flop, make a minimum bet (nuisance bet) often, especially when you're playing against a tight-passive player who will fold. When playing against a "calling station," I prefer to check-fold when I miss the flop.

When the flop comes and you hit a piece of it against a passive player, be relentless when betting for value. Also, you should never leave the hand (where you have a piece of the flop) unless you and the other player are both non-pot committed and you have a good indication that you are beaten, such as a large re-raise when you only have bottom pair.

When you are playing head's up and dealt the above-average starting hand, you should raise pre-flop for value. Against an aggressive player, your confrontation with them will result in a game of tug-of-war. When in this situation, push your stronger starting hands and call or fold your weaker ones. The more often they re-raise your limp in, the more you should fold hands that are too weak to push onto them.

No poker strategy fits every circumstance or player, but here are some exercises I've employed, or have seen used in numerous head's up matches.

Play a Great Deal of Hands: Chris Ferguson mentions that he plays about 70-80% of the hands in a head's up situation. While I'd certainly advocate playing any Ace, or any King, Ferguson suggests playing anything Jack or higher.

Keep Applying Pressure: Keep raising pre-flop with any hand that has any strength, and one that has an Ace or King. Raise with any reasonable starting hand if you are in the small blind, since you will have position for the rest of the hand, which is very important playing head's up.

If you hit the flop, there is already a large pot to be won. If the flop doesn't hit, you are in a position to pick up the pot with an additional bet, because you've already represented a strong hand

Position, Position, Position: Being aggressive while in position means you have the opportunity to control the last bet that goes into the pot. So, when you're ahead, you can increase the pot, winning bigger pots than the other player. When behind, you can check down, keeping the size of the pot under control. The main concept of "medium ball" is staying aggressive and limiting your risk.

Also, you have the chance to watch for weakness, and pick up the occasional pot. Position and your chip stack size are the most valuable aspects in a head's up match.

When Catching Part of the Flop: This will have you in the lead before the turn card. Calling with something like middle pair will seldom lead to good results at a full ring game, but in head's up, catching any part of the flop can put you ahead of the other player.

The All-in: Of course patient players are in no hurry to win the match, but not all poker players are patient. Simply put, if you find yourself with the nuts, you must go all-in.

It may not work the first time, but players don't like the feeling of having to lay down a hand that was contested in an all-in bet. If you've gone all-in before, they are more likely to think they can catch you bluffing the second time, and will make the call.

One of the first things that comes to mind when thinking of head's up poker is how you handle the other players' strategy. Are they aggressive, tight, or a mix of both? Take notes on the other player and decide which style their strategy falls into. Are they not raising most of the time? They may be a tight player that is too afraid to make a raise with a mediocre hand.

Once you have determined the other player's style of play, you can take advantage of it. If they always check, you should definitely limp in or raise, depending on your cards. While the blinds are low at the beginning of the match, try to see as many flops as possible. If the other player is aggressive and raises a lot of the time, you may need to throttle back and play better hands than you would if they were timid.

You should force the other player to pay to see the next card. By letting the other player limp into a pot for the minimum amount of chips, you are just asking for a bad beat. Think aggressively and keep them from seeing a flop for free. If you have a suited connector on the big blind and the other player calls, don't be afraid to bet the amount of the pot. If they call, you can halfway assume that they have a decent hand. If they fold, then you know that they were a limping to suck out on you. In my opinion, it is better to have some money in the pot when the flop comes. It makes the other player's decisions that much more difficult.

How much should you be betting? I have always been able to tell how much of a bet a player will call in a head's up match, but it is not always easy.

In your starting hand you have:

Let's say you just flopped:

and the other player is only in for $500 chips. You don't want to go all-in because it will send up a red flag. Make a solid bet for 2 or 3 times the pot and see if they call. Your goal here is to maximize the amount of chips you can take from the other player when you know you have the winning hand.

Please don't misunderstand me. I'm not suggesting that you start slow playing all of your good hands. You may be up against an inexperienced player who will call you on a straight or flush draw and end up catching their card. Then you will be committed to the pot and end up with a big chip loss. Remember that reading your opponent is of the utmost importance in head's up poker; it is just as important as being aggressive. Find the right balance of betting, and you will wear down the other player quickly.

During head's up play, you can now concentrate on exploiting the other player's weaknesses that hopefully you picked up on earlier in the game. Of course, gaining experience playing head's up poker helps your overall poker game tremendously.

Let's do some head's up hand examples:

The blinds are $2,000/$4,000, heads up. You have $26,000 in tournament chips and your hole cards are:

in the big blind. The player on the button has a huge chip lead, $162,000 in tournament chips. He is an extremely loose-aggressive player who has been raising and taking down pots almost every hand. He now raises all-in, pre-flop. Do you call or fold?

The answer is call. The reason I say this is because with having pocket 5's, the chances of the other player having a higher pair 6's through A's is unlikely, making it favorable for you to call here. Since you are getting better than even money, this presents your best chance at doubling up. You are far in the tournament and have a small stack, and this will have to be the time to make a stand against a big stack. Otherwise, you will probably be blinded out on a much lower ranked hand.

Another thing I would like to discuss in this chapter is trapping in head's up play, since this is very different from regular ring game play. In a nine-handed poker game, the hands that you trap with have to be a lot stronger than a hand you would trap with in a head's up poker game

Here is an example. Let's say you have:

You are out of position pre-flop, and you raise. You're called by the button and you see the flop:

You're first to act. Checking here would be a bad move, as your vulnerable top pair needs to be protected from giving the other player a free draw at a straight. In a full ring game, top pair is a hand that you want to win the pot with right away, before you give the other player a chance to catch up by catching an ace on the turn, since a hand containing an ace is likely.

Now, let's look at this same hand but apply it to head's up play. You raise from the big blind head's up, and the button/small blind calls. The flop comes down the same:

You are the first to act. There is still a straight draw possible. An ace can still come off on the turn, but checking to let the other player see another card isn't that bad of a plan here. You are so strong head's up that you want to shield that from the other player by pretending to be weak

What's the difference you may ask yourself?

In head's up, it's difficult to make a pair. Most of the time you only connect with the flop about a third of the time, and when you connect with top pair, it is considered a monster hand head's up. You want to show plenty of weakness, so that the other player might either bluff the turn or pick up a little something to match his hand so they can call you on the river. It's safe to try to act weak to gain extra bets later in the hand.

Another consideration in head's up play is position. The big blind will be out of position for the whole hand, except for pre-flop play. This gives the small blind a huge advantage. You'll be at the disadvantage of being out of position for the rest of the hand, and you'll need to raise more pre-flop to make sure you won't have to make too many difficult decisions later on in the hand.

You want to either end the hand pre-flop or end it with a solid continuation bet on the flop, should the other player call your pre-flop bet. I'd suggest a range of four to six times the big blind. You should also take into account the other players' style because, as always, each poker situation is unique to whom you're up against. This is something you will pick up over time and with head's up experience. If you are playing against an opponent that frequently calls your raises no matter how big or small, then it is worth more it to just let him do the heavy betting when you have a hand you want to play.

NO

The final aspect that I would like to mention in head's up play is pot control. Chipping away at the other player in head's up is the strategy that many pros like to use. This holds true regardless of whether you are the chip leader or the small stack. Being aggressive enough to raise pre-flop on the button with a wide range of hands, continuation betting, betting out small, or even check-calling, keeps the pot in your control and also keeps the pot small and manageable when it suits your interests.

If you have played enough head's up, you will really start to develop a sense for when the other player has a hand or not. I have come to the conclusion that head's up poker is the fastest road to learning how to read the other players, and in doing so, your post-flop play will begin to get better as you mature. This will apply to cash games, big tournaments, and even when you are in a sit-n-go.

With better post-flop play, you want to keep the pots small. Since your skill advantage is superior, you don't need to get into big confrontations unless you have the monster hand, of course.

In head's up poker, it is sometimes difficult to control pot size as you will run into the player that has heard aggressive play is the only way to win head's up poker. While it is a strong strategy, it's often misinterpreted to mean that you should try to bulldoze over people, which is not usually the case. If you can just focus on taking more pots than the other player when you both have nothing, then this will present you with a cushion for the pots that will turn into big altercations. This way, if you lose that pot, you're not out of the game just yet, and if you win, then you've broken the other player.

Always remember, head's up poker is just as much about the other player as it is about your cards. Once you gain a feel for what they are trying to do, counter attack and the chips should and will fall your way. Trust me on this concept, I have seen and done this so many times that I have lost count over the years.

❝ I never go looking for a sucker. I look for a Champion and make a sucker of him. ❞

—Thomas "Amarillo Slim" Preston, 1972 W.S.O.P. Champion, has a total of four WSOP bracelets, including two in Omaha and is a poker book author.

PART FIVE

More Games To Get Addicted To...

CHAPTER EIGHTEEN:

H.O.R.S.E.

H.O.R.S.E. is a form of poker commonly played at the high stakes tables of casinos. The game changes each hand, rotating between:

Limit Texas Hold'em,
Omaha eight or better,
Razz,
Seven–Card Stud, and
Seven–Card Stud Eight or better.

H.O.R.S.E. is a limit game, including Hold'em. However, in some tournament situations (such as the 2006, 2007, & 2008 World Series of Poker event), the final table has been played as NL Texas Hold'em. So far only professional players have won this event. Michael DeMichele did come close to pulling off this accomplishment in 2008's event.

A **H.O.R.S.E.** tournament was held at the World Series of Poker in 2004 and was won by Scott Fischman. The 2006 World Series **H.O.R.S.E.** tournament had a record-setting $50,000 entry fee and was won by Chip Reese. The $50,000 buy-in tournament returned for the 2007 WSOP, along with seven satellite events with a $2,250 buy-in whose winners earned seats to the event. The $50,000 event was won by poker professional Freddy Deeb.

Separate **H.O.R.S.E.** events with $2,500 and $5,000 buy-ins were also on the 2007 WSOP program. The tournament returned for its third straight year in 2008, but without one of its previous champions, Chip Reese, who died earlier in December. The future winners of this event will receive a trophy named after the late David "Chip" Reese.

Reese was a true gentleman and was the youngest person admitted to the Poker Hall of Fame; he has been recognized by his peers as the most successful player in the biggest mixed cash games of all time. He three WSOP bracelets, including one for his historic victory in the inaugural $50,000 buy-in **H.O.R.S.E.** tournament in 2006

The WSOP 2008 H.O.R.S.E. World Champion was Scotty Nguyen and Michael DeMichele was the runner up.

The H in H.O.R.S.E. is for Limit Hold'em

Well, my friend, you just read most of this great book on NL Texas Hold'em so we are going to assume for assumptions sake that you have a firm grasp on the "H" of **H.O.R.S.E.** It's time now to give you the basics on the other games included.

You should know that playing these games by themselves is often not only a great learning experience but a good way to round out your game with some variety. In an **H.O.R.S.E.** Poker tournament, the game changes after the blinds are raised. The game type changes every 8 hands during a **H.O.R.S.E.** cash game. In all of the **H.O.R.S.E.** poker games, the play cycles back to Limit Hold'em Poker after the final hand of Eights or Better (Seven-Card Stud High-Low.)

When transitioning between Omaha high-low and Razz, the button is frozen. This is done so that when the game switches to Hold'em once again, blinds are not missed and extra blinds are not paid. Each game in **H.O.R.S.E.** is fixed limit. Let's go through all of these game variations in an **H.O.R.S.E.** tournament.

The O in H.O.R.S.E. is for Omaha Eight or Better

Nine or ten players are customary in Omaha high-low split, which has a rotating blind system (meaning for every hand, a certain player must contribute a set amount of money to start the betting). Usually, a score of eight or better is placed on the low hand, and the best high hand will split the pot with the best low hand. This means for a hand to qualify as a low, it must have five cards not paired that are ranked eight or lower. For example, a hand consisting of ace, two, three, seven, and eight qualifies as a low hand, but a hand of ace, two, three, seven, and nine does not.

Each player is dealt four down cards, called "hole" cards. Then three community cards are dealt face up in the center of the table. These cards are called the "flop." Another card is dealt face up, which is called the "turn," followed by the last card being dealt face up, called the "river." Rounds of betting are before the flop, after the flop, after the turn, and after the river.

Each player must use exactly three cards from the five community cards and two from his or her hand in any combination to form a high and/or low hand. The same five cards do not have to be used for the high and the low. Note that if there are not at least three community cards ranked eight or below, there will be no low hand, and the entire pot will be awarded to the best high hand. The two most important rules are:

Each player must use exactly three community cards and two hole cards.

The order of ranking for low hands is from the highest of the five cards.

The easiest way to rank low hands is to read them backward as a number with the lowest number winning.

For example:

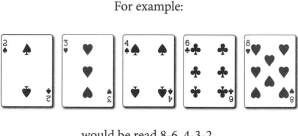

would be read 8-6, 4-3-2.

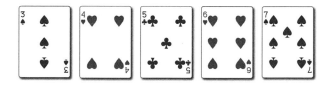

would be read 7-6, 5-4-3, and would be the lower of the two hands. Many times two players will have the same low hand and split the low half of the pot. This is often called "getting quartered."

Omaha eight or better games, especially on most poker (was)sites and card rooms, are filled with players who don't know how to play the game. Almost all Omaha eight or better players are current or former Texas Hold'em players who use the same thought process and mentality while playing Omaha eight or better as when they played NL Texas Hold'em. This is why Omaha eight or better can be profitable. Because there are four hole cards instead of two, many players think they see more possibilities to win and thus play far too many hands.

Another weakness in the games of many beginning players is not folding after the flop when the only hope they have is a split pot or a runner-runner (that is, needing the turn and river cards to win, which is a statistically weak position). In Omaha, after the flop, your hand is well defined. You see 7 out of the 9 cards you will use, almost 80 percent. In contrast, after the flop in NL Texas Hold'em you have seen only 5 of 7 cards, which is just over 70 percent. Omaha eight or better tends to be a much more straightforward and mathematical game than NL Texas Hold'em.

For this reason, Omaha eight or better tends to have less short-term variance (luck) than NL Texas Hold'em. Many players enjoy playing Omaha eight or better more than NL Texas Hold'em because of the reduced variance. The problem is that it can sometimes be hard to find a good Omaha eight or better game, while there never seems to be a shortage of NL Texas Hold'em games.

An important skill to master in Omaha eight or better is reading the cards. You must be able to look at the cards and consider what the best possible hand is, the likelihood of someone having the best hand, how close your hand is to the best hand, and what chance you have to improve to the best hand. As will be discussed shortly, you must often have the best hand possible to win. Reading the cards is a skill that will become easier as you gain experience. A good way to improve your skills is to read the cards on every hand even when you have folded. This not only improves your skills but also will help you learn what types of hands your opponents are playing. You need to determine if there is a possible low, flush, straight (which will be possible on most hands), full house.

Starting Hand Selection

As in NL Texas Hold'em, the most important decision you will make in Omaha eight or better is on which hands to enter a pot and on which hands you should run for the hills. Omaha eight or better is a game of scoops (winning both the high and low pots on the same hand or the high when no low is possible) and redraws (having a good hand with the opportunity to improve to a better hand with community cards).

A hand containing an ace that is suited to another card in the hand is a good example of both scooping and the redraw hands. You can win low with the ace, and you can win high with an ace high flush if your three suited cards hit on the board. For these reasons, your starting hand selection should include mostly hands that have the possibility to scoop and that offer redraws. Hands that have an ace are the most common starting hands because an ace can be used for a high hand and a low hand.

Another important concept is having counterfeit protection. For example, let's look at two hands, one with:

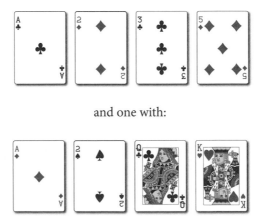

and one with:

If the flop comes:

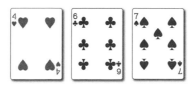

both players have the best possible low hand. You might raise the bet here, thinking you have a good shot at the low hand. However, if an

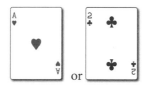

or

falls on the turn or river, the hand with **A-2-Q-K** no longer has the best possible low, while the other hand still does. Remember, you have to use two cards from your starting hand. If you have to throw out your A or 2 because you made a pair on the turn or river (and consequently no longer have the lowest hand), you would have to play your K or Q (making your low hand very weak). The first hand has counterfeit protection because it can fall back on the 3 or 5.

Most experts agree that in NL Texas Hold'em, you should see the flop only about 20 percent of the time. Many players believe because you have four hole cards in Omaha eight or better instead of two, you can see more flops. This is only true if you want to be a losing player. The fact is, you should see only about 20 percent of the flops as well. Starting hand selection is at least as important in Omaha eight or better as it is in NL Texas Hold'em, perhaps even more so.

At the lower limits, position is not nearly as important in Omaha eight or better as it is in NL Texas Hold'em. While it is nice to act last, it can be almost as good to act first, and even acting between players is not as bad as doing so in NL Texas Hold'em. Due to the straightforward way Omaha eight or better plays and the fact that you should have a very good idea of your chances to win after the flop, you should be able to play almost any hand in any position. As you become more experienced and move up in limits, position plays a more important role.

Particularly at the lower limits where the majority of players see the flop, you will often have to start with the best possible hand to win either the high or the low half of the pot. For example, if a flush is possible, you have almost no chance of winning the high pot unless you can beat a flush as one or more of your opponents will have one. If you have a flush and the board pairs, like

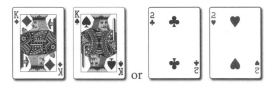 or

then you have probably lost to a full house. This is one of the reasons it is important to have hands that have both high and low potential.

Looking at low possibilities, most players will play any hand containing an

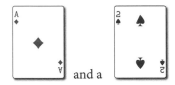 and a

If you have a low that cannot beat one that has A-2, then you probably won't win the low half of the pot unless the ace or two is counterfeited. If you are playing only toward half of the pot after the flop, it is imperative to draw only to the best possible hand.

Game Selection

If you have the choice of more than one game of Omaha eight or better to play in, you should look for these types of games:

A game that has over 50 percent of the players seeing most flops. In most poker games, especially Omaha eight or better and NL Texas Hold'em, the player who starts with the best hand will win a higher percentage of the time than any other player. If you follow the starting hand guidelines above, on average you will be entering the pot with a stronger hand than the other players. Omaha eight or better a game with little or no pre-flop raising. You will learn to prefer a game full of passive players. Sometimes in a card room it may be difficult to find these games, but if you play on certain poker sites, these games are abundant.

Now that you've bet before and after the flop, it's time to enter the nitty-gritty. Betting on the turn and river can mean the difference between gaining chips and going to the rail. Here's a look at my strategies for both.

How to Play on the Turn:

Play on the turn is straightforward and simple. If you have the best hand, bet. If you have a draw to the best hand, check and call (once again, assuming the pot odds are correct). If you have the best possible high or low hand and a chance at the other (low or high) pot, you should raise to the size of the pot accordingly.

How to Play on the River:

Play on the river is the most straightforward situation you will find. If you have the best high hand, raise as much as possible. High hands are almost never quartered. If you are heads-up or have three players and have the best low hand but no chance at the high hand, it is usually best to just call due to the possibility of being quartered. Realize that against three players, if you have the best low hand and are quartered, you will recoup at least every bet you place on the river. When you are against four or more players, have the best low hand, and are quartered, you will be making money on every bet you place, so it is often best to raise. If you are against two players and have the best low hand, you should check and call.

Sometimes you will be in a hand at the river against two players while you have the best low hand and they are both raising. It is extremely likely that you will be quartered in this situation, and you must decide if there is enough money already in the pot to warrant calling all of the raises. Against two players, if you have a low and it is quartered, every dollar you put into the pot will return only 75 cents to you.

In some cases, if the pot is small, your best play may be to fold. As you are learning to play, you may never fold in this situation because you want some of the money you contributed to the pot returned to you. Just bear in mind that this can actually cost you more. This is something you will learn with experience.

Omaha poker can be a fun and profitable game. By mastering the basic concepts in this chapter, you will play better than the average player, and with some experience you should become a consistent winning player.

Scotty Nguyen's Ace Deuce Controversial Theory

Scotty Nguyen is a Vietnamese-American professional poker player who has five (WSOP) bracelets, and is most well known as the winner of the 1998 World Series of Poker Main Event. He's also considered one of the best Omaha players.

His advice for Omaha eight or better players is very simple. He thinks you should only play starting hands that include A-2 in it and nothing else. How remarkable is that! This is an extremely super-tight strategy, if you ask me. He believes that if you play this way, you'll always put yourself in a good position to win. Scotty would fold any hand with A-A in it since he thinks big pairs in Omaha eight or better are useless. He also mucks the usual high hands like T-J-Q-K. He also advises that all players who want to win should stick with the A-2 strategy.

Phil Hellmuth mentions this strategy in one of his books and feels it's a little too eccentric. Phil also advises that you should play a little more like Miami John Cernuto would. I think Scotty's strategy is more practical for cash games when you have the time to play tight. If you use it in tourney play, I think you risk getting chipped down.

For specific Omaha eight or better information and strategy, please refer to:
CHAPTER TWENTY: Omaha (Omaha Eight or Better Section)

The R in H.O.R.S.E. is for Razz

Did you ever wish your "bad" hands could make you money? Then Razz could be the game for you. Part lowball, part 7-card stud, the goal is to make the worst hand possible. Razz is dealt just like basic Seven-Card Stud, but strangely enough the purpose is to make the lowest hand.

In Razz, each player starts with two hole cards and one up-card: there are then three more rounds of up-cards, with betting after each card, and a final down card. Each player ends up with seven cards: four face up and three face down. Flushes and straights don't count against you and have no value. Three of a kind and pairs are terrible too; this is because they make it more difficult to make a five-card low hand. Aces are always low, and the player holding the best low hand using any five of their cards wins the pot.

The best possible hand in Razz is **A-2-3-4-5,** and is also referred as "Wheel." The second best is **A-2-3-4-6**, and is called "Six-Perfect. It is easy to tell the difference which hand is the "best" in similar showdowns in playing Razz.

For specific Razz information and strategy, please refer to:
CHAPTER TWENTY ONE: Razz

The S in H.O.R.S.E. is for Seven-Card Stud, the E is for Seven-Card Stud Eight or Better

Seven-Card Stud is a variant of stud poker with two to eight. Until the recent increase in popularity of NL Texas Hold'em, Seven-card stud was the most popular poker variant in home games as well as in eastern US casinos. Seven-card stud is also played in western American casinos, but NL Texas Hold'em is far more popular there.

In casino play, it is common to use a small ante and bring-in. In home games, it is typical to use an ante only. The game begins with each player being dealt two cards face down and one card face up. If played with a bring-in, the player with the lowest-ranking up-card pays the bring-in, and betting proceeds after that in normal clockwise order. The bring-in is considered an open, so the next player in turn may not check. If two players have equally ranked low cards, suit may be used to break the tie and assign the bring-in (see high card by suit). If there is no bring-in, then the first betting round begins with the player showing the highest-ranking up-card, who may check. In this case, suit should not be used to break ties. If two players have the same high up-card, the player first in clockwise rotation from the dealer is the first player to act.

After the first betting round, another up-card is dealt to each player (after a burn card, and starting at the dealer's left as will all subsequent rounds), followed by a second betting round beginning with the player whose up-cards make the best poker hand. Since fewer than five cards are face up, this means no straights, flushes, or full houses will count for this purpose. On this and all subsequent betting rounds, the player whose face-up cards make the best poker hand will act first, and may check or bet up to the game's set limit.

The second round is followed by a third up-card and betting round, a fourth up-card and betting round, and finally a down-card, a fifth betting round, and showdown if necessary.

Seven-card stud can be summarized therefore as "two down, four up, and one down." Upon showdown, each player makes the best five-card poker hand out of the seven cards that he was dealt.

Note that seven cards to eight players plus four burn cards makes 60 cards, and there are only 52 in the deck. In most games this is not a problem because several players will have folded in early betting rounds.

But there are certainly low-stakes home games where few if any players fold. If this is the case in your game, you may want to limit the game to seven players. If the deck does become exhausted during play, previously-dealt burn cards can be used when only a few cards are needed to complete the deal. If even those are not sufficient, then on the final round instead of dealing a down-card to each player, a single community card is dealt to the center of the table.

Under no circumstances can any discarded card from a folded hand be "recycled" for later use. Unlike draw poker, where no cards are ever seen before showdown, stud poker players use the information they get from face-up cards to make strategic decisions, and so a player who sees a certain card folded is entitled to make decisions knowing that the card will never appear in another player's hand.

For specific Seven-Card Stud information and strategy, please refer to:
CHAPTER TWENTY TWO: Seven Card Stud

For specific Seven-Card Stud Eight or Better information and strategy, please refer to:
CHAPTER TWENTY TWO: Seven Card Stud (Eight or Better Section)

In conclusion, H.O.R.S.E is my favorite game. It does take a significant level of skill to be successful, but once you have it down the rewards are plentiful. I recommend playing low-limit H.O.R.S.E games online. When you start to crush low-limit games consistently, then it is time to move up into middle stakes and live games.

"2-7 Triple draw lowball is a game for donkeys and morons.**"**

—Mike "the mouth" Matusow, a nice guy who can't stop talking trash, and has great poker talent. He started working as a poker dealer, and then as professional player. His successes include being a three-time W.S.O.P. bracelet winner, and the winner of the 2005 W.S.O.P. Tournament of Champions. One thing's for sure, no table featuring him will ever be boring.

CHAPTER NINETEEN:

2-7 TRIPLE DRAW LOW-BALL

Triple draw lowball is referred to as "crack for poker players," most professional cash game players understand that poker is a long-term grind. There are hundreds of sessions, thousands of hands, millions of decisions.

In the present poker era, a strong majority of players are making their hourly rate almost exclusively at the NL Texas Hold'em tables. While NL Texas Hold'em is still an incredibly profitable game, especially online, sometimes it can get exceptionally boring just looking at two hole cards all day long. In the interest of breaking the repetitiveness, I would like to remind you that yes, there are many games other than NL Texas Hold'em that are bizarre, wild, and brilliant poker variants like Badugi, Deuce-To-Seven, and Razz that will challenge a player to think outside the flop, turn and river. To make the changeover from NL Texas Hold'em to any one of these more specialized games necessitates a little more than an unyielding understanding of the game rules, a few starting hand requirements, and some good poker sense.

Professional poker players have a common misconception that triple draw is nothing more than a game of pure luck. That's simply not the case. While luck plays a role in any given hand, playing correctly will minimize any hazardous swings that luck may bring, allowing skill to triumph.

Deuce-To-Seven Triple Draw Lowball is a game loaded with action. You may need firm grip on the poker table when playing this game. All the action and constant decision making you will endure throughout this game would equate to a ride on a large roller coaster ride. To better prepare you for this excitement, this chapter will give you all the strategies that you'll need to become a successful Deuce-To-Seven Triple Draw Lowball player. This game can drive players crazy. All of the variables of poker are represented in this game, and the pots are almost always monsters. So if you are the type of player that likes to gamble and rake in monster pots, this is the game for you. Just don't rip all of your hair out when you miss your draws.

Triple draw is often played live as part of a higher-stakes mixed game; it is unusual to see a pure triple draw table spread.

After reading this chapter, you will have a firm grasp of this game. And if you apply these simple strategies to your game, this should be enough to enable you to beat almost any triple draw game around.

Deuce-To-Seven Triple Draw Lowball Rules

Deuce-To-Seven triple draw is a moderately new game, only emerging in the last decade. In today's casinos, it is primarily spread only in high-limit mixed games. However, I have found that there are low-limit games available online at Ultimate Bet and PokerStars. True poker junkies love triple draw for its wild action. It's a naturally shorthanded game limited to six players dealt in at once due to the amount of discards and the four betting rounds can lead to huge pots. It is possible to play this game seven or eight-handed, but only if players sit out on every deal. When playing seven-handed, the player to the left of the big blind is forced to sit out one hand. Eight-handed, the players in first and second positions sit out.

How to play Deuce-To-Seven Triple Draw Lowball

Much like limit Texas Hold'em, triple draw is played in a two-tiered limit structure with a button, small blind and big blind. Five cards are dealt face down to each player; there are no up-cards or community cards. There are four betting rounds, after the deal and after each of the three draws. In these rounds players may either "stand pat" or discard between one to five cards and draw new ones in their pursuit to make the best low hand. After the second draw, the betting limit doubles in size.

While in razz and in A-5 lowball an A-2-3-4-5 wheel is the absolute nuts, this is the best possible hand in 2-7 triple draw:

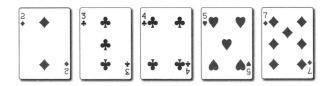

Betting in Deuce-To-Seven Triple Draw Lowball

In some areas of the South, they play spread-limit, meaning that in a $50/$200 game, you can bet from $50 to $200 at any time, but fixed limits are more popular. If you are seated in a $50/$100 triple draw game, the small blind posts $50 and the big blind $100. If you are first to act, you can fold, call the $100, or raise it to $200. Every player after you has the same options: fold, call, or raise. Once that action is complete, there is another betting round, also in $100 increments, after the first draw. After the second draw, the bet doubles. You can now bet or raise $200. Finally, after the third draw, the bet is once again $200.

So there are four betting rounds in total. In a $20/$100 game, they would be:

1. $100 before the first draw;
2. $100 after the first draw;
3. $200 after the second draw; and
4. $200 after the third draw.

Now that we've got that out of the way, let's look at what types of hands we should be starting with.

First and most important: Don't get involved with a hand without having a deuce. In deuce-to-seven triple draw, the lowly deuce is more powerful than any other card. Your goal in deuce-to-seven triple draw would be to make a seven, and in order to do so, you must have a deuce in your hand. There are four possible sevens, all of which contain a deuce:

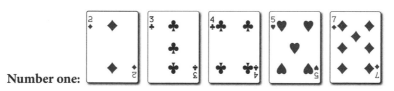

Number one:

This hand is also referred to as a wheel in Deuce-To-Seven triple draw. Not **2-3-4-5-6**, which would be a straight. Many players new to triple draw tend to forget that and I've seen a shocking number of deuce to seven players turn over **A-5** and **2-6** straights expecting to have the pot sent their way, only to be totally shocked when their opponent takes the hand with a raggedy Jack low. After the 2-7 wheel, the next best low hands are:

Number two:

This hand is also referred to in Deuce-To-Seven triple draw.

Number three:

This hand is also referred to in Deuce-To-Seven triple draw.

Number four:

This hand is also referred to in Deuce-To-Seven triple draw.

There are two variations of triple draw that are played today; Ace-to-Five (A-5) and Deuce-to-Seven (2-7). In A-5 aces are low and straights and flushes do not count against you. The opposite is true in the more popular 2-7. Your objective in 2-7 triple draw is to make the worst hand possible without hitting a straight or a flush. Pairs are bad, trips are even worse. Also, in Deuce-To-Seven triple draw, an ace can only be used for high. This leads to the rare case of the worst traditional poker hand winning. So always keep in mind that you should discard aces immediately!

Deuce-To-Seven Triple Draw starting hands:
Just like Omaha, 2-7 triple draw is a game of the nuts. You should always be drawing to the nuts (**2-3-4-5-7**), or something close to it. Playing this game in a tight controlled manner is the key to success, especially as a beginner, and you should rarely play a starting hand without a deuce in it.

Deuce-To-Seven Triple Draw made (no need to draw) hands:
When you have any five cards to a 7-low or an 8-low, this is an excellent deuce-to-seven hand. When you're lucky enough to pick up a hand like that after the deal, it's best to "stand pat" and stick with what you have, drawing no cards. 7-lows like **2-3-4-5-7, 2-3-4-6-7, 2-3-5-6-7, and 2-4-5-6-7** are premium hands and instead of trying to slow play these hands, you should be trying to get in as many bets and raises as you possibly can against the other players who are on a draw. This is because once you decline new cards, your secret is out and the other players will already know that you have a big hand. A made 8-low or "pat 8" is also powerful. Hands with a **5-8, 6-8** or **7-8** low such as **2-3-4-5-8, 2-4-5-6-8,** and **2-4-6-7-8** are all strong enough to stand pat. However, since the other players will likely be drawing to some sort of 8-low, these hands are a bit more vulnerable than the monster pat sevens.

One Card Draws in Deuce-To-Seven Triple Draw Lowball:
Four cards to a 7 or 8-low that include a deuce or a trey are strong one-card drawing hands. The exception would be open-ended straight draws like 3-4-5-6 (only an 8 or

higher could help this hand, as the **2** or **7** will fill the straight) or **4-5-6-7** (a **2** is the only way to improve, as a 3 or 8 fills this straight). Like in every other poker variant, draws to the nuts should be played aggressively, so think about constantly raising your 7-low draws like **2-3-4-7, 2-3-5-7** and **2-4-5-7**. One card draws to an 8-low that do not contain straight possibilities are also strong draws to play aggressively, such as **2-3-4-8, 2-3-5-8, 2-4-5-8, 2-3-7-8 or 3-4-5-8.** You should not fold these hands, they are simply too good for that. And playing them be sure to target the other player or steal the blinds. Any time you are playing a hand that has a one-card draw, regardless of its ranking, you should be raising and re-raising before the first draw.

In other words, any hand you decide to play before the first draw, plan on putting in a raise. There are few situations where limping is correct. If your hand is strong enough to play, play it aggressively. If it's not, fold it immediately. In triple draw, your strategy before the draw should be similar to that used in Limit Texas Hold'em before the flop, tight but smart-aggressive.

Two Card Draws in Deuce-To-Seven Triple Draw Lowball:

There are several two-card draws that are also playable hands before the first draw. **2-3-4, 2-3-5, 2-3-7, 2-4-5, 2-4-7,** and **2-5-7** are the strongest two-card draws (all drawing at a wheel). Two-card draws containing a 6, such as **2-3-6, 2-4-6** and **2-5-6** are also great starting draws, but remember, the presence of the 6 in your hand means you are not drawing at the all-important nuts (the **2-3-4-5-7** wheel). Two-card draws to an 8-low like **2-3-8, 2-4-8** and **2-5-8** can also be worth playing, but are much more vulnerable hands. Think about playing these sorts of draws from late position.

Three, Four and Five Card Draws in Deuce-To-Seven Triple Draw Lowball:

Play these hands only if you want to lose a lot of money. I suggest folding these. Period!

When You are Fortunate to be Dealt Pat Hands

If you are dealt a pat hand, you want to protect it by putting in every bet you can. Any pat seven is a monster, and while a pat eight is great, it is also vulnerable. For the most part, if you are dealt a pat seven or eight you won't be drawing at all, and depending on the action, you'll probably see the hand through to the end.

Once you've decided to stay pat with your seven or eight, there is no need to slow-play your hand. Bet and raise at every opportunity before the draw and after the first draw. With a pat hand, smooth calling before the draw is pointless, as your secret will be out soon.

A nine, however, is more difficult to play. In some situations, it may be okay to stay pat with a nine, but in general you want to avoid even playing a rough nine. You'd be better off placing a hand like **9-8-7-6-4** in the muck than hoping it holds up in a multi-way pot.

However, if you held something like **9-7-4-3-2**, you would have a dynamite draw. You would discard the nine and have three chances at a seven. You are certainly a favorite to make at least a nine or better with a draw like this, since you'd have fifteen outs three times! That makes you a big favorite over a foolish player who stays pat with the same nine.

Playing Deuce-To-Seven Triple Draw Lowball from the Blinds

Playing out of the big blind can be tricky. Though you will usually get excellent pot odds, if you start with rough draws, you will make rough hands and receive rough hits to your chip stack. You certainly want to stretch you're starting requirements some, but if you go too far, you are going to be left with too many difficult decisions. For example, drawing two out of the big blind with a hand like **4-6-5** is just asking for trouble. What are you looking to catch?

How about if you have **2-7, or 2-8?** Even if you catch this miracle draw, your hand is still not in the clear. Fold your hand because this draw will cause some major headaches.

The hands you should add to your playable list are the excellent three-card draws (**2-3, 2-4, 2-5, and** 2-7) and some of the two-card eight draws (**3-4-8, 3-5-8**). Since you are being laid such great pot odds, you should also add the seven draws that don't contain a deuce (**3-4-7, 3-5-7, 3-6-7, and** 4-5-7). With rough draws like these, you want to get to the draw as cheaply as possible. Calling one raise is fine; calling two raises is suicide. Every once in a while you'll pick up a really strong draw in the blind, such as a one-card draw to a non-straight eight-or-better or a two-card draw to a wheel containing a deuce. If you are holding one of these and find yourself up against a late position raiser, you should punish him by re-raising.

If everyone folds to you in the small blind, don't get carried away trying to steal the big blind's money. In fact, since you don't have position, you should play tighter than you would if you were the button. Good three-card draws, one containing a 2, **3, 4, 5, or 7**, are still playable. Against a loose-aggressive player you should probably limp with these weak hands, but if the big blind plays conservatively, you should raise it. Remember, the small blind acts first on all subsequent rounds of betting, so it's the worst position at the table. If anyone else has joined the pot, you'd need a solid starting hand to play from the small blind.

If you are in the big blind head's up against the small blind, you should call one more bet with anything remotely playable. That even includes a three-card draw to a 3-4! There are many reasons why having position is so valuable when playing head's up. That, in addition to the 3 to 1 odds you're getting to defend your big blind against the small blind, makes calling the right play with almost any three-card draw to a wheel.

Playing Deuce-To-Seven Triple Draw Lowball Against a Raise

If you are the button and facing a raise, usually you should re-raise and take the hand head's up with the power of position. Hands like 2-3-4, 2-3-7, one-card draws, and pat hands are all strong hands that you don't want to fold. Take control by three-betting it. If your hand isn't good enough to three-bet, seriously consider folding. If you're outside the blind, hands like 2-3-8 are good enough to raise with if no one has entered the pot, but not quite good enough to call a raise.

Playing After the First Draw in Deuce-To-Seven Triple Draw Lowball

Depending on the draw you start with, you'll generally want to bet and raise when you improve your hand and check and call or check and fold. Again, it all depends on your initial draws. If you were dealt 2-3-4-7 and were up against any player who drew two, you would bet whether you improved or not. In fact, it would be fine to bet without even looking to see if you improved..

When You Miss in Deuce-To-Seven Triple Draw Lowball

What to do when you don't improve depends on your position, the number of cards you draw, and the numbers of cards the other players draw. If you draw one and the other players draw two or more, you should always bet. In fact, anytime you are a card ahead of the other players, it's safe to bet, with one exception. Here it is: if you draw two and don't improve, then are called by two players drawing three, you should check. Chances are that one if not both of them improved, so it would be wise to take the free card rather than risk being raised or check-raised.

When out of position and drawing an equal number of cards as the other players, what you do depends heavily on whether or not you improve. Generally speaking, you should play the hand straightforward, betting when you improve and checking when you miss.

For example, in the small blind with **2-5-6-7**, a late position player raises you, and you re-raise. You draw one, as does the other player. If you don't improve, betting would be silly. The other player will almost never fold here, but will likely raise you if he improves. Sure, you may have a marginally better draw than he does, but that doesn't justify losing an extra bet if he did improve.

Even if the other player draws to a **3-4-5-8**, it wouldn't be a disaster if the betting round went check, check. In the best case scenario, you'll get a bet in as a marginal favorite. In the worst case scenario, you'll get two bets in as either a significant underdog or drawing dead, while the other player is drawing smoother.

Now, if you are drawing two cards to a premium hand in a raised multi-way pot, you should still call a bet whether you improve or not, since the pot is already sizeable.

However, you should rarely call a bet or raise if you don't improve your two-card draw, as you will likely find yourself up against two one-card draws, one-card draw, pat hand, or two pat hands. If you do decide to call a double bet, you won't even know for sure whether it will cost you more to see your next draw. If the first bettor does have a pat hand, he will likely re-raise, putting you in a horrible position, drawing two against a pat hand with two draws left.

When You Improve in Deuce-To-Seven Triple Draw Lowball

When you do improve after the first draw, it's time to get aggressive. Whether you improve to a one-card draw or a vulnerable pat hand, you'll want to narrow the field as much as possible in multi-way pots. Being aggressive in head's up situations isn't quite as important. Let's look at an example.

You raise in first position with 2-4-7. You are called by the button and re-raised by the big blind. The big blind draws one, while both you and the button draw two. Now you catch a 5 and a king. The big blind bets and it's up to you. Should you call or raise?

The correct answer would be raise. While it's true that you may be up against a pat hand, you'd still have two draws to make a seven or possibly an eight, depending on the other players' hand. Forcing the button out is the most important thing. If you just call, he would be getting good enough pot odds to draw two cards. That's not what you want. You want to secure last position by chasing the button out, and then take the hand heads up. If the big blind didn't improve, you'll have an even better chance against just one player.

What if you are heads up the whole time? Same scenario, except this time there is no third player. In this case, a raise wouldn't be horrible, but calling would be better. Since you don't have to worry about knocking out a player, you can simply call here and draw to your hand cheaply. The one key drawback to raising is the risk of the other player making his hand. It would then cost you three bets rather than one to outdraw him. As I mentioned earlier, you may be giving up little value since you have the better draw, but that won't make up for the times you pay extra against a made hand.

Keep the 8 or Draw to the Wheel in Deuce-To-Seven Triple Draw Lowball

This is probably one of the most difficult decisions you'll have to make in a triple draw hand. When drawing to a hand like 2-3-7, should you keep the 8 after the first draw and draw rough, or discard it and draw to the wheel?

The reason it is such a difficult decision is because it depends on several variables, including the number of players, the number of cards the other players need, your position, and the discards you made.

Number of Players You are Up Aagainst in Deuce-To-Seven Triple Draw Lowball

The more players in the pot, the more you should lean toward discarding the 8 and going for the wheel. The problem with keeping the 8 with more players drawing is that it will get beat too often by an 8-6, an 8-5, or a seven.

If you are up against just one other player, you might decide to keep the 8, but you should consider other factors, like the number of cards the other player is drawing and your position.

Number of Cards Being Drawn in Deuce-To-Seven Triple Draw Lowball

If the other players are drawing three or more, you should keep the 8. They need a lot of help, and if you make an 8-7 here, it will usually be good enough to win. If you go to the deck and again draw two, you will be giving them a better shot of getting back into the hand. Draw to the 8-7 and punish them for their loose play.

Discards in Deuce-To-Seven Triple Draw Lowball

We are going to cover this subject in greater detail near the end of the chapter. But for now, we'll say that generally, the more paired wheel cards you have in your hand, the stronger the hand. While 2-3-4-K-Q and 2-3-4-3-4 appear to be the same draw (2-3-4), the latter is a much stronger hand.

Why? Because that extra 3 and 4 might be cards that the other player is looking for but can now no longer catch! Additionally, it makes it less likely that you will pair. Furthermore, if the other player holds 2-5-7, your discard makes it less likely that he will make his draw now that two of his cards are dead.

So how does that apply to keeping an 8? Simple. The more paired cards you have, the more you should lean toward keeping the 8.

Making an Eight on the First Draw

When you start out playing triple draw lowball, you are usually going to stay pat if you make an eight at any point. Once your reading ability improves, however, you will be able to break an eight and draw to the seven under the right circumstances. An 8-7 can be broken, but if you make an 8-6 or better, you're better off staying pat. Being in position will also play into your decision of whether or not to break an eight. How so?

If you are holding 2-3-6-7-8 and the player in front of you stands pat after the first draw, you have to ask yourself, "What can I beat?" You ask yourself, would the other player stay pat with his nine here? Or could he possibly have a worse 8-7?

In this case, with the other player standing pat in front of you, you will usually break the eight, since you have such a smooth draw to a seven (2-3-6-7). If no one yet has stood pat, you should stay pat until the game changes

Playing After the Second Draw in Deuce-To-Seven Triple Draw Lowball
When to Check

After the second draw, you should always check to a player that is one card ahead of you. For example, if you are drawing two and the other player is drawing one, you can even check in the dark. Or if you are drawing one and the other player is pat, again you can check in the dark. In these situations, you won't be risking a free card because the other player will surely bet. If the other player doesn't make this normally automatic bet, then he will often give you a free card.

If after the first draw, both you and the other player draw one and you fail to improve to a pat hand, you should probably check, especially when out of position and most of the time when in position. Even if you feel like you have the best draw going into the last card, it is usually only a slight advantage, so it's probably best to avoid the possible check-raise.

When to Bet

If you had this hand out of position however, you should still check despite the powerful draw you have. The other player isn't going to fold here; he'll either raise or call. If he does raise, you have now lost an extra bet and are probably an underdog to win the pot. This is an important concept to understand. When out of position, you need to think about minimizing your losses by avoiding marginal value bets. They have value when the other player happens to miss, but when the other player completes his draw; you give up way too much equity when he raises you. In position, you should also bet some of your premium one-card draws for another reason. If the other player is perceptive, he will know that you don't have a pat hand when you check behind him going into the last draw. If he has a hand like 2-3-4-8-10, he might decide to stay pat knowing that your hand is not complete. However, had you bet your draw, he would have a really tough time staying pat with a ten.

If you don't have a pat hand, you want the other player to break the ten. The ten is a favorite over even 2-3-4-7-7. If you can get him to break the ten with a bet, your 2-3-4-7 will become the favorite over his draw to the 2-3-4-8.

When to Call

When drawing one to a wheel or any seven, you should always call one bet going into the last draw. In fact, sometimes you may even raise with a draw like this, but we'll get to that. Let's cover situations where you would simply call.

If both you and the other player draw one going into the last draw and you don't improve but he bets, you should usually just call. The other player's bet should tell you that he has a pat hand. So unless you have reason to believe he'd fold to a raise, you should just call and try to outdraw him. Also, if you draw two and improve to a one-card draw, and the other player draws one going into the second draw, you should just call. If you get really lucky and make a pat hand, then consider raising.

There is one more interesting situation where calling might be better than raising. Suppose the other player draws one and you, though still drawing two, have position on him. You find yourself with a hand like 2-4-6-7-8. Should you raise or just call?

Let's think about what may happen if you just call. If you call, the other player will assume that you are still drawing at least one, if not two. If he makes a hand like 10-7-4-3-2 he will probably stay pat ahead of you. After all, a pat ten is a favorite over any draw. Now, if you smooth call, you've just ensured yourself the pot. Since there are no draws left, you are protecting what's in the middle. In a sense, you're tricking the other player into thinking he has the best hand because you didn't raise.

So what would have happened if you raised? Well, you'd certainly be taking the best of it, as your pat eight is a favorite over his wheel draw. The problem is, you don't want the other player to be drawing live at all. If you raise and force the other player to break the ten, he'll now be drawing live to a five, six, or even an eight. Why risk the whole pot to get in one extra bet in on the turn? You might even be able to win that bet on the river when the pot is secured. This play is a valuable tool that has to be added to your tool chest if you want to be a winning triple draw player.

Finally, and this should go without saying, you should call when you are a card behind. If you improve from a two-card draw to a one-card draw, and the other player was already on a one-card draw, you should simply caller. If you are up against a player who was already pat and you are on a one-card draw, you should usually just call unless you have reason to believe he has a weak hand, in which case you may choose to raise.

When to Raise

The most obvious reason to raise is that you have the best hand. For the most part, with a seven, 8-5, or even 8-6, you should raise since you probably do have the best hand.

In a multi-way pot, it's even more important to raise with one of these pat hands in order to put pressure on the other players trying to outdraw you. They will call one bet drawing to a wheel or a good eight, depending on the players you may be able to get them to lay it down.

Even when head's up, you should raise with a seven or an 8-5, then follow through with a bet on the river. Hands ranked one through five are difficult to outdraw. The other player can't possibly have too many outs if he is still drawing. Even if the other player is drawing to a 2-3-4-7 against your 2-3-4-5-8, he can only win the pot with a 6 or one of three remaining fives, a total of seven outs. If the other player has a pat eight, chances are he won't break it, thinking you might be making a play at the pot.

Making a Play at the Pot

What do I mean by making a play at the pot? Sometimes if you have an excellent draw, you might be better off spending an extra bet, hoping to force the other player to break a pat hand, rather than just calling in the hopes of outdrawing him.

For example, say you are on the button with:

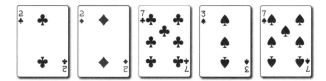

The other player raises before the first draw, and you re-raise him. Then the other player draws one and you, of course, draw two. Your two new cards are

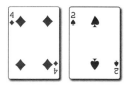

giving you a wheel draw,

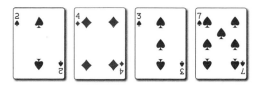

Next, the other player bets. Because of your position, your strong draw, and the valuable discards you've mucked, you decide to raise it. The other player calls and decides to stay pat.

Right there you can assume that the other player doesn't have a very strong hand. If he did, he probably would have re-raised once more. Also, since you have seen three deuces and two sevens, it's a lot more likely that the other player has a hand like :

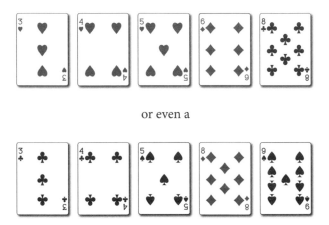

or even a

On the second draw, the other player is pat and you draw one to the wheel. This time, you catch another

Unless the other player has both the last

2♥ and the last 7♥

he definitely doesn't have a pat seven. The other player bets. What should you do?

It all depends on your read of the other player. You have a pretty good idea as to the strength of his hand, most likely an eight or a nine. Will the other player fold? Will the other player come off of a nine and draw? If you think there is a reasonable chance that the answer to either question is yes, then you should go ahead and raise.

By investing one more bet, you may either win the pot right there or go from an underdog to a sizeable favorite. If it doesn't work out, it adds more deception to your game at little cost, deception that you can exploit later. After all, you have one more draw and could still make your hand. In order for a play like this to work, you have to know the other player. If you know him to be stubborn enough not to break, or fold, you should save your money.

However, if he is a thinking player, he'll ask himself, "What can I beat?" Since you played the hand so aggressively before and after the first draw, a thinking player would know that you have a strong draw. If he is looking down at 3-4-6-8-9, what could he possibly break and draw to? He has to simply hope and pray that you are making a play and that you will miss on the last draw. Based on all of this, a thinking player may decide it's not worth seeing the hand through and fold. Remember, though; do not try this play against a calling station. Trying to bluff a bad player will make you the fool.

When to Fold

There are several situations where you should fold, even with one draw remaining. If you are still drawing two with only one draw remaining, you should usually fold to a bet, especially out of position. The only time you should consider drawing two going into the last draw is when you have position, you think the other player is still drawing, there is a lot of money in the pot, and you have made valuable discards. Otherwise, it's just too difficult to make a hand drawing two with just one draw left. Even 2-3-4 is an underdog to beat **K-Q-J-10-8**.

Here's another situation where you should consider folding: say you are up against a pat hand drawing to a rough eight. If the other player stays pat after the first draw and you are holding 2-6-7-8, two things need to happen for you to win the pot:

You would need to make your hand.

You would need to be drawing live.

Since the other player stayed pat after just the first draw, chances are he has at least an eight made, so you will be drawing dead here too often to make calling correct. You should fold when you make either a rough eight or nine and get raised after the second draw. The only way your hand could be playable is if the other player is making a bluff-raise and is still drawing.

Finally, you should fold when facing two bets going into the last draw, even when drawing to the nuts. This bit of advice may come as a shock to some, so let's look at the reasoning behind it. With one draw left, you have 2-4-5-7 on the button. In front of you, it's bet and raised. Fold. You know that a 6 will give you number four, a strong hand, but one that still might not be good enough considering the action in front of you. This leaves you needing a 3 to give you the nuts. Considering that you are facing two players who obviously have five low cards already, what are the chances that all four threes are still live? In addition, there's always the chance that the first bettor will re-raise once more. All of a sudden, your monster wheel draw doesn't look so hot now, does it?

When to Stay Pat

We know for sure that a pat jack is a small favorite over any draw. Even a hand like J-10-9-8-6 against 2-3-4-7 with one draw left is a 55 percent favorite. From this, can you assume that you should always stay pat with a jack or better with one draw left. There are too many chances to lose here.

Head's Up

If you are heads-up with position and know that the other player is drawing, then you could consider staying pat, even with 2-3-4-7-J. However, if you are out of position and don't have the luxury of knowing whether or not the other player is drawing or staying pat, that changes things dramatically. In this case, you should always draw. Even after the other player draws one card, you should probably draw one as well when you figure you're drawing better. That's because you have almost as big an advantage in the one-card versus one-card match-up as you do standing pat, assuming you just showed down the results without betting. In addition, you'll have the opportunity to gain ground through the final betting, considering your superior draw and the fact that you'll act last.

The opportunity to make more money outweighs your slightly diminished chances of ending up with the better hand. So it's usually correct to draw a card. In doing so, you'll also rule out the possibility of being bluffed out by the other player. Again, it's interesting to note that in a showdown situation, where there can be no future betting, the jack is the favorite over any draw, and it's correct to stand pat with such a hand.

As you see, this is what makes position so important in triple draw. With position in a showdown situation, you would know for certain that the correct play is to stand pat behind the other player who drew one, hoping he missed.

How to Snow

Snowing is something that you should not do frequently. If you do it too often it will lose its effectiveness, but not doing it at all will make you too predictable. If you get caught snowing again and again, you will get a few loose calls here and there, but that will also make this bluffing weapon useless to you.

In order to pull this off, you need to have earned respect from the other players without becoming predictable. As a general rule, snowing only when you have three deuces, three sevens, and so on would establish a decent snowing frequency.

There are several ways to snow, and I could go on and on about all of them. But if you have a good understanding of the ones I describe below, you'll do fine. As you have learned already, the information you receive from paired cards should heavily influence your decision of whether or not to snow. Generally speaking, snowing is more effective if you've stayed pat on the first or second draw. Staying pat so early in a hand represents strength. Finally, and as is the case with most poker strategies, this one works best when played in position.

So with the 2-2-2-2-3, you could raise it up and stay pat right off the bat. If you get any callers, you would be forced to bet the hand the whole way through and hope that the other player doesn't make a hand he is willing to call you with. Many times, when you stay pat right off the bat, alarm bells go off in the other players' heads. They may suspect a snow and call you on the river to find out. To avoid this, you can draw one to your 2-2-2-2-3, and stay pat after the first draw. This approach is generally more believable and looks less suspicious. If somewhere along the way, someone stays pat as well, it's time to abort the mission. You should fold to a bet or, naturally, draw if it's not bet to you.

Conclusion

Let me repeat this: the deuce is the key card in this game. Most of the hands you choose to play should contain a deuce with few exceptions. You might see others drawing to hands that don't contain a deuce, but don't fall into that trap.

For the most part, you want to play strong hands that can make the nuts. When you are drawing smooth, you are going to make smooth hands when you hit. If you are drawing rough, you'll often be drawing to a loser or often drawing dead.

Now that you have read this whole chapter, I recommend that you practice this strategy at PokerStars or Ultimate Bet, before playing in the high stakes games area of certain casinos.

❝...Just as Hold'em supplanted Seven-card Stud as the most popular variation of poker in the world, I believe Omaha will be supplanting Hold'em in the very near future.**❞**

—Sam Farha, runner up in the 2003 W.S.O.P. Main Event. He also has two W.S.O.P. bracelets, which were Pot Limit Omaha and Limit Omaha eight or better.

CHAPTER TWENTY:

OMAHA

Omaha is another fun variation of poker. In my opinion, it involves a little bit more thought, more scrupulous hand selection, and a tighter style of play than Texas Hold'em. While it's not my favorite poker game, Omaha can be tons of fun once you've mastered it.

As mentioned in chapter 18, each player is dealt four hole cards face down with 5 community cards dealt in turn on the board. To form a hand a player uses two hole cards and three community cards. Between six and ten total players form the table with the blind set-up and betting system emulating Texas Hold'em. Players can bet, check and call pre-flop, post flop and subsequently after the turn and the river. When compared to Texas Hold'em, the only difference in Omaha is that each player holds four hole cards instead of two.

Starting hand selection is of utmost importance in Omaha because players each get four hole cards, thus lowering your odds of hitting your best hand.

The Most Desired Starting Hands in Omaha and Pot-Limit Omaha are as Follows:

1. **A-A-K-K** double suited is best
2. **A-A-J-10** double suited is best
3. **A-A-Q-Q** double suited is best
4. **A-A-J-J** double suited is best
5. **A-A-10-10** double suited is best
6. **A-A-9-9** double suited is best
7. **A-A-x-x (x)** = Can be any card
8. **8-9-10-J** double suited is best
9. **K-K-Q-Q** suited is preferred
10. **K-K-J-J** suited is preferred
11. **K-Q-J-10** double suited is best

12. **K-K-10-10** double suited is best
13. **K-K-A-Q** suited is preferred
14. **K-K-A-J** suited is preferred
15. **K-K-A-10 suited is preferred**
16. **K-K-Q-J** suited is preferred
17. **K-K-Q-10** suited is preferred
18. **K-K-J-10** suited is preferred
19. **Q-Q-10-10** suited is preferred
20. **Q-Q-A-K** suited is preferred
21. **Q-Q-A-J** suited is preferred
22. **Q-Q-A-10** suited is preferred

When you're new to the game don't be scared to raise with:

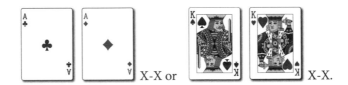

X-X or ... X-X.

Or any two pair greater than nine.

Intermediate and advanced players might also consider limping into the pot pre-flop with any pair less than nine.

Intermediate skilled players should considering playing:

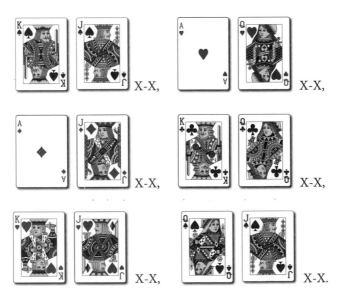

X-X, ... X-X,

X-X, ... X-X,

X-X, ... X-X.

These hands are strongest when suited. Use caution, as these hands are not as strong as in Hold'em, because someone else probably has a pocket pair, or a strong flush draw or straight draw. In Omaha, one pair (even a high one) will almost never be enough for you to win a hand.

Starting Hands that should be Folded Immediately:
- If all four of your hole cards are under nine.
- Four cards of different suits.
- Four cards of the same suit (since you already have four, odds that you will get three on the board out of the nine left in the deck are slim)
- Four cards that could make a straight with one more card (remember that you can only use two of them!)

I usually only play the above mentioned hands with at least a pair. I will fold if I only have one ace, unless I have a decent kicker, in which case I will limp into the pot.

As mentioned earlier, play is similar to Texas Hold'em, except that each player has four hole cards instead of two. Assuming that you have the basics of playing poker from this book, I will outline some common situations that you will encounter in Omaha and guide you on how to play them.

If you are in a hand with a pocket pair and hit your set on the flop, bet twice the pot post-flop immediately, since each card that follows has an increased possibility of making the other players' superior flush or straight. If you don't flop your set or end up with a significant flush or straight draw, and the other player(s) are aggressively raising, you should fold.

Here is a personal example:

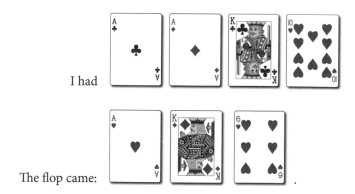

I had

The flop came:

I bet twice the size of the pot post flop, and was raised to all-in. I called with my set of Aces, as there was no significant straight or flush draw on the board.

The turn came:

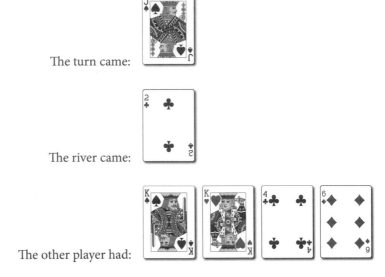

The river came:

The other player had:

My set of aces doubled me up. Slow-playing is only advised in Omaha if you have the absolute nuts.

Here is a one more example that I want to share with you:

I limped into a pot with:

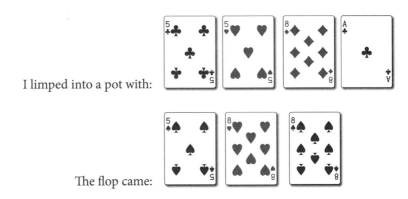

The flop came:

I slow played this hand and went all-in after the river in order to make the most out of my full house.

Beware of low flushes and low straights as chances are good that someone has a one. Beware of your set if there is a flush or a straight draw on the board. If the other player is betting/raising hard, it's likely that they have already hit their flush, straight or full house.

Note that in Omaha, bad beats come often, because players have four hole cards, therefore increasing their chances of making monster hands. Each player's "best hand" changes with each additional card that comes on the board.

Here are Some more Great Tips to Think About When Playing Omaha

- In Omaha, play tight and exercise patience. The ability to wait for the good hands is what separates riches from rags. If you've played a lot of Texas Hold'em, you may be swayed to play some great Texas Hold'em starting hands that are actually pretty iffy for Omaha.

- Play hands that go together. In other words, hands with multiple possibilities. A three-card straight that includes a pair or two pairs are examples of this.

- Don't play hands that have danglers. Danglers are cards that just don't belong with the others. For example, in the hand K-Q-10-8, the 8 is a dangler. You might make an exception if the cards are suited.

- You really want to avoid "fishing" in Omaha; let the other players' do the betting for you when you have a monster hand. Otherwise fold. Patience will pay off.

- High pair with an over-card is a good flop in Texas Hold'em, but not in Omaha. In this game you need to flop two pair, a set, or better.

Don't be discouraged by the bad beats. They only emphasize that in Omaha, you have to calculate your odds and select your hands very carefully, realizing that your odds are lowered due to the increased number of hole cards dealt to each player. Omaha is a fun, exciting, edge-of your-seat type of game. Once you master the rules and become comfortable playing Omaha, I think you will find it an entertaining game.

Omaha Eight or Better (High-Low Split) Strategy

Omaha Eight or Better (High-Low Split) is a very difficult game to learn, but learning it is undeniably worth the time needed to muddle through this chapter. What "high-low" split means, is that half the pot goes to the high hand and half the pot goes to the low hand. If there is no low qualifying hand the whole pot goes to the high hand, which is also called "scooping" the pot.

Rules You Should Become Familiar with in Omaha Eight or Better (High-Low Split)
What Qualifies as a Low Hand in Omaha Eight or Better (High-Low Split).
This information will apply to some aspects of Seven Card Stud Eight or Better (HIGH-LOW SPILT) as well. You will need to have eight low, which basically means you have five low cards, the highest of them an eight. Also in this hand, any of the five cards can't have any pairs in them, but straights, flushes don't count against you. A seven low basically means five low cards containing a seven or less. A six low means five low cards containing a six or less. A five low, also known as the wheel, is the same as razz 5-4-3-2-A. This is the best low hand you can get, as it entitles you to have a great chance at winning the high as well because it is a straight. Aces are great because they have two purposes: they count as a high card and a low card. To further emphasize, the wheel is one of the most desired hands to have in this game.

Now that you are staring to grasp this concept of high-low split, let me refresh you on all of the possible low qualifying hands. The worst qualifying low is **8-7-6-5-4**. The best qualifying low is **5-4-3-2-A**.

This might seem confusing at first, but with practice and keeping an open mind, this game is quite interesting to play and beating others until they learn it is very rewarding. When playing this game, if you have three unpaired cards under eight on the board, and any two cards under eight in your hand, with none of them paired, this will give you a qualifying low.

one of 65
should be a 7

Let's do some examples:

With a board that looks like:

After seeing this, can you determine what the best possible low hands could be? All you have to do is decide which would be the lowest two non-paired low cards in the other players' hands, and this will give you the best low hand. In this situation, if a player had an **A-2**, that would be the best low hand **8-7-6-2-A**. The second best low hand could be **8-7-6-3-A**. Hopefully you can see that all it takes is the three lowest cards on the board plus the two lowest cards in your hand to make the best low hand. In Omaha Eight or Better (High-Low Split), the five lowest cards win.

When you can decide which hand is lower than the other one, this game is much easier to understand. A hand having **8-7-3-2-A** will lose to an **8-6-5-4-3**. A hand having **8-6-5-4-3** will lose to an **8-6-5-4-A**, and so on. One thing to remember about Omaha Eight or Better (High-Low Split) is that it promotes action and big pots, with all sorts of unusual hands winning a pot or two in this game.

When this Isn't a Low Hand Present
In Omaha Eight or Better (High-Low Split), the low hand only gets half the pot, by way of being a qualifying low hand. This also points out that if there is no low hand, the entire pot goes to the high hand. For there to be a low hand the board must have three cards under eight; some examples of boards that will not have a low hand no matter what are as follows: **9-7-7-5-5, 4-4-5-5-4, 7-7-9-6-6** etc..

Most Omaha players might confuse these boards as low boards, but they are not. It's easy to see a no low board when they look like this: **Q-K-10-9-J**. Just always remember you can only use 2 cards from your hand to make a hand, the other three must come from the board.

When Two Players have the Same Low Hand

While playing Omaha Eight or Better (High-Low Split), there are rare occurrences that you and another player might have the same low hand. If you ever sense that they might have the same hand as you, stop betting and raising. Why, you ask? This is because you and another player have the same low hand, and another player wins the high hand. You are only going to win one-quarter of the pot and actually lose money in the process. This is referred to as "being quartered;" it happens time and time again.

A-2 is an Important Starting Hand

A-2 makes so many great low hands in Omaha Eight or Better (High-Low Split), the times you can win the low hand pot are endless. You should always play this starting hand when you have **A-2** in it. **A-2** is better than **A-A**, because most board combinations will have 3 low cards on them such as **4-6-8**, **3-4-5**, **3-7-8**, and **4-5-7**. So, having the **A-2**, will give you a low hand almost every time and that is what you want. There will be times when you can win the high hand as well, if you can river a set, straight, full house, and even a flush.

Here are the best and decent starting hands in Omaha Eight or Better (High-Low Split)

Best Starting Hands	Decent Starting Hands
A-A-2-3	A-2-Q-Q
A-A-2- any card	A-3-4-any card
A-A-3- any card	2-3-4-5
A-2-3-4	J-Q-K-A
A-2-3- any card	A-A-K-J
A-2-K-K	A-A-any card-any card
A-3-4-5	A-2- any card-any card
A-A-4-5	9-10-J-Q
A-2-Q-K	2-3-4- any card
A-3-K-K	Any four cards between 10 through Ace

Conclusion

Hopefully by reading this chapter you have gained a great deal of information about Omaha Eight or Better (High-Low Split). There are several different strategies out there, but the one that I have had the most success with is always to get into a flop without and I mean without having an ace. You can experiment with several different hands, but if you tighten up your play and only play starting hands with ace-two, I think you will be very surprised at how successful you will become at this game.

"Honey! Honey! I was supposed to go broke on that hand, honey, except they forgot one thing: I can dodge bullets, baby.**"**

—Phil Hellmuth, one of the most successful poker players of all time. He is a 1989 W.S.O.P. champion. He has won eleven W.S.O.P. bracelets and countless large buy-in tournaments from all over the world. He also holds the records for most W.S.O.P. cashes and most W.S.O.P. final tables.

CHAPTER TWENTY ONE:

RAZZ

Razz is attractive to many players who get "burned out" playing a lot of NL Texas Hold'em and consistently finds them knocked out early. It's a nice change of pace that offers a style similar to Seven-Card Stud which many of us grew up on before the NL Texas Hold'em craze but Razz is completely different from your daddy's Seven-Card Stud game.

In Razz, you get dealt two hole cards and one up card just as in Stud and each round of betting can give you valuable information not only about your own hand, but more importantly, everyone who is in the hand. How you interpret other players' hands and controlling your hand is seen by other players is the main objective in Razz.

I also would like to emphasize if NL Texas Hold'em is a game of infinite patience that Razz is a game that takes that same patience to the EXTREME! You must lay in wait for those golden hands and then milk them for all they are worth and if you start catching bricks you must be just as ready to toss them directly into the muck. Folding a terrible hand (ironically any hand that contains a lot of cards, which are 8 or higher) is the most important thing you can in this game!

Razz Basics:

The best hands in Razz are the worst hands. In reality it should be stated that the "lowest" hand wins. This is the ultimate game of lowball. Razz, is a Seven-Card Stud low game. It means that it is played like Seven-Card Stud, however the lowest wins. Straight, flushes, and the like don't matter anymore, however they don't hurt either.

In this game every player recieves seven cards from which they can only use five as their final hand. Also unlike Texas Hold'em, there are no flops or community cards.

The "Nuts" in Razz is also called "the wheel" in other poker games and consists of **A-2-3-4-5** of any suit.

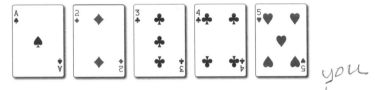

you

The Ace is played as the lowest card. Most winning hands in Razz will be 8 and under. The winning hands can end up higher when in head's up play, but generally want to have a hand of 8 and below. Razz is dealt just like Seven-Card Stud. Here is a brief overview of dealing cards and action in Razz:

Ante

Every player must ante up before the hand begins (before the cards are dealt). Ante is usually 1/5 of the low limit bet size. Also, the ante does not count toward any future bets or calls.

How Razz is Dealt

Three cards are dealt to each player. Two are face down and one face up.

Bring In- One player (the player with the highest card showing) has to make the first bet. This is called "bringing in" and it is mandatory.

- If there are two or more players with the same high card (suit doesn't matter), the player closest to the dealer has to bring it in.

- The player with the highest card has to bring in a bet 1/5 of the low limit bet size in the pot.

- This does count towards the betting and calling in the game. So if you don't get raised, you don't have to place any more bets in the pot.

Betting Rounds- There are 5 betting rounds in this game.

- In the first two rounds of Razz the bets are equal to the low limit bet size.

- In the last three rounds the bets are equal to the high limit bet size.

- For example in a $5/$10 limit game, during the first 3 betting rounds, the bets are $5 and during the last 3 rounds the bets are $10. *That 6 Betting rds not 4*

- A maximum of three raises are allowed per each betting round.

- All bets and raises are done clockwise at the poker table.

The First Betting Round in Razz- This occurs after all the players get their first three cards, two face down and one face up. All bets and raises are in small bet amount.

two?

The Second and Third Betting Rounds in Razz- Three more cards will be dealt face up to players (one at each round) and there is a betting round after each card is dealt. All bets are still in small bet amount.

The Fourth Betting Round in Razz- One more card is dealt face up to each player. There is a betting round just like the previous ones after the card is dealt but, the bets are in large amount.

The Fifth Betting Round in Razz- The last card is dealt to players face down. Then, there is the final betting round.

The Showdown in Razz- Anyone who has not folded will have to show their cards to win the pot. Usually, the person who made the last bet shows his hand first and it proceeds clockwise from him. The person with the lowest hand wins.

Evaluating Razz Hands

In Razz, there are no requirements for a low hand. To put it another way, a low hand can be **2-5-9-J-Q**. It doesn't happen often that some player would win with that hand, but it is still qualified.

In a Razz game, to determine the lowest hand, you must look at the highest card in each player hand (keep in mind every player gets to only play 5 cards from his hand and it can not contain a pair). The player with the lowest high card wins. So **5-6-9-10-J** is better than **1-2-3-5-Q**. *what if everyone left has a pair two guys w/2 full Boats*

The Most Favorable Hands in Razz (suits do not matter)

5-4-3-2-A	7-4-3-2-A	7-6-4-2-A
6-4-3-2-A	7-5-3-2-A	7-6-4-3-2
6-5-3-2-A	7-5-4-2-A	7-6-5-2-A
6-5-4-2-A	7-5-4-3-A	7-6-5-3-A
6-5-4-3-A	7-5-4-3-2	7-6-5-3-2
6-5-4-3-2	7-6-3-2-A	

Starting Hands and the Importance of "The Boards"

The very first thing you have to decide once your cards are dealt to you, assuming your hand is not the "bring in" (Highest up card player must bring in the blind) is whether to fold, call, or complete/raise. Betting hand selection should be simple; you are dealt two cards face down and one card up. If all three cards are 8 or less, with no pairs or trips remain in the hand. If there are cards higher than an 8, fold immediately. If you stayed with this strategy alone however you wouldn't last very long, as you would constantly be losing your ante and bring-in's. It's actually best to mix up your play and attempt to steal the antes with a 2 card 8 or better when you have a nice low up-card and the other players' up-cards are of inferior quality.

An example would be holding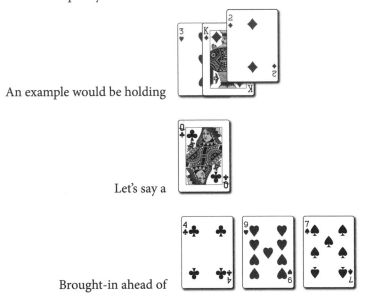

Let's say a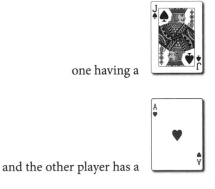

Brought-in ahead of

with all of them folding over to you. You look to your left and see two other players after you;

one having a

and the other player has a

You could go ahead and complete raise. The jack should fold and the ace would probably call. Then you hope for a small card to a brick (card higher than 8) for him which if you bet would definitely encourage him to fold. This strategy works best if you don't have a lot of inexperienced players who will call anything or bet back aggressively. If that is the case simply try to wait for better opportunities.

The cards showing for each player in the hand are "the Boards". It's very important to pay attention to all the visible cards as they can tell you just how strong your hand may be.

If you have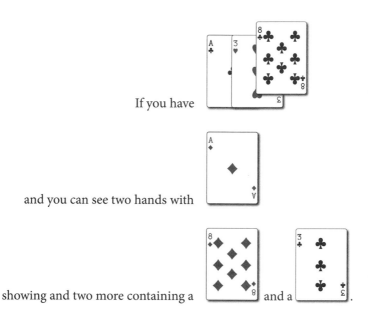

and you can see two hands with

showing and two more containing a and a .

After seeing these cards exposed, you can now relax knowing your hand has a less chance of pairing and therefore giving you a **VERY** strong hand.

Holding that same hand, you see several

You now can determine that your hand is pretty weak, as a lot of the cards that you wanted to land in your hand are already taken and the chances of pairing your Ace, 3, and 8 are increased. How the other players interpret your board cards, can be very important as well.

Let's use that last hand of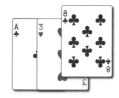

the other players see that you have an 8 showing. They have no clue what's hidden in your two hole cards. Sure this is good, but say you got the same cards but in this order:

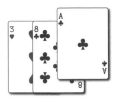

This is a much more powerful starting board especially, if you start landing some babies

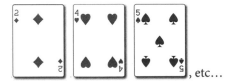, etc...

In the later stages of the hand, your board is giving your opponent information telling the other player to bet or fold and giving you the same info. You must learn to recognize when you have the other player beaten and vice versa. You absolutely know your 8 low on Sixth Street can **NOT** be beaten if the other player is showing:

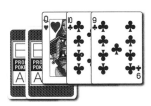

Push with a vengeance here and make the most of your nut hand. The other player should fold, but if they are inexperienced enough to keep committing chips. You should go ahead and take em' all.

Know When to fold...

It can definitely be painful to keep folding hand after hand or to start with wonderful hands like:

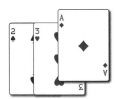

only to land ,

and some other high card killing it. Discipline and patience are key and you must remember a bad starting hand will always be bad.

Take this for example:

It is not going to just turn into the automatic winning hand. If you notice you already have 3 cards with only 4 to come. That means that hand could only possibly end up a 9 low with a great chance it wouldn't even be close to that. Fold garbage hands immediately and if you have the bring-in go ahead and fold when it comes back around.

Remember again, folding bad hands time and time again is the most important part of Razz, if you want to stay alive and have a chance at winning this game. Never waste your chips and every chip you keep is an ante you can fold around until you get better cards to actually make a hand with. Remember, to combine both attention to the cards on the other players' board cards and attention to what others see in your hand and eventually you will be raking in the chips.

Razz Cash Game Strategy

There is nothing more profitable than a loose razz game, remember that. To start, you should follow a very tight-aggressive approach to this game. If you come up to the poker table and see that there are plenty of players, **DON'T** play anything higher than a 7. If the game, later on becomes shorthanded, you should loosen up your starting hand requirements a little, but don't go crazy.

If you have a good starting hand you should usually raise it up, but only re-raise if you believe you are definitely ahead and have the best of it. The one exception to the above would be if you only have a good low door card showing and there is nothing, but high cards before and behind you.

Say you have

(a horrible hand in reality) and the other players in the hand are showing a King, Jack, a Queen, and a 9. RAISE THAT HAND UP! Also try to keep in mind, no matter how good your hole cards may look, don't defend your bring-in, especially if there are several players in the hand. It will cost you more to play as the odds are stacked against you.

Razz Tournament Strategy

You should approach Razz tournaments in much the same way as you would any other long lasting tournament. Be relaxed, refreshed, and ready to play and even more ready to fold! The number one reason players get busted out of razz tournaments is they panic the minute they think their chip stack size is diminishing. With the ante and bring-in system of Razz tournament play, your stack is likely to be in better shape than you think, and the chip and a chair philosophy is never truer than in the game of Razz.

You can be down to just a few bets and within the span of two really great hands be up with the chip leaders! Just wait for those playable hands and a little luck and you will do just fine! If the tables are staying full, that means you will be paying less bring-ins and mostly just paying the ante. Do your best not to panic when you're short-stacked. Panic can lead to bad decisions and have you putting all your chips in a multi-player pot with just a marginal hand. We want the odds on our side, so it's imperative in Razz to just fold and wait for a good hand.

Solid basic play is most important in cashing in Razz tournaments. Even if there are several professional players in the tournament, it doesn't mean you won't get any further than they do. Many professional poker players play Razz during H.O.R.S.E. events and will join Razz tournaments just to get experience to improve their H.O.R.S.E. game. Many do not have the patience and determination to actually do well in razz as a whole, if they do not play it regularly.

Razz tournaments are a closed type of game that at times leaves you with more limited options than the cash game. There are usually no chances to do a re-buy, if you go out early. In some tournaments you might play as many as 15 hour's straight dealing with the ups and downs of the game. Just as if you were playing a high stakes cash game, you must be ready to adjust to the different player personalities as they come and go from your table in the game. You must remain focused and play your patient game to survive the ups and downs to make the final table.

To get to the final table, one important step (hopefully the first step) is at your first table, you must lay back and watch how the others are playing, giving you a feel for the table, or as some would say, "Take the table temperature" to see if its hot or cold. You must adjust your play accordingly, so give it a few hands before mixing it up. Remember that you will be folding a high percentage of hands anyway. Make the time that you're not in hands useful to you. Watch how other players wager and how they may pressure other players. Also, take time to see the showdown to see if they truly "had it" or just fronted it. Razz is a game chock full of information you can use to your advantage to destroy the other players down the line.

If you encounter those wonderfully loose players who will bet aggressively even with junk in the hole, just wait for your best hands to go up against them. Do NOT turn into them.

Sit back and wait for your strong hands so that you can play aggressively from Third Street all the way to the showdown unless you start drawing bricks. There is no shame in folding if you're beat. In fact, it's a necessity. Even if you start with a 3 card 7, (3 cards under 7) you still have to "catch" 2 more out of the 4 remaining dealt cards. If you think about it, even with "the best" starting hands, you only really have just over 50% chance to finish with a hand 8 and under. That is why folding when you're beaten is so important. If you teach a man to fold when he's beaten, I think he will make the money every time, at least in Razz.

Once a tournament reaches the middle stages, it's time to think a bit differently. Don't bother seeing who the chip leaders are at this point, because it's not really of any consequence, as everyone is paying the ante, and good hands are coming with the bad, so it's not likely that they will make the final table. Just keep playing a solid game and you will be fine. Players will start dropping at a more rapid rate, but don't concentrate on that, because it isn't your place to put them out. Most of the time, it is bad play equaling their exit. Once the bubble approaches, play less aggressively, as no one wants to double up the ones that are getting desperate, just to watch them go on a streak and win. If you have a healthy stack you can "afford" to fold into the money.

Once the bubble busts, it's still a game of infinite patience. Getting bricks? It's OK, just keep folding until you get that great hand while other players drop left and right, because they are in the money and are making stupid plays. You might even move up a few money levels because of stupid plays by desperate players with marginal hands. Remember, as the number of player's decreases, the number of good player's increases, and you must always keep the feel of the table and the players. Be the tortoise instead of the hare; don't let others dictate your play.

There is one more major thing to keep in mind once you're in the final stages of a Razz tournament. Keep an eye on the players' stacks around you. If they are good players, then you should know how fast their stack can disappear if they misplay a hand. There will be no bluffing going on. If they are pushing at you aggressively, then they truly think they have you beaten. Make sure that you have the advantage before keeping the hand going.

Once it gets to head's up, then of course, all bets are off. You will play much more marginal hands, but you will also keep an eye on your opponents' board, and fold immediately if you think you're beaten. If you think you still have the edge, monster aggression is what you need! Don't be afraid to go toe to toe if you think you have them beaten!

Razz is a game of complete manipulation mixed with aggression when its head's up, and many players cannot make that change and adjust for head's up. Be aggressive, but also fold aggressively if you are not holding a good hand. If you have a good hand but the bring-in doesn't complete it, let the other player complete it and then re-raise them. Or, if you wish to keep the mystery, just simply call and re-raise on the next card. Never be hurried by the head's up player. Take your time to make a decision or, if you just want to be irritating, take your full time. This can really get on some players' nerves and perhaps set them a bit on Tilt. Take every advantage you can, and hopefully you can find yourself final tabling in tournament after tournament!

❝ You call...gonna be all over, baby...**❞**

—Scotty Nguyen, 1998 W.S.O.P champion and 2008 W.S.O.P. $50,000 H.O.R.S.E. champion. He is the first and only player to win both the W.S.O.P. Main Event and $50,000 H.O.R.S.E. events, giving him a total of five W.S.O.P. bracelets. He has a WPT title as well.

CHAPTER TWENTY TWO:

SEVEN-CARD STUD

Before there was NL Texas Hold'em, anyone who played poker most likely played Seven-Card Stud. Seven-Card Stud is a clever game of complete deception. It takes a certain level of skill, and a memory like an elephant to be successful. Professional poker players who have won bracelets in Seven-Card Stud throughout the years are: Phil Ivey (2002), Chris "Jesus" Ferguson (2000), and Ted Forrest (1993). Lets look at a combination of strategies that will steer you in the right direction to become a great Seven-Card Stud player and someday, a champion.

Before I go any further, I just wanted you to know that Seven-Card Stud is my worst game. However, I still felt that it needed to be included in this book so I asked two of my good friends to contribute to this chapter, Danielle Adams-Benham and Glenn "Bignutz515" Franco, to contribute their expertise.

Seven-Card Stud is a variant of stud poker with two to eight. Until the recent increase in popularity of NL Texas Hold'em, Seven-card stud was the most popular poker variant in home games as well as in eastern US casinos. Seven-card stud is also played in western American casinos, but NL Texas Hold'em is far more popular there.

In casino play, it is common to use a small ante and bring-in. In home games, it is typical to use an ante only. The game begins with each player being dealt two cards face down and one card face up. If played with a bring-in, the player with the lowest-ranking up-card pays the bring-in, and betting proceeds after that in normal clockwise order. The bring-in is considered an open, so the next player in turn may not check. If two players have equally ranked low cards, suit may be used to break the tie and assign the bring-in (see high card by suit). If there is no bring-in, then the first betting round begins with the player showing the highest-ranking up-card, who may check. In this case, suit should not be used to break ties. If two players have the same high up-card, the player first in clockwise rotation from the dealer is the first player to act.

After the first betting round, another up-card is dealt to each player (after a burn card, and starting at the dealer's left as will all subsequent rounds), followed by a second betting round beginning with the player whose up-cards make the best poker hand. Since fewer than five cards are face up, this means no straights, flushes, or full houses will count for this purpose. On this and all subsequent betting rounds, the player whose face-up cards make the best poker hand will act first, and may check or bet up to the game's set limit.

The second round is followed by a third up-card and betting round, a fourth up-card and betting round, and finally a down-card, a fifth betting round, and showdown if necessary. Seven-card stud can be summarized therefore as "two down, four up, and one down." Upon showdown, each player makes the best five-card poker hand out of the seven cards that he was dealt.

Note that seven cards to eight players plus four burn cards makes 60 cards, and there are only 52 in the deck. In most games this is not a problem because several players will have folded in early betting rounds.

But there are certainly low-stakes home games where few if any players fold. If this is the case in your game, you may want to limit the game to seven players. If the deck does become exhausted during play, previously-dealt burn cards can be used when only a few cards are needed to complete the deal. If even those are not sufficient, then on the final round instead of dealing a down-card to each player, a single community card is dealt to the center of the table.

Under no circumstances can any discarded card from a folded hand be "recycled" for later use. Unlike draw poker, where no cards are ever seen before showdown, stud poker players use the information they get from face-up cards to make strategic decisions, and so a player who sees a certain card folded is entitled to make decisions knowing that the card will never appear in another player's hand.

In Seven-Card Stud there are Antes to pay

Unlike NL Texas Hold'em and Omaha, Seven-Card Stud has a fifth and extra round of betting. After playing those games for so long, jumping into Seven-Card Stud is difficult to acclimate to. In Hold'em you post a small blind or big blind, but Seven-Card Stud is an ante game. Before the cards are dealt, all the players must ante in. The amount of the ante varies by the casino but is normally ¼ of a full bet. Seven-Card Stud allows you to play as low as $1/$2 where your ante is 25 cents or you can play a high roller and take on Larry Flynt in his casino. If you're in the higher stakes, after making a $200,000 buy-in and playing $2,000/$4,000 Seven-Card Stud your ante would be $1,000.

With five rounds of betting in Seven-Card Stud, the size of a pot can be huge, depending on the players you're up against. The first two rounds of betting and raises are in the smaller amount, if you're playing in the hand.

SEVEN-CARD STUD STRATEGY

BY DANIELLE ADAMS-BENHAM

 I wanted to begin by stating that in no means am I a professional Seven-Card Stud player; I am merely a well-known writer and analyst in the poker world as well as a person who loves the game. With the amount of live, home style games and the research that I have done paired with successful outcomes to my bank roll, my strategy in this game is definitely helping me on my way to eating pro's alive! My usual game of choice is NL Texas Hold'em and Razz online. My advice for a minimal bank roll in Seven-Card Stud is 200 big bets.

As I am not a professional poker player yet, I advise that these concepts and strategies be used in low to medium limit cash games. Seven-Card Stud like all other poker based games; you must be able to play both the player and the table. This is definitely the key to success. When playing Stud, remember opposites attract payoffs. If the table is tight, play loose and vice versa. Like all other things in poker, this is just a guideline. The best general strategy advice I can give on Seven-Card Studs is…If you have position to make a great play, and then do it! Unlike many other variants of poker, in Seven-Card Stud I have found only one type of play style applies: Tight and Aggressive. Strong play and successful play in my experience, equates to two words: PLAY or FOLD.

Third Street: the Best Starting Hands in Seven-Card Stud
- Rolled trips: three of a kind; a rare hand in this game but a great start.
- Large pairs: ten's or better.
- Small pairs: deuces to nine are being described here, bluffing may be required.
- Three suited connectors: these are great drawing hands in multi-player pots.
- Combination of three A-K-Q-J-10, any suit: these look for high pairs or a straight (Broadway).

These hands need help to stand but the previous table action and the showing cards (up-cards) should dictate precisely what your move should be. When in early position, it is a great play to bet out on all of these hands. My opponent's up-cards certainly have some weight in my decision in whether to play. The only thing that would alter my decision would be if a paired door card comes into the equation. There are a few situations that could happen where I would fold to a small bet, but remember, Seven-Card Stud is a game of draws and folding. With hands like this you want to be the ultimate sly fox and bluff with a weaker hand. Stay aggressive in late position on fourth and fifth streets, and apply pressure to those who may only have small pairs.

On Fifth Street there is a major choice to make, raising or folding aggressively. As mentioned earlier, these are the two key elements.....PLAY or FOLD. When you catch a blank card (card of no assistance), I recommend checking instantly. If the other player responds with a strong bet, I would follow my checking pattern and fold. As with all poker variants, sometimes folding is winning.

Small and Mid Pairs: Deuces to Nines

Small and medium pairs from deuces to nines are the weakest starters in Seven-Card Stud, excluding rubbish hands. However, with some deception you can use them to turn a profit. Keep in mind my prior points before deciding to attempt this. The key concept is to play or fold, deceptive play takes a little more time to master. Don't feel bad when choosing to fold because next time you may have the big pair and receive the payout.

Big Pairs: Ten's to Ace's

I like to play fast and straight to the point with big pairs. Try to raise others out of a pot when in a multi-player situation, because **Q-Q** or **K-K** doesn't hold up too often. Again, I emphasize that Seven-Card Stud is a game of drawing. Trying to bet the other players out of the hands on early streets is a must to avoid them drawing the ultimate hand. Using a check-raise as a way to narrow the amount of players is an option but a risky one. You should be extremely cautious making this move on Fourth Street.

Three Suited Connectors

Having this hand is great in multi-player pots, and a raise on Fourth Street is the best play when playing aggressively. This is a move that should definitely be made when you have caught a fourth required card. If you're in early position, a check-raise is a great way to build the pot especially with an open-ended straight or flush draw. It gives you the image of being loose and when you make your hand, you catch the other player completely off guard.

Being overly aggressive on Fourth Street is a great play in a multi-player pot. This will build the pot and give others equity to call with on later streets.

When head's up with a player, it may be in you better interest to use a different approach. In this situation, there is less value in suited connectors, so you should use some discretion and control the size of the pot. Managing pot size is essential with these types of drawing hands

Rolled Trips

Having a set dealt to you in Seven-Card Stud doesn't happen very often and you should always make the most of it. If it's a lower or middle set in a multi-player pot, DO NOT slow-play it. I suggest betting your hand. Again, this differs when you're playing head's up. In which case you should get creative and add value to the pot by check-raising on Fifth

Street. A lot of players using the check-raise on Sixth Street in multi-player situations end up losing a huge chunk of money. You must be very alert and cautious making this move here. Playing fast is the key but knowing when to play fast, fold, and act on feelings is what separates the fish from the sharks, or should I say the pros from the amateurs.

"Keeping it simple and play your hands as they are dealt."

Other Thoughts

As with all games of poker, it is vital to always keep pot odds in mind. I recommend PokerTracker or Hold'em Manager software to help you with this when playing online. It's an easy way of keeping track of sessions and looking back to see against whom you were profitable. This will also help you locate the weaker players and start your fishing trip. Don't get frustrated with yourself or your game, and always look for improvements to plug the leaks.

Here are further points that have made my presence even stronger in the world of poker. Great success doesn't happen overnight. In order to obtain it takes knowledge, understanding, patience, planning, confidence, self management, performance, and a lot of ambition. A lot of the great NL Texas Hold'em players began playing Seven-Card Stud. Poker is a process and developing yourself is the key. Poker has a lot of variance, so just stay with it and most of all stay positive about your self.

SEVEN CARD STUD EIGHT OR BETTER (HIGH-LOW SPLIT) STRATEGY

BY GLENN "BIGNUTZ515" FRANCO

Seven-Card Stud Eight or Better is similar to the strategy in the previous section; it is dealt the same way as Seven-Card Stud. This game is a high-low split game, which basically means that half the pot of chips will go to the winning high hand, and the other half goes to the low hand. This is true if there is a low hand, which is an eight-low or better qualifying hand. In low hands, aces count as the low. No pairs can exist but a straight and/or a flush may. The lowest possible hand is A-2-3-4-5. The highest possible qualifying low hand is 8-7-6-5-4. When there is no low hand, the high hand will take the whole pot. This is also referred to as "scooping" the pot, which basically means that you win both pots, the high and low combined.

Just like in Seven-Card Stud, you can use any five of the seven cards that you have for making the high hand and any five of the seven cards that you hold to make a low hand. The main objective in the game of Seven-Card Stud Eight or Better is to make both a five card high hand, and five card low-hand with any combination of the seven cards you are dealt.

Forced Bets Antes

Seven-card stud is normally played with an ante that is approximately 1/5 of the low limit bet size. Every player must ante up before the hand begins. The ante does not count towards any future bets.

The Bring In

After the initial deal when every player has one card showing and the person with the lowest card must "bring in" meaning he must place the low limit bet size in the pot. If two or more players share the lowest card, the one closest to the dealer's left side must bring in. This bet counts as first round betting, so as long as nobody raises, you don't have to place any more money in the pot to see the next card.

Betting Rounds

There are five rounds of betting. In limit Seven-Card Stud Eight or Better, all bets and raises must be equal to either the low limit or high limit bet size, depending on what round it is. In the first two rounds, all bets and raises must be equal to the low limit bet size. In the third, fourth, and fifth rounds, all bets must be equal to the high limit bet size. If, for example, you're playing $3/$6 Seven-Card Stud, all bets in the first two rounds will be in increments of three dollars, and all bets in the last three rounds will be in increments of six dollars. A maximum of three raises are allowed per betting round.

Third Street: Two cards are dealt face down to every player, followed by another card face up. The player with the lowest card must bring in, by betting ½ of the low limit bet. He may choose to raise by betting full the low limit bet. Play proceeds clockwise around the table, with each player choosing to fold, call, or raise. All bets and raises must be equal to the low limit bet size.

Fourth Street: A fourth card is dealt face up to every player. The player with the highest hand showing (at this point, the highest possible would be a pair of aces) is the first to act. He may choose to fold, check, or bet. If two or more players are tied for the highest hand, the one closest to the dealer's left will be the first to act. Play proceeds clockwise around the table as before. If a player is showing a pair at this point, then he and all the other players have the option to bet either the low limit bet size or the high limit bet size. Otherwise, all bets and raises must be equal to the low limit bet size.

Fifth Street: A fifth card is dealt face up to every player. Play proceeds as in the previous round, with the highest hand betting first, except now all bets and raises must be equal to the high limit bet size.

Sixth Street: A sixth card is dealt face up to every player. Play proceeds as in the previous round. All bets and raises must be equal to the high limit bet size.

Seventh Street: A seventh and final card is dealt face down to every player. Play proceeds as in the previous round. All bets and raises must be equal to the high limit bet size. In the rare event that all eight players remain in the hand at this point, there would not be enough cards for each player to receive another one. If this occurs, instead of every player receiving a card face down, a single card is placed in the middle of the table face up as a community card.

The Showdown: All who have not folded after the last round of betting will now have the option of showing their hand in hopes of taking down the pot. The person who bet last is the first to show their hand, and then it proceeds clockwise, with each remaining player choosing to show their hand or muck it. Often times a player will muck their hand if they aren't going to win the pot and don't want their opponents to see what they played. In Seven-Card Stud Eight or Better, it's important to remember that THIS IS NOT HOLD'EM.

There are several major differences that one must account for, primarily:

Dead Cards:

In any stud game you have a lot more information at your disposal, namely, the dead cards. Keep track of the cards that have been shown and you will have a HUGE advantage over the other players. It's very difficult to remember each and every card, so concentrate on remembering those cards that either you or your opponents may have needed example: straight cards, flush cards, dead low cards, etc. This is the absolute most important part of the game and I cannot stress how valuable this information can be!

Fluid Position:

In stud, position is apt to change with each round of play. Keep in mind that raising for a free card when you are in late position may backfire if you pair off and are suddenly in first position. Position in stud games is very difficult to understand as it is not something a beginner can pick up on quickly. There is no community board of cards to help you, only what the dealer sends your way. It can almost feel like you're always on a drawing hand in Seven-Card Stud Eight or Better because basically you are! Many times you can start out with four to a low on Fourth Street and have many high options as well (straight, boat, flush, etc) only to catch useless bricks the next three cards. Your attention must focus not only on your hand but the visible boards of all the hands around you. The only information you have other than physical tells is what other player's boards are showing. You must use this information wisely in order to determine the best way to play the hand you hold.

Watch all of the other players in the hand and their cards. This will help you determine the relative strength of your hand and what cards are still available in the deck to help you. If you are on a heart draw but see hearts on the boards of the other players, the chances of you catching one are much slimmer. Same holds true if you are aiming for the low pot and many of the low cards you need are on the table around you.

Always assume that any hand you go into at a Seven-Card Stud Eight or Better table is going to be split. Too many split pots lend no profit except to the card room taking the rake. Not to mention all the ante money spent waiting to catch the winning hand. Maximum profitability for the time and energy involved in this game should never be taken lightly!

If you have a playable starting hand, complete the bet if it has not been done already and do not give the bring-in a free card. This is all-to-often seen at the tables that would probably not have been split if the bring-in were raised out. If you are the high draw calling to play the hand, by not completing the bet it encourages being counterfeited on later streets.

I do encourage an open three-bet rule at a Seven-Card Stud Eight or Better table to maximize profit. **This is a standard for professional play** and is not often seen at the tables online. This is because most players are shy on draws and do not bring the bankroll necessary to handle the variances that occur with this type of play.

The best hands in Seven-Card Stud Eight or Better are:

- Any Rolled up Trips, (A-A-A, K-K-K, 9-9-9, etc.)
- Pair of aces with a low card (A-A-2)
- Three to a low straight flush
- Three to a low straight or flush (2-3-8 or 2-3-4)
- Three low cards with an ace (like A-2-6, A-4-7)
- High pairs (K-K and Q-Q, preferably buried with a low door card)
- Low pairs with an ace (like 4-4-A, A-6-6)

Don't play anything else until you have some experience and first and foremost, PLAY TO SCOOP! You want the WHOLE POT. Hands that have two way potential can be played much stronger than one way hands, even if you're behind in one or both directions. Do not draw to second best hands:

If you're drawing to a low, be sure that it will be the best low if you make it. Don't draw to a straight when someone else looks to be drawing to a flush, etc. The only exception is if you're playing for both ends. If you have a low straight draw to an 8 high straight, and there appears to be a flush draw and a better low draw out there, go ahead and play, maybe even get aggressive to knock out one of the others.

Some hands do better head's up, while others do much better multi-player. Pairs, Aces, Kings, Queens, and low pairs with an ace, do better heads up. Try to thin the field with strategic raises on third and Fourth Street but remember, you want the WHOLE POT.

Use raises throughout the hand to knock out other hands if a good opportunity arises. You really want to knock out the low draws if you're going high (so you can win the whole pot) but it's also very important to raise to knock out other draws. If you have a high pair and someone else appears to be drawing at a straight, make them call two bets for the chance.

Remember that until it is made, even a good low draw (such as 2-3-4-7) is behind even a pair of queens or kings. You don't want to be heads up against a high hand if you only have a draw to half the pot. Fold and save some Big Blinds. Once it is made however, you will often be free rolling for the high end so be very aggressive and try to get the WHOLE POT.

Check-raising and three betting are very important in Seven-Card Stud Eight or Better. If there are good players at the table do not be afraid to jam them yourself if you feel that you have a lock for the high, low, or both! Slow playing is generally a very bad idea in a loose Seven-Card Stud Eight or Better game. Don't do it unless you have a high rolled set or another real monster. NO FREE CARDS! Take them yourself when offered them but NEVER give them out, especially on the all important Fifth Street! The ability to read hands and analyze opponents and their strategy is, in my opinion, more important in Seven-Card Stud Eight or Better than any other form of poker. Experience will help in the long run but concentrate yourself first on whether the other players are shooting for the high or low pot as this is the basic information you must gain quickly.

"Be tight, be aggressive, play good hands and play them hard. Play for the SCOOP!"

~~~ PART SIX ~~~

Tournaments

CHAPTER TWENTY THREE:

HEARTLAND POKER TOUR

My experience with the Heartland Poker Tour was both challenging and rewarding. The tournament was well organized. I placed sixth, but felt should have given a better performance, but went all-in with Quad 5's to receive a bad beat by the chip leader at the table. He turned up quad 8's. Yet, I was happy with the fact that I lasted longer than 50 other players who all put up a good fight. Furthermore, I want to emphasize that if you are truly passionate about the game of poker and aren't well-to-do, the Heartland Poker Tour is money well spent as you further your career or entertainment as a poker player. There are good people there, and they have my outmost respect in being a leader in the poker scene. The Heartland Poker Tour is mid limit poker with televised events. You can start by entering the Heartland Poker League (HPL). The Heartland Poker League is weekly sanctioned low limit tournaments in which you can play locally or nationally. By signing up at Heartlandpokerleague.com, I entered a Heartland Poker Tour qualifier at the Oneida casino in Green Bay, Wisconsin.

Participating Casinos:
Here is a list of which casinos host Heartland Poker League (HPL):

Oneida Casino . . . . 2522 W. Mason Street Green Bay, WI 54313
Phone: (800) 238-4263

Majestic Star Casino . . . . 1 Buffington Harbor Drive Gary, IN 46406
Phone: (888) 225-8259

Diamond Jo Casino . . . . 777 Diamond Jo Lane Northwood, IA 50459
Phone: (877) 323-5566

Dubuque Greyhound Park. . . . . 1855 Greyhound Park Rd Dubuque, IA 52001
Phone: (800) 373-3647

Four Winds Casino Resort. . . . . 11111 Wilson Rd New Buffalo, MI 49117
Phone: (866) 494-6371

Golden Gates Casino: Poker Parlour . 300 Main St Black Hawk, CO 80422
Phone: (303) 582-2906

Grand Casino Mille Lacs . . . . 777 Grand Avenue Onamia, MN 56359
Phone: (800) 626-5825

Greektown Casino Hotel . . . . 555 East Lafayette Boulevard Detroit, MI 48226
Phone: (888) 771-4386

Shooting Star Casino and Hotel . . . . 777 Casino Rd Mahnomen, MN 56557
Phone: (800) 453-7827

Win-River Casino . . . . 2100 Redding Rancheria Rd. Redding, CA 96001
Phone: (800) 280-8946

Jackpot Junction Casino Hotel . . . . . 39375 Co. Hwy 24 Morton, MN 56270
Phone: (800) 946-2274

Meskwaki Bingo & Casino . . . . 1504 ~ 305th Street Tama, IA 52339
Phone: (800) 728-4263

Midnight Rose Casino . . . . 256 E. Bennett Ave Cripple Creek, CO 80813
Phone: (800) 635-5825

Northern Lights Casino . . . . 6800 Y Frontage Rd. N.W Walker, MN 56484
Phone: (800) 252-7529

Here are the casinos that host Heartland Poker Tour (HPT) televised events:

Majestic Star Casino . . . . 1 Buffington Harbor Drive Gary, IN 46406
Phone: (888) 225-8259

Turning Stone Casino . . . . 5218 Patrick Road Verona, New York 13478
Phone: (315) 361-8525

Greektown Casino Hotel . . . . 555 East Lafayette Boulevard Detroit, MI 48226
Phone: (888) 771-4386

Island Resort & Casino . . . . W399 US Highway 2 & 41 Harris, MI 49845
Phone: (906) 466-2941

Golden Gates Casino: Poker Parlour . 300 Main St Black Hawk, CO 80422
Phone: (303) 582-5600

Meskwaki Bingo & Casino . . . . 1504 ~ 305th Street Tama, IA 52339
Phone: (800) 728-4263

Grand Casino Mille Lacs . . . . 777 Grand Avenue Onamia, MN 56359
Phone: (800) 626-5825

Soaring Eagle Casino . . . . 6800 Soaring Eagle Blvd Mount Pleasant, MI 48858
Phone: (888) 732-4537

Poker is a competition of people. While countless other games of probability match players against the house or even machine, poker puts competitors face to face with their opponent. The poker match-up presents all the excitement, energy, and passion that humans possess. The Heartland Poker Tour (HPT) has been, and always will be about the people. This is a poker tournament where someone would be able to win and win big. HPT poker tournaments are held at exclusive casinos, attracting hundreds of people to the opening round and always boiling down to a final table of six remaining players.

HPT tapes this final table and creates two, one-hour episodes with extensive commentary to be aired at a later date. HPT started with modest expectations and will have hosted over 50 events by the end of 2008.

How It All Began

Long-time friends, Todd Anderson and Greg Lang started HPT early in 2005. These independent television producers harnessed their collective experiences in broadcast television, regional and national business development, marketing and branding to establish the Heartland Poker Tour. Its ascension within the industry was almost immediate. The growth comes from its uncomplicated approach, quality production, and substantial purses. It is currently viewed in over 50 million households nationwide with new audiences tuning in each week. Anderson and Lang consider HPT to be the "minor leagues" of poker with major league potential. The show is part drama, part reality television. It is younger, funnier, and more energetic than current poker shows. They have a great set, dynamic announcers, and fresh faces. Industry insiders have declared it to be the "third best poker show on television."

Anderson and Lang have three very simple and straight-forward objectives for the Heartland Poker Tour:

- Create and host well organized, fair, and fun poker tournaments that offer both reasonable opening buy-ins and large prize pools, all while welcoming any poker player regardless of experience or background.

- Provide a quality experience for the participating Casino. HPT views its relationship with the host Casino as a partnership and strives to create a product that delivers exceptional players, generates traffic, and produces ample buzz about the property.

- Produce a quality television program that features real people, can't-miss-a-minute poker action, and cleverly insightful commentary.

When a college student moves all-in with A-Q suited in heads-up poker play, and gets called by a construction worker holding K-J off suit. The two players are surrounded by an audience and camera. They know that hole cameras reveal what they hold to the audience at home. On the line is a top prize of $30,000, bragging rights, and a brief reign in the poker spotlight of "flyover country." No, we're not talking about the World Poker Tour or World Series of Poker here. Instead, it's the Heartland Poker Tour, a poker tournament TV show featuring everyday players with reasonable buy-in tournaments at casinos most people outside America's heartland have never heard of.

On the surface, it sounds like a strange format. No "poker brat" to taunt players? No "Devilfish" to grace the table in a suit? No boxful of hundreds of thousands of dollars brought out to the table when head's-up play begins? Who would watch it? Surprisingly a lot. Since many people who are looking for an alternative to the poker tournaments that fill the airwaves. They would like to see casinos they might play at, opponents they can relate to, and a tournament with a buy-in that is not a quarter of many people's yearly salaries. By watching the Heartland Poker Tour, a new poker show featuring casinos off the beaten path and players you are more likely to run into at the VFW than the high-stakes games at the Bellagio

Beginnings
The Heartland Poker Tour wasn't some Hollywood TV producer's idea, and didn't come out of Las Vegas or Atlantic City. The idea for the program came from the unlikely spot of Fargo, North Dakota, when friends and independent television producers Todd Anderson and Greg Lang teamed up. According to Anderson, he and Lang were coming home one evening from a tournament last winter, shooting the breeze about a new television show. Lang's first idea was for a home improvement show, but Anderson felt that it would not

gather a very large audience. A few days later, Greg Lang suggested a poker show and over 3 or 4 weeks, Todd Anderson worked on a plan to launch the show.

After Christmas of 2004, Anderson and Lang started laying the groundwork for the show. Anderson even quit his job to focus on the program. He said that one of the stations he worked at was broadcasting an "unwatchable" poker show. If this could air, there was certainly a market for better poker programming, and plenty of casinos that would like to host some tournaments. At first glance, the Heartland Poker Tour looks like any other poker show: two commentators, a final table under the lights, hole cameras, and a person on the floor to interview players as they exit. But you won't find the big names in poker at the final table. What you will find are "real people," whom Anderson feels there is a genuine interest in seeing. "Part of our show's appeal is that there are a lot of real people out there who are interesting. You don't need a $10,000 buy-in or Phil Hellmuth. Poker is a great game to watch, no matter who might be playing," said Anderson. Anderson repeated pro golfer Lee Travino's comment that the pressure of making a big putt to win a lot of money was nothing compared to the pressure a golfer putting for a few hundred dollars might be under when he has no real money of his own. "It's interesting to see how real people handle pressure," he said. Phil Hellmuth, he pointed out, doesn't need more money, but a college student winning $22,000 in a tournament does. Winning $22,000 from a $30 buy-in satellite could pay for his first four years of college.

The Format

The Heartland Poker Tour highlights the casinos of the heartland, including those in Minnesota and Wisconsin. Future stops may include Iowa, Michigan, Ohio, Illinois, Oklahoma and Nevada. The tour has six to eight events near Minnesota and Wisconsin and four to six events outside the region. Tournaments include about 200 to 400 players, with the final table broadcasted over two episodes. The featured poker hands include percentages, (so the viewer knows who the favorites are at each stage of the hand) updates on chip counts and blinds, hole cameras, and constant on-air commentary. Buy-in's are in the $300 to $500 range, with the casinos hosting the event with satellite tournaments as well.

Hosts include Chris Hanson, a morning host on a Fargo radio station, and Fred Bevill, a full-time comedian who tours every week. The two might seem to be an odd pairing for a poker program, as neither is a professional player. Anderson, however, has been pleased by their performance. He says that he and Lang both started the project on a shoestring budget, and had to find people who would be committed to the show but be able to work for nearly nothing. Anderson said they were looking for people who might not be poker experts, but who were funny, interesting, and had some broadcast experience.

Ratings Success

Anderson says he has been quite pleased with the ratings of the Heartland Poker Tour thus far. In Minneapolis, the HPT has been the top rated show on Saturday night on the WB affiliate, hitting as high as a 2.4 ratings share. Ratings seem likely to continue to rise as the HPT expands. The show is not limited to cable, and is being on broadcast stations in Minneapolis, Fargo, Cincinnati, Duluth, and Bismarck. The program also airs on cable in Chicago, Detroit, and Denver. Anderson noted that in Chicago, HPT is on the Comcast network, on the Chicago-equivalent of Fox Sports Net. The show will be entering even more homes, as a deal was recently signed with America One Sports, a satellite feed that is beamed into 140 different stations (mainly low-power networks). According to Anderson, the HPT is available in million homes currently, and adding another 8 to 10 million homes by the end of 2008. The ability to be on broadcast stations in some markets is a big plus, according to Anderson. He cited the World Poker Tour as being a great show, but if you want to watch it in certain markets you have a problem: The Travel Channel and now the Game show network is not on in many markets. Broadcast stations, available to the millions of viewers without cable subscriptions, greatly expand the TV audience.

The Future

The HPT is currently filming its fourth Season and will have 100 original episodes at the end of 2008. About 17 to 20 are shown in each hour-long episode. Season 5 will kick off in February of 2009.

Impressions

With a local production you might expect a sub-par set. The HPT, however, is even better than some. The table is well lit, and the hole cameras work great. Hanson and Bevill work very well together. They are quick to recognize how many outs each player has, and to comment on the how tight or loose the betting of players at the table is. Anecdotes about the players were also provided, so the viewer has a chance to get to know the players a little better. These players are ordinary people, who don't have several homes and don't travel the world to play in poker tournaments. They are people you're likely to run into in low stakes games online or at your local casino, such as college students, businessmen, and construction workers. You'll also see bits and pieces you won't see on tournaments with professionals as well. In one episode, for instance, a player inadvertently flipped his cards up. I wouldn't expect to see Johnny Chan do that at a final table. It's also fascinating to see how people not used to the spotlight react to being on TV. The learning value of a show like the Heartland Poker Tour is greater than other poker shows on the air. .

It's much more helpful to see how amateurs play at these levels than it is to see Phil Ivey and Annie Duke, who aren't going to show up at your table (unless you're one of the elite players of the world, or can afford the expensive buy-ins of major tournaments).

The bottom line? The Heartland Poker Tour is a surprisingly good production that has a lot of potential to be a mainstay on the airwaves for years to come.

Viewing Times

The HPT has different airtimes based on the network serving your area. As to be expected, the website is top-notch. Just go to HeartlandPokerTour.com and click on the TV tab and you'll get a handy listing of networks, dates, and times. .

Awarded To Date - By TPP

Event	Place	Final Table	Prize Pool
1	Northern Lights Casino Walker, MN	June 26, 2005	$100,000
2	Jackpot Junction Casino & Hotel Morton, MN	Aug 7, 2005	$100,000
3	St. Croix Casino & Hotel Turtle Lake, WI	Aug 28, 2005	$180,000
4	Grand Casino Mille Lacs Onamia, MN	Sept 25, 2005	$100,000
5	Seven Clans Casino Thief River Falls, MN	Oct 30, 2005	$90,000
6	Grand Casino Hinckley Hinckley, MN	Nov 27, 2005	$145,000
7	Shooting Star Casino Mahnomen, MN	Dec 18, 2005	$120,000
8	St. Croix Casino & Hotel Turtle Lake, WI	Feb 25, 2006	$57,000
9	St. Croix Casino & Hotel Turtle Lake, WI	Feb 26, 2006	$228,500
10	Grand Casino Mille Lacs Onamia, MN	Mar 26, 2006	$171,300
11	Seven Clans Casino Thief River Falls, MN	April 23, 2006	$108,300
12	Leelanau Sands Casino Peshawbestown, MI	May 21, 2006	$216,900
13	Jackpot Junction Casino & Hotel Morton, MN	July 23, 2006	$130,320
14	St. Croix Casino & Hotel Turtle Lake, WI	Aug 20, 2006	$274,400
15	Chukchansi Gold Resort & Casino Coarsegold, CA	Oct 1, 2006	$78,520
16	Grand Casino Mille Lacs Onamia, MN	Oct 22, 2006	$155,710
17	Majestic Star Casino Gary, IN	Oct 29, 2006	$436,910
18	Royal River Casino Flandreau, SD	Nov 26, 2006	$173,410
19	Hooters Casino Hotel Las Vegas, NV	Jan 29, 2007	$167,325
20	Lucky Nugget Card Club Deadwood, SD	Mar 4, 2007	$270,878
21	Meskwaki Bingo Casino Hotel Tama, IA	Mar 18, 2007	$297,804
22	Majestic Star Casino Gary, IN	Mar 25, 2007	$506,440

Event	Place	Final Table	Prize Pool
23	Shooting Star Casino Mahnomen, MN	April 12, 2007	$192,181
24	Leelanau Sands Casino Peshawbestown, MI	May 20, 2007	$229,244
25	Turning Stone Casino Verona, NY	June 16, 2007	$164,000
26	Turning Stone Casino Verona, NY	June 17, 2007	$260,850
27	Majestic Star Casino Gary, IN	July 30, 2007	$816,612
28	Grand Casino Mille Lacs Onamia, MN	Aug 27, 2007	$280,572
29	Northern Lights Casino Walker, MN	Sept 16, 2007	$192,998
30	Golden Gates Casino Black Hawk, CO	Oct 14, 2007	$463,500
31	Lucky Nugget Card Club Deadwood, SD	Oct 21, 2007	$232,046
32	Meskwaki Bingo Casino Hotel Tama, IA	Nov 4, 2007	$307,280
33	Casino Del Sol Tucson, AZ	Nov 18, 2007	$204,118
34	Majestic Star Casino Gary, IN	Dec 10, 2007	$835,200
35	Grand Casino Mille Lacs Onamia, MN	Feb 24, 2008	$251,806
36	Meskwaki Bingo Casino Hotel Tama, IA	Mar 9, 2008	$271,881
37	Golden Gates Casino Black Hawk, CO	April 13, 2008	$602,700
38	Majestic Star Casino Gary, IN	April 28, 2008	$603,100
39	Island Resort & Casino Harris, MI	May 11, 2008	$106,266
40	Greektown Casino Detroit, MI	June 8, 2008	$717,100
41	Turning Stone Resort & Casino Verona, NY	June 29, 2008	$375,000
42	Majestic Star Casino Gary, IN	July 28, 2008	$692,777

Updated: 30 July 2008   Total Awarded $11,907,948

CHAPTER TWENTY FOUR:

WORLD POKER TOUR

Mike Sexton, HOST
Vince Van Patten, CO-HOST
"All the way from Persia to France to the mighty Mississippi river, poker has a long and much-disputed history. Let the World Poker Tour take you throughout the growth of the most exciting card game in the world."

There are as many views on the origin of poker as there are combinations of hands. Card games from Persia (As Nas), India (Ganjifa), France (Poque), and Germany (Pochen) are all believed to be forerunners of the modern game. Decks with face cards are believed to have first been developed in France, and then later brought to America. Modern poker was born and spread on the Mississippi river by steamboat and quickly spreading into the interior by wagon and train; heading west with the California gold rush. By the late 1850s, the game was fast evolving into its modern day form.

In 2003, the World Poker Tour revolutionized televised poker and brought Texas Hold'em, the Cadillac of Poker, to the forefront of international excitement. WPT introduced the world to the "WPT Cam," a new, lipstick-sized camera that enables the TV audience to see the players' hole cards. This tiny camera plays a crucial role in revealing the drama of the poker players' high-stake bets and bluffs. WPT's expert commentary and educational content enables viewers to improve their own poker play. Mike Sexton and Vince Van Patten use poker lingo, and pop-up boxes appear on the screen with more information about the terminology. Such phrases, including the "flop," "turn," and "river," help familiarize new enthusiasts with the game.

The World Poker Tour has transformed poker into a sporting event that draws the young, old, men, women and people of all nationalities into the game. It has reshaped the face of poker and has raised the competitive bar to a new level. The World Poker Tour established the WPT Walk of Fame at Commerce Casino to honor top poker players, starting with Doyle "Texas Dolly" Brunson, Gus Hansen, and James Garner. With over 100 episodes filmed and over 90 Poker-Made Millionaires ™ to date, the World Poker Tour continues to popularize and evolve the sport. You can even play poker online with the WPT. And the rest, as they say, is history...

Meet The Hosts:

Mike Sexton is poker's accomplished promoter. He's well-known for his contributions to the sport and his commitment to raising poker's profile around the world. A former European poker champion with his own coveted World Series of Poker bracelets, Sexton is one of the premier ambassadors of poker.

His hard work and dedication have allowed him to successfully achieve his goals. He attended Ohio State University where he received a full four-year scholarship after winning a state championship title in gymnastics. It was during his time at college where Sexton developed his life-long passion for the sport of poker. Upon graduation he joined the 82nd Airborne Division in Ft. Bragg as a paratrooper. After completing his service, he stayed in North Carolina working as a salesman and playing poker at night. Realizing that he could make a living playing cards, he left his day job to become a professional poker player.

In 1985, Sexton made the jump to Las Vegas where his dedication to the sport prevailed. Mike won a WSOP bracelet in Limit Seven Card Stud Hi/Lo event in 1989. From there, he has amassed well over $2.7 million in prize money and become a regular fixture in tournaments.

Recently, in June 2006, Sexton battled it out on the felt with Daniel Negreanu at the WSOP Tournament of Champions to win his second gold bracelet and pocket $1 million. However, he elected to donate half his winning to several charities. As a sound commentator for the WPT and successful player in the poker circuit, Sexton has become, and always will be a great ambassador of the sport and a pioneer for charities outside of poker.

Vince Van Patten successes have come in many forms for this actor, producer, director, author, and former tennis player. The son of actor Dick Van Patten, Vince has thrived in all his endeavors through a winning combination of talent, ambition, and dedication.

As an actor, Vince launched his career at the age of 9, staring in a Colgate commercial. He went on to guest star in over three dozen classic television shows, including "Bonanza," "High Chaparral," and "Adam 12." He also starred in such television specials as "The Bionic Boy, "Gidget's Summer Reunion," and "Dirty Dozen III."

Graduating from television to film, Vince appeared in a number of movies along side such major actors as Kurt Russell and Charles Bronson. Prior to that, he starred in and co-produced the feature film, "The Break," playing the role of Nick, a washed up tennis pro whose bookie (Martin Sheen) forgives his gambling debts in exchange for coaching his 17-year old son. Vince wrote and directed another feature film, "The Flunky," starring Farah Fawcett, Dean Stockwell, and Vince's brother, James Van Patten.

For his work, he was awarded the prestigious award of Best Director at the Port Hueneme International Film Festival in 2000. Vince and his brother have also written a screenplay about a young poker player entitled, "California Kid," which is currently with Universal Studios. Vince co-authored the fictional poker novel, "The Picasso Flop," with Robert Randisi, which hit shelves in February of 2007.

Beyond his achievements in the entertainment industry, Vince is a remarkably talented tennis player who competed professionally through the mid-1980s. At his peak he ranked 25th in the world, scoring wins over almost every major player including John McEnroe.

Vince's passion for poker started at the young age of 13, when his father taught him how to play poker at the LA Tennis Club. Soon Vince was playing in side games in between tennis matches. By the time he turned 16, Vince had accumulated enough skill to play in his Dad's poker game. One night on a winning streak, he played until 7AM, when he finally had to throw in the cards to go to school. Vince continues to play poker every week with his buddies in a pot-limit game in Beverly Hills. He has tried his hand at the World Series of Poker three times, and brings solid experience hosting both televised sports and poker broadcasts to the World Poker Tour.

CLUBWPT.COM
Their motto: **No Buy-ins. No Deposits. No Risk.**
This new poker client and club allows players to win seats to WPT Buy-in events and even win their way onto TV on special FSN televised CLUBWPT events coming soon. You also have the chance to win over $100,000 in cash every month with your membership. They are currently offering new members who sign up a two-week free trial.

WPT BOOT CAMPS
To date, hundreds of poker players from around the world have participated in these amazing events and their testimonials clearly show that participation in WPT Boot Camp is any player's profitable poker decision.

The two-day WPT Boot Camp Tournament Edition is geared up for any poker player from the beginner to the advanced and features an integrated curriculum that includes live lecture, archived footage from the WPT, and interactive game playing. This camp will give you the tools to fully understand the tells, reads, and strategies integral to improving your own game. As a student, you will play in a private multi-table tournament to win an all-inclusive weeklong poker trip and other exciting prizes!

Each event has limited seating. A high instructor-to-student ratio maximizes your learning experience and provides you with one-on-one interaction, insight and feedback within an intimate hands-on experience. This is what separates WPT Boot Camp and allows their instructors the ability maximize your learning experience.

Your participation includes a seat in two private WPT Boot Camp tournaments. In each case, you will only play against fellow WPT Boot Camp students. On day one, you will participate in a single table Tune-Up Tournament where each winner will receive an exclusive chip set.

You will then conclude with a chance to win an all-inclusive weeklong poker trip or other exciting prizes! By placing you in this exciting, yet challenging position, the opportunity for you to complete "Your Fast Track to Your own Final Table" is unmatched anywhere else.

During your event, your all-star instructors will teach you, discuss your own experiences, share many of their own, enjoy meals with you and will be in attendance for the complete event. Their instructors do not just make guest appearances for a brief lecture and leave. They will guide you through this amazing event from start to finish!

Trainers were hand picked by none other than the World Poker Tour's Mike Sexton. With their complimentary knowledge and critical review of today's most distinguished players and experts, WPT Boot Camp has retained several of the most dynamic players and poker insiders in the world today.

WPT Boot Camp's all-star staff of instructors currently includes Mike Sexton, Linda Johnson, T.J. Cloutier, Mark Seif, and Clonie Gowen. These individuals are regarded as some of the most talented, knowledgeable, and skilled poker experts in the world. Each instructor utilizes the exclusive WPT courseware combined with their own understanding of the strategies and expertise to provide you with an unmatched opportunity to reach your dream of making it to your own final table.

WPT Cruises

Beginning in 2008, a new experience in poker cruises featured new destinations, tournaments, and special events. Compete to win a $10,000 seat into a WPT main event tournament on every sailing. Enjoy live, tournament poker while sailing on the newest and largest ships of Norwegian Cruise Line and the "eat when and where you want" dining experience of Norwegian's Free Style Cruising.

WPT Cruises can be Contacted by Mail:
WPT Cruises
5240 S Eastern Ave Las Vegas, NV 89119
Phone: (702) 740-2256 or (877) 736-8516
Fax: (702) 736-8889
Email: cruiseinfo@casinocenter.com

Cabin space is limited so don't delay. You must book your stateroom directly with WPT Cruises to be eligible to compete for the valuable $10,000 seat awards. If you want to be guaranteed a chance to enter these exciting tournaments make your reservations today.

WPT – Amateur Poker League

WPTAPL™ hosts Free Live Texas Hold'em Tournaments at your favorite locations throughout the world allowing you to learn the game, test your poker skills against others in your area, sharpen the skills you have already mastered, and enjoy the "Poker Night" food and drink specials at participating WPTAPL™ Venues.

More info can be found at: http://www.amateurpokerleague.com

World Poker Tour Season 1 (2002–2003)

Event	Winner	Prize
Five Diamond World Poker Classic	Gus Hansen	$556,480
Legends of Poker 2002	Chris Karagulleyan	$258,000
Ultimate Poker Classic - Amateurs	Juha Helppi	$50,000
Ultimate Poker Classic - Pros	Phil Gordon	$250,000
Costa Rica Classic	Jose Rosenkrantz	$108,730
Gold Rush	Paul Darden	$146,000
World Poker Finals - 2002	Howard Lederer	$320,400
World Poker Open - 2003	Dave Ulliott	$589,175
Euro Finals of Poker	Christer Johansson	$500,000
LA Poker Classic	Gus Hansen	$532,490
WPT Invitational - Season 1	Layne Flack	$100,000
Party Poker Million II	Howard Lederer	$289,150
World Poker Challenge III	Ron Rose	$168,298
WPT Championship - Season 1	Alan Goehring	$1,011,866

World Poker Tour Season 2 (2003-2004)

Event	Winner	Prize
Grand Prix de Paris 2003	David Benyamine	€357,200
Legends of Poker 2003	Mel Judah	$579,375
WPT Ladies' Night I	Clonie Gowen	$25,000
Borgata Poker Open 2003	Noli Francisco	$470,000
Ultimate Poker Classic II	Erick Lindgren	$500,000
World Poker Finals 2003	Hoyt Corkins	$1,089,200
Five Diamond World Poker Classic 2003	Paul Phillips	$1,101,980
Bad Boys of Poker	Gus Hansen	$25,000
Battle of Champions - Season 1	Ron Rose	$125,000
PokerStars Caribbean Poker Adventure 2004	Gus Hansen	$455,780
World Poker Open 2004	Barry Greenstein	$1,278,370
LA Poker Classic 2004	Antonio Esfandiari	$1,399,135
WPT Invitational - Season II	Phil Laak	$100,000
Bay 101 Shooting Star 2004	Phil Gordon	$360,000
PartyPoker Million III	Erick Lindgren	$1,000,000
World Poker Challenge IV	Mike Kinney	$629,469
WPT Championship - Season 2	Martin De Knijff	$2,728,356

World Poker Tour Season 3 (2004-2005)

Event	Winner	Prize
Grand Prix de Paris 2004	Surinder Sunar	€679,860
The Mirage Poker Showdown	Eli Elezra	$1,024,574
Legends of Poker 2004	Doyle Brunson	$1,198,260
WPT Ladies' Night II	Isabelle Mercier	$25,000
Borgata Poker Open 2004	Daniel Negreanu	$1,117,400
Ultimate Poker Classic III	Eric Brenes	$1,000,000
Festa Al Lago III	Juan Carlos Mortensen	$1,000,000
World Poker Finals 2004	Tuan Le	$1,549,588
Poker By The Book	David Sklansky	*
Five Diamond World Poker Classic 2004	Daniel Negreanu	$1,795,218
Young Guns of Poker	Scott Fischman	**
PokerStars Caribbean Poker Adventure 2005	John Gale	$890,600
World Poker Open 2005	Johnny Stolzmann	$1,491,444

World Poker Tour Season 3 (2004-2005) *Continued*

Event	Winner	Prize
LA Poker Classic 2005	Michael Mizrachi	$1,859,909
WPT Invitational - Season 3	Alex Brenes	$100,000
Bay 101 Shooting Star 2005	Danny Nguyen	$1,025,000
Party Poker Million IV	Michael Gracz	$1,525,000
World Poker Challenge V	Arnold Spee	$663,880
WPT Championship - Season 3	Tuan Le	$2,856,150

* Bragging Rights #1 Poker Author
** $25,000 Entry to WPT World Championship

World Poker Tour Season 4 (2005-2006)

Event	Winner	Prize
Battle of Champions II	David Benyamine	$25,000
Battle of Champions III	Tuan Le	$25,000
The Mirage Poker Showdown	Gavin Smith	$1,128,278
Grand Prix de Paris 2005	Roland De Wolfe	€479,680
Legends of Poker 2005	Alex Kahaner	$1,125,000
WPT Ladies' Night III	Jennifer Tilly	$25,000
2005 Borgata Poker Open	Al Ardebili	$1,498,650
UltimateBet Aruba Poker Classic	Kassem Deeb	$1,000,000
Doyle Brunson N. American Championship	Minh Ly	$1,060,050
World Poker Finals 2005	Nick Schulman	$2,142,000
Five Diamond World Poker Classic	Rehne Pedersen	$2,078,185
PokerStars Caribbean Poker Adventure	Steve Paul-Ambrose	$1,363,100
Gold Strike World Poker Open	Scotty Nguyen	$969,421
2006 Borgata Winter Poker Open	Michael Mizrachi	$1,173,373
LA Poker Classic	Alan Goehring	$2,391,550
Celebrity Pro Invitational	Barry Greenstein	$100,000
Bad Boys of Poker II	Tony G	$25,000
Bay 101 Shooting Star	Nam Le	$1,172,800
World Poker Challenge	Mike Simon	$1,052,890
Foxwoods Classic	Victor Ramdin	$1,331,889
WPT Championship	Joe Bartholdi Jr	$3,760,165

World Poker Tour Season 5 (2006-2007)

Event	Winner	Prize
Battle of Champions IV	Nick Schulman	$25,500
Mirage Poker Showdown	Stanley Weiss	$1,294,755
Mandalay Bay Poker Championship	Joe Tehan	$1,033,440
Grand Prix de Paris	Christian Grundtvig	€712,500
Legends of Poker	Joe Pelton	$1,577,170
Ladies Night IV	J. J. Liu	$25,500
Borgata Poker Open	Mark Newhouse	$1,519,020
Festa Al Lago	Andreas Walnum	$1,090,025
North American Poker Championship	Soren Turkewitsch	$1,352,224
WPT Canadian Open Championship	Scott Clements	$250,027
World Poker Finals	Nenad Medic	$1,717,194
Bellagio Five Diamond World Poker Classic	Joseph Hachem	$2,182,075
PokerStars Caribbean Adventure	Ryan Daut	$1,535,255
World Poker Open	Bryan Sumner	$913,986
Borgata Poker Classic	John Hennigan	$1,606,223
L.A. Poker Classic	Eric Hershler	$2,429,970
WPT Invitational	Adam Weinraub	$125,000
Bay 101 Shooting Star	Ted Forrest	$1,125,500
World Poker Challenge	J.C. Tran	$683,473
Foxwoods Poker Classic	Raj Patel	$1,298,405
WPT Championship	Carlos Mortensen	$3,970,415
Poker by the Book: Chapter II	Barry Greenstein	$25,000

World Poker Tour Season 6 (2007-2008)

Event	Winner	Prize
Mirage Poker Showdown	Jonathan Little	$1,066,295
Mandalay Bay Poker Championship	Shawn Buchanan	$768,775
Bellagio Cup III	Kevin Saul	$1,342,320
Legends of Poker	Dan Harrington	$1,600,365
Ladies Night V	Kristy Gazes	$25,500
Gulf Coast Poker Championship	Bill Edler	$747,615
Borgata Poker Open	Roy Winston	$1,575,280

World Poker Tour Season 6 (2007-2008) *Continued*

Event	Winner	Prize
Turks & Caicos Poker Classic	Rhynie Campbell	$436,675
Spanish Championship	Markus Lehmann	€537,000
North American Poker Championship	Scott Clements	$1,387,224
World Poker Finals	Mike Vela	$1,704,986
Doyle Brunson Five Diamond World Poker Classic	Eugene Katchalov	$2,482,605
World Poker Open	Brett Faustman	$892,413
Borgata Winter Open	Gavin Griffin	$1,401,109
L.A. Poker Classic	Phil Ivey	$1,596,100
WPT Celebrity Invitational	Van Tuyet Nguyen	$125,500
Bay 101 Shooting Star Championship	Brandon Cantu	$1,000,000
World Poker Challenge	Lee Markholt	$493,815
Foxwoods Poker Classic	Erik Seidel	$992,890
2008 WPT Ladies Championship	Nancy Todd Tyner	$68,640
2008 WPT Championship	David Chiu	$3,389,140

World Poker Tour Season 7 (2008-2009)

Event	Winner	Prize
Spanish Championship	Casper Hansen	€655,720
Bellagio Cup IV	Mike Watson	$1,673,770
Legends of Poker	Bon Phan	$1,116,428
Borgata Poker Open	Vivek Rajkumar	$1,424,500
North American Poker Championship	Glen Witmer	$1,254,152
Festa Al Lago	Bertrand Grospellier	$1,411,015
World Poker Finals	Jonathan Little	$1,120,310

These are the latest results as of 11/15/2008

" I've often thought, if I got really hungry for a good milk shake, how much would I pay for one? People will pay a hundred dollars for a bottle of wine; to me that's not worth it. But I'm not going to say it is foolish or wrong to spend that kind of money, if that's what you want. So if a guy wants to bet twenty or thirty thousand dollars in a poker game that is his privilege. "

—Jack Binion, successor to the founder of the World Series of Poker.

CHAPTER TWENTY FIVE:

WORLD SERIES OF POKER

The **World Series of Poker*** (WSOP) * is the largest set of poker tournaments in the world. It is held annually in Las Vegas, and since 2007 consisted of 55 events, all but the "Main Event" is finished in just over a month.

The winner of each event receives a World Series of Poker bracelet and a prize based on the number of entrants. Most of the major poker variants are featured; though in recent years, over half of the events have been variants of Texas hold 'em. The series culminates with the $10,000 NL Hold'em "Main Event" that since 2004 has attracted entrants numbering in the thousands, with the victor receiving a multi-million dollar prize. Since 2005, the WSOP has been sponsored by Harrah's Entertainment and since 1971; all WSOP events have been tournaments with cash prizes. In 1973, a five-card stud event was added.

* WORLD SERIES OF POKER and WSOP are trademarks of Harrah's License Company, LLC ("Harrah's"). Harrah's does not sponsor or endorse, and is not associated or affiliated with "Eat Professional Poker Players Alive!" or its products, services, or promotions.

In 2006, there were 45 events at the WSOP, covering the majority of poker variants. Currently, Texas hold 'Em, Omaha hold 'em and Seven-card stud and their low-ball variants (if any) are played. Even H.O.R.S.E. and S.H.O.E. has made an appearance. Other events played in the past include Chinese Poker, Five-Card Stud and many others.

Like most tournaments, the sponsoring casino takes an entry fee (a percentage between 6% and 10%, depending on the buy-in) and distributes the rest; hence the prize money increases with more players. In the 2005 main event $52,818,610 in prize money was distributed among 560 players, with $7.5 million to first prize.

Highlights
The number of participants in the WSOP has grown almost every year, and in recent years the growth has exploded. In 2000 there were 4,780 entrants in the various events, but in 2005, the number rose to over 23,000 players. In the main event alone, the number of participants grew from 839 in 2003 to 8,773 in 2006.

Phil Hellmuth holds the record for the most bracelets after winning eleven. Runners-up Doyle Brunson and Johnny Chan have each won ten bracelets. Doyle's son, Todd Brunson, won a bracelet in a $2,500 Omaha Eight-or-better event in 2005, making them the first and (so far) only father/son pair to win at least one event at the WSOP. Crandell Addington is the only player to place in the top ten of the World Series of Poker Main Event eight times.

Four players have won the main event multiple times: Johnny Moss (1971, 1974), Doyle Brunson (1976, 1977), Stu Ungar (1980, 1981, and 1997) and Johnny Chan (1987, 1988).

Bracelet winners who first achieved fame in other fields include French actor/singer Patrick Bruel (in 1998), Danish soccer player Jan Vang Sørensen (in 2002) and American actress Jennifer Tilly (in 2005).

History
The World Series of Poker began in 1968 as an invitational event sponsored by Tom Moore of San Antonio, Texas, and was held at the Holiday Hotel and Casino in Reno, Nevada. This inaugural event was won by Crandell Addington. The set of tournaments that the World Series of Poker (WSOP) would evolve into was the brainchild of Las Vegas casino owner and poker player Benny Binion.

In 1970, the first WSOP at Binion's Horseshoe took place as a series of cash games that included five-card stud, deuce to seven low-ball draw, razz, seven-card stud, and Texas hold 'em. The format for the Main Event as a freeze-out Texas hold 'em game came the next year. The winner in 1970, Johnny Moss, was elected by his peers as the first World Champion of Poker and received a silver cup as a prize.

In 2004, Harrah's Entertainment purchased Binion's Horseshoe, kept the rights to the Horseshoe and World Series of Poker brands, sold the hotel and casino to MTR Gaming Group, and announced that the 2005 Series events would be held at the Harrah's-owned

Rio Hotel and Casino, located just off the Las Vegas Strip. The final two days of the main event in 2005 were held downtown at what is now the MTR operated "Binion's" in celebration of the centennial of the founding of Las Vegas. It also added a made-for-television $2 million "free roll" invitational "Tournament of Champions" (TOC) event first won by Annie Duke as a "winner-take-all" event.

Starting in 2005, the WSOP began a tournament "circuit" at Harrah's-owned properties in the United States where in addition to the $10,000 buy-in tournament at each site, qualifying players became eligible for a revamped Tournament of Champions. The 2005 TOC, made up of the top twenty qualifying players at each circuit event, along with the final table from the 2005 Main Event and the winners of nine or more bracelets (Johnny Chan, Doyle Brunson, and Phil Hellmuth) would participate in the revamped TOC at Caesars Palace. Mike "The Mouth" Matusow won the first prize of $1 million, and all the players at the final table were guaranteed a minimum of $25,000 for the eighth and ninth place finishers. During a break in the final table of the 2005 Main Event on July 16, Harrah's announced that eleven properties, including the recently added Bally's and Caesars properties, would host 2005-06 WSOP Circuit events that started on August 11 in Tunica, Mississippi. One event that was scheduled for Biloxi, Mississippi was canceled after the Grand Casino Biloxi, which was scheduled to host the event, suffered major damage from Hurricane Katrina.

The Rio also hosted the 2006 World Series of Poker, which began on June 25 with satellite events and formally began the day after, with the annual Casino Employee event, was won in 2006 by Chris Gros. 2006 featured the "Tournament of Champions" on June 25 and 26, won by Mike Sexton. Various events led up to the main event, which was held from July 28 until August 10. The first prize of $12 million was awarded to Jamie Gold.

Main Event
The Main Event of the WSOP has been the $10,000 buy-in NL Texas Hold 'Em tournament since 1972. In 1971, the buy-in was $5,000. Winners of the event not only got the largest prize of the tournament and a gold bracelet, but additionally, their picture is placed into the Gallery of Champions at Binion's.

World Series of Poker: World Champions

1970	Johnny Moss*	Prize (Silver Cup)	Entrants = 7
1971	Johnny Moss	Prize $30,000	Entrants = 6
1972	Thomas "Amarillo Slim" Preston	Prize $80,000	Entrants = 8
1973	Walter "Puggy" Pearson	Prize $130,000	Entrants = 13
1974	Johnny Moss	Prize $160,000	Entrants = 16
1975	Brian "Sailor" Roberts	Prize $210,000	Entrants = 21
1976	Doyle Brunson	Prize $220,000	Entrants = 22
1977	Doyle Brunson	Prize $340,000	Entrants = 34
1978	Bobby Baldwin	Prize $210,000	Entrants = 42

World Series of Poker: World Champions *Continued*

1979	Hal Fowler	Prize $270,000	Entrants = 54
1980	Stu Ungar	Prize $385,000	Entrants = 73
1981	Stu Ungar	Prize $375,000	Entrants = 75
1982	Jack Straus	Prize $520,000	Entrants = 104
1983	Tom McEvoy	Prize $540,000	Entrants = 108
1984	Jack Keller	Prize $660,000	Entrants = 132
1985	Bill Smith	Prize $700,000	Entrants = 140
1986	Berry Johnston	Prize $570,000	Entrants = 141
1987	Johnny Chan	Prize $625,000	Entrants = 152
1989	Phil Hellmuth Jr	Prize $755,000	Entrants = 178
1990	Mansour Matloubi	Prize $895,000	Entrants = 194
1991	Brad Daugherty	Prize $1,000,000	Entrants = 215
1992	Hamid Dastmalchi	Prize $1,000,000	Entrants = 201
1993	Jim Bechtel	Prize $1,000,000	Entrants = 220
1994	Russ Hamilton	Prize $1,000,000	Entrants = 268
1995	Dan Harrington	Prize $1,000,000	Entrants = 273
1996	Huck Seed	Prize $1,000,000	Entrants = 295
1997	Stu Ungar	Prize $1,000,000	Entrants = 312
1998	Scotty Nguyen	Prize $1,000,000	Entrants = 350
1999	Noel Furlong	Prize $1,000,000	Entrants = 393
2000	Chris "Jesus" Ferguson	Prize $1,500,000	Entrants = 512
2001	Juan Carlos Mortensen	Prize $1,500,000	Entrants = 613
2002	Robert Varkonyi	Prize $2,000,000	Entrants = 631
2003	Chris Moneymaker	Prize $2,500,000	Entrants = 839
2004	Greg Raymer	Prize $5,000,000	Entrants = 2,576
2005	Joe Hachem	Prize $7,500,000	Entrants = 5,619
2006	Jamie Gold	Prize $12,000,000	Entrants = 8,773
2007	Jerry Yang	Prize $8,250,000	Entrants = 6,358
2008	Peter Eastgate	Prize $9,119,416	Entrants = 6,844

* awarded by vote

World Series of Poker: Final Tables 2000 – 2008

2000 Prize Pool $5,120,000 - 512 Entries

1. Chris "Jesus" Ferguson $1,500,000	2. T.J. Cloutier $896,000
3. Steve Kaufman $570,500	4. Hasan Habib $326,000
5. Jim McManus $247,760	6. Roman Abinsay $195,600
7. Jeff Shulman $146,700	8. Captain Tom Franklin $97,800
9. Mickey Appleman $74,980	

2001 Prize Pool $6,130,000 - 613 Entries

1. Juan Carlos Mortenson $1,500,000	2. Dewey Tomko $1,098,925
3. Stan Schrier $699,315	4. Phil Gordon $399,610
5. Phil Hellmuth Jr. $303,705	6. Mike Matusow $239,765
7. Henry Nowakowski $179,825	8. Steve Reihle $119,885
9. John Inashima $91,910	

2002 Prize Pool $6,310,000 - 631 Entries

1. Robert Varkonyi $2,000,000	2. Julian Gardner $1,100,000
3. Ralph Perry $550,000	4. Scott Gray $281,400
5. Harley Hall $195,000	6. Russell Rosenblum $150,000
7. John Shipley $120,000	8. Tony D $100,000
9. Minh Ly $85,000	

2003 Prize Pool $7,802,700 - 839 Entries

1. Chris Moneymaker $2,500,000	2. Sam Farha $1,300,000
3. Dan Harrington $650,000	4. Jason Lester $440,000
5. Tomer Benvisitsi $320,000	6. Amir Vahedi $250,000
7. Young Pak $200,000	8. David Grey $160,000
9. David Singer $120,000	

2004 Prize Pool $24,224,400 - 2,576 Entries

1. Greg Raymer $5,000,000	2. David Williams $3,500,000
3. Josh Arieh $2,500,000	4. Dan Harrington $1,500,000
5. Glen Hughes $1,100,000	6. Al Krux $800,000
7. Matt Dean $675,000	8. Mattias Andersson $575,000
9. Michael McClain $470,400	

2005 Prize Pool $52,819,610 - 5,619 Entries

1. **Joseph Hachem** $7,500,000	2. **Steven Dannenmann** $4,250,000
3. **John Derick "Tex" Barch** $2,500,000	4. **Aaron Kanter** $2,000,000
5. **Andrew Black** $1,750,000	6. **Scott Lazar** $1,500,000
7. **Daniel Bergsdorf** $1,300,000	8. **Brad Kondracki** $1,150,000
9. **Mike Matusow** $1,000,000	

2006 Prize Pool $85,512,162 - 8,773 Entries

1. **Jamie Gold** $12,000,000	2. **Paul Wasicka** $6,102,499
3. **Michael Binger** $4,123,310	4. **Allen Cunningham** $3,628,513
5. **Rhett Butler** $3,216,182	6. **Richard Lee** $2,803,851
7. **Douglas Kim** $2,391,520	8. **Erik Friberg** $1,979,189
9. **Dan Nassif** $1,566,858	

2007 Prize Pool $59,784,954 - 6,358 Entries

1. **Jerry Yang** $8,250,000	2. **Tuan Lam** $4,840,981
3. **Raymond Rahme** $3,048,025	4. **Alex Kravchenko** $1,852,721
5. **Jon Kalmar** $1,255,069	6. **Hevad "Rain" Khan** $956,243
7. **Lee Childs** $705,229	8. **Lee Watkinson** $585,699
9. **Philip Hilm** $525,934	

2008 Prize Pool $64,333,600 - 6,844 Entries

1. **Peter Eastgate** $9,152,416	2. **Ivan Demidov** $5,809,595
3. **Dennis Phillips** $4,517,773	4. **Ylon Schwartz** $3,774,974
5. **Scott Montgomery** $3,096,768	6. **Darus Suharto** $2,418,562
7. **David Rheem** $1,772,650	8. **Kelly Kim** $1,288,217
9. **Craig Marquis** $900,670	

Player of the Year

Since 2004, a Player of the Year Award has been given to the player with the most points accumulated throughout the World Series. Only "open" events in which all players who participate, count in the standings. Beginning with the 2006 World Series of Poker, the Main Event and the $50,000 H.O.R.S.E. competition had no effect on the outcome of the winner of the Player of the Year award. However, in the 2008 World Series of Poker, the $50,000 H.O.R.S.E. event counted toward the Player of the Year award.

Year	Winner	Bracelets	Final Tables	Money Finishes
2004	Daniel Negreanu	1	5	6
2005	Allen Cunningham	1	4	5
2006	Jeff Madsen	1	3	5
2007	Tom Schneider	1	3	5
2008	Erick Lindgren	1	3	5

The winner of the Main Event has traditionally been given the unofficial title of World Champion. However, the game's top professionals have stated that the recently-added $50,000 H.O.R.S.E. event is the one which ultimately decides the world's best player. The $50,000 buy-in, five times larger than the buy-in for the Main Event, has thus far deterred amateurs from playing in the H.O.R.S.E. The H.O.R.S.E. tournament was won by Chip Reese in 2006, Freddy Deeb in 2007, and Scotty Nguyen in 2008. Since Reese's death in December 2007, the winner of this event wins the David 'Chip' Reese Memorial Trophy in addition to the bracelet and the prize money.

Another point that I would like to bring up is that when you win big at the World Series of Poker, The taxman does also…

The 2008 World Series of Poker winner of the main event won $9,152,416 but would he actually end up with all that money? This year's winner was Peter Eastgate from Denmark. The United States and Denmark have a tax treaty. Because of the treaty Mr. Eastgate doesn't owe a penny to the IRS. That just leaves the Danish tax authorities.

Denmark's tax agency is called SKAT. Denmark, like the United States, does tax gambling winnings. For casino gambling the tax rate is 45% on the first 4 million Danish Kroners; it's 75% on income above that. Today $1 is worth 5.88907 DKK; Mr. Eastgate won 53,899,250.70 DKK before taxes. Mr. Eastgate will owe about 39,224,438 DKK in tax ($6,660,545). Put another way Mr. Eastgate will keep 14,674,813 DKK ($2,491,871) of his winning, just 27.23% of his prize. Yes, he faces an effective tax rate of 72.77%, which is ridiculous.

Ivan Demidov of Moscow, Russia finished second and won $5,809,595. The United States and Russia also have a tax treaty and Mr. Demidov won't have any of his winnings withheld by the IRS. Russia has a 13% flat tax rate, so Mr. Demidov will owe about $755,247 to the State Taxation Service of Russia.

Third place went to an American, Dennis Phillips of Cottage Hills, Illinois. Mr. Phillips won $4,517,773 for his efforts. He was an amateur gambler so he won't owe self-employment tax on his winnings. Still, he can expect to pay $1,568,950 to the IRS and $135,533 to the Illinois Department of Revenue.

Ylon Schwartz of Brooklyn, New York, finished in fourth place for $3,774,974. He is a professional gambler so he will owe self-employment tax on his winnings. He'll also owe state and New York City income tax. His likely tax bite is $1,396,304 to the IRS and $387,966 to the New York Department of Tax and Finance.

Two Canadians finished in fifth and sixth place. Scott Montgomery of Perth, Ontario finished in fifth place for $3,096,768. The US-Canada tax treaty specifies that 30% of his win will be withheld to the IRS. Thus, $929,030 was withheld. Mr. Montgomery is a professional gambler so he will owe tax on his win to Revenue Canada. However, he will be able to take a credit on his Canadian tax return for the money withheld to the IRS. As Canada's tax rate is 29% he likely won't have to pay any additional funds to Revenue Canada. However, when provincial taxes are included the tax rate becomes 46.41%. Thus, Mr. Montgomery will owe tax in Canada: about $491,728 after the credit for the tax withheld to the IRS.

The sixth place finisher was Darus Suharto of Toronto. Mr. Suharto is an accountant, so he won't owe tax to Revenue Canada on his won. However, of the $2,418,562 he won, $725,569 was withheld per the US-Canada tax treaty. He may be able to claim a credit on his Canadian tax return for years to come based on this withheld money and eventually get it back.

David Rheem and Kelly Kim these two Californians finished in seventh and eighth place, earning $1,772,650 and $1,288,217 respectively. Mr. Rheem will owe about $651,262 to the IRS and $170,302 to the Franchise Tax Board; Mr. Kim will owe about $470,995 to the IRS and $121,074 to the Franchise Tax Board.

Craig Marquis of Arlington, Texas finished in ninth place. He is also a professional gambler, and of the $900,670 he won he'll have to dish out about $328,911 to the IRS.

The taxation of the final table winners is a bit unfair, the amount won at Final Table $32,731,625

- Tax to SKAT (Denmark) $6,660,545
- US Tax Withheld to IRS $1,654,599
- Add'l Tax Owed to IRS $4,416,422
- Total Tax to IRS $6,071,021
- Tax to State Taxation Service (Russia) $755,247
- Tax to Revenue Canada $491,728
- Tax to NY Dept of Tax and NYC $387,966
- Tax to California FTB $291,376
- Tax to Illinois Dept of Revenue $135,533

Total Taxes $14,793,416

" Most of the money you'll win at poker comes not from the brilliance of your own play, but from the ineptitude of your opponents. **"**

—*Lou Krieger, one of the most influential gaming writers of the past 100 years and a valued poker book author.*

PART SEVEN

Online Poker

CHAPTER TWENTY SIX:

GREAT ONLINE POKER ROOMS

bodog **Bodoglife.com** offers all the excitement of great multi–player poker, served up with typical Bodog flair and the best customer service in the poker world.

The Bodog Poker software features clean, stylish graphics, easy–to–use and reliable features. It's even customizable, you can even choose between a dozen different felt colors. Multi–tabling has never been easier as you stake your claim in Texas Hold'em, Omaha, Omaha Hi/Lo, 7–Card Stud, 7–Card Stud Hi/Lo, and 5–Card Stud.

The Bodog Poker Room features daily tournaments with a monthly guaranteed prize pool of $5 million, and its $100,000 guaranteed tournament each Sunday provides massive overlays, giving online players exceptional value for their tournament dollars. Its Bodog Poker Open tournament series is quickly becoming one of the most popular online poker series in the industry with players battling it out in different formats of Texas Hold'em, including No Limit, Pot Limit, Limit, No Limit with Re-buys, and Six-Handed No Limit.

For new players, Bodog gives an unrivaled sign-up bonus, and for each friend you refer to Bodog, you instantly receive 20% of their initial deposit (up to $100).

To put their bonuses to work, players can take advantage of Bodog's weekly Player's Choice Package qualifiers, where winners receive a $12K prize package to cover their buy-in and travel expense to the international tournament of their choice. Whether you choose a mainstream event in a place like Las Vegas or you want to go somewhere more exotic like Turks & Caicos, let your poker skills take you to the destination that suits you. That's right – you can choose to play in EPT, WPT or WSOP events all around the world. Some of the other international tournament locations include: Melbourne, London, Dublin, Barcelona, Prague, Baden and Copenhagen. Could there be anything cooler than paying for a wicked vacation and large tournament entry fee by winning an online qualifier?

In addition to its poker room, Bodog offers the best horse racing from around the globe in its race book, an industry-leading sports book with play-by-play wagering through Bodog Live. In 2008, Bodog announced its newest innovation, a mobile casino client that puts Bodog's top casino games in the palm of your hand.

With all of the above considered, the key to Bodog's success is the importance placed on quality customer service - players are never more than a mouse click or phone call away. Bodog makes it easy for players to request information, services and support 24 hours a day, 365 days a year.

SpadeClub.com powered by Card Player, is a brand-new online poker community that is poised to revolutionize the world of poker. SpadeClub Exclusive membership offers a brand-new way to play poker and win real cash without any risk. Exclusive members have access to more than 350 tournaments a week with prize pools totaling more than $100,000 every month.

SpadeClub is a completely risk-free poker site because it will:

- Never require a deposit.
- Never charge an entry fee.
- Never take a rake.
- Always offer an abundance of community features and poker tips.

SpadeClub offers a unique way to play poker and with no risk and no deposits. The site offers $100,000 in freerolls to its Exclusive members each month, the biggest of which has a $40,000 prize pool and awards $10,000 to the first-place finisher.

SpadeClub's software is bright and colorful and easy to navigate. The software allows for users to upload their own avatars (and has the option to turn off other players' avatars). The site also offers a four-color deck that gives the table a fun feeling.

Exclusive members at the site have both a Hand Helper and an odds calculator inset into each table for easy access. The Hand Helper allows players to input their hole-cards, their position at the table, and the number of players at the table to get a ranking of the hand's pre-flop value. The odds calculator allows players to input two sets of hole-cards and anywhere from zero to four board cards (from pre-flop up to the turn) to see the odds of winning the pot. Both of these tools are helpful for members to improve.

SpadeClub also offers extensive community tools like personal profiles, blogs, and a friend-tracking system. A player's profile shows their bio and interests along with any badges of achievement they've earned. Badges are earned by achieving certain milestones, such as hands played, first-place finishes, or bounties (players eliminated).

Here is a list of the features available on SpadeClub:

Membership Type	Exclusive	Basic
Price	$19.99/month or $149.95/year (a savings of $89.93, or 37 percent) 14-day free trial available	Free
Game access*	-$100,000 worth of freerolls -All tournaments -All sit-and-go's -All play-money ring games	-$10,000 worth of freerolls - All play-money ring games
Can earn and redeem points	Yes	No
Player profiles	Yes	Yes
Friend tracking	Yes	No
Badges of achievement	Yes (all badges)	Yes ("Hands Played" badge)
Hand Helper	Yes	No
Odds calculator	Yes	No
Leader boards	Yes	No
Uploadable avatars	Yes	Yes
Ad-free tables	Yes	No
Money earned can be used for membership	Yes	Yes
Free digital Card Player subscription	Yes	No

*No purchase necessary

The site has tournaments constantly running, and they're all freerolls. The flagship tournament for the site is the $40,000 Mega Monthly free roll. Players qualify for that tournament, as well as the weekly $5,000 tournaments, by playing in free satellites that offer entry-tokens. There are also freerolls that award cash payouts running throughout the day.

Points and tokens are the currency on SpadeClub. Tokens are earned through the qualifiers mentioned above. Points can be earned in almost any tournament (aside from the token-awarding events), including tournaments that already award cash prizes. Players then cash in the points in to enter bigger tournaments. The site also offers sit-and-go tournaments to its members. Players can play sit-and-go's to earn points at both single-table and multi-table events at all hours of the day.

Spade Club is providing new ways for poker players to take advantage of their skill without risk. It will be interesting to see how the site fares over the coming months. Spade Club currently accepts, PayPal, Master Card, and Visa.

Special Features
- All tournaments are freerolls
- Badges of achievement
- Odds calculator and Hand Helper inset in table (members only)
- Friend tracking (members only)
- Personal profiles with blogs
- Leader boards (members only)

Promotions
- 14-day free trial
- $40,000 Mega Monthly
- 5,000 weekly freerolls
- Refer-a-friend program which awards free membership

FullTiltPoker.com launched in 2004, continues to showcase its ambition through massive growth and a reputation as one of today's market leaders. Full Tilt has a virtual armada of sponsored pros, counting the much-lauded Team Full Tilt which sports 13 big-name pros, including: Phil Ivey, Chris "Jesus" Ferguson, Howard Lederer, Mike Matusow, Jennifer Harman, Phil Gordon, and Allen Cunningham. Team Full Tilt has a combined 32 WSOP bracelets. Team Full Tilt members and the other 47 sponsored pros are easy to find playing on the site (their screen names and the tables they sit at show up red in the lobby) and will often chat with observers.

The Full Tilt software sports a sleek lobby and fun, cartoonish tables and avatars. While users cannot import their own images for avatars, they do have a choice from 58 different characters that Full Tilt offers. Each avatar has a set of four "emotions" that it can convey to further personalize the experience, including: normal, happy, angry, and confused. The software allows for a high amount of customizability in various other ways as well. There are seven different table themes users can choose from ranging from the Vegas skyline to outer space. A stripped-down "racetrack" view without avatars can be chosen as well, which caters to users who prefer a classic tabletop over cartoonish trappings. The table windows can also be resized (either shrunk or expanded), which is a feature that few sites offer but one that is very welcome.

The main lobby conveys an abundance of information about each table, all of which is individually sorted. Cash games can be filtered by poker variant, limit type, hands per hour, or stakes (high, medium, or low). The tournament tab features a highly-customizable filtration system that lets users get very specific in dictating which tournaments they wish to view. Tournaments in the lobby are also labeled with icons for re-buy, deep-stack, turbo, shorthanded, and so on, to aid players in quickly finding their ideal table. The lobby provides a legend for these icons.

Specific tournament lobbies are rife with useful information, including: blind/payout structure, biggest/smallest/average stack, time until next break, time until next blind level (and what it will be), and total/current number of players.

The lobby also displays a running list of the current rank of every player in the tournament (many poker sites only rank the top 100 and those already eliminated). Every displayed list is sorted, making it easy and efficient to find desired information. FullTilt does not currently support final table deal-making, although players are, of course, allowed to make deals and transfer money on their own terms. (FullTilt does not oversee or guarantee such deals.)

While the software does have "auto-post blinds" and "sit out next hand" checkboxes, it does not have checkboxes for "Wait for next blind and auto-post" when entering a table or "sit out at next blind" when preparing to leave a table.

Almost all of the poker variants offered in cash-game form are also offered as tournaments (the exceptions being H.O.S.E., H.A., and H.O.). Single-table, low-buy-in Hold'em sit-and-go tournament fill up in less than two minutes. Full Tilt offers sit-and-go's for up to 90 players. There are plenty of guaranteed prize pool tournaments at Full Tilt and buy-ins range from as little as $1 to as much as $500. Such tournaments regularly go well beyond their respective guarantees.

Players can find a cash game to their liking and start playing within seconds. Full or nearly full tables abound in the Hold'em section and the other poker variants' sections are heavily populated as well (yes, even razz).

Stakes: $0.25-$0.50 up to $1,000-$2,000
Game Variety
- Hold'em (limit, no-limit, capped no-limit, pot-limit, six-handed, heads up)
- Omaha (high, eight-or-better, six-handed, eight-or-better heads up)
- Seven-card stud (high, eight-or-better, heads up)
- Razz (low, heads up)
- H.O.R.S.E. (including: Hold'em, Omaha, razz, stud, and stud eight-or-better; six-handed available)
- H.O.S.E. (including: Hold'em, Omaha, stud, and stud eight-or-better)
- H.A. (including: Hold'em and Omaha high)
- H.O. (including: Hold'em and Omaha eight-or-better)

Special Features
- Team Full Tilt and sponsored pros.
- A lot of noteworthy live-poker pros play on Full Tilt, and many are willing to chat with observers.
- Loyalty programs that allow players to earn customized Full Tilt jerseys or online avatars.
- One of the few sites to have true high-stakes tables that can be observed by any player.
- Choice from 58 avatars and seven table backgrounds.
- Capped no-limit games.
- Special "Pro Chat" allows a player to chat with selected pros each week.
- E-mail newsletter with strategy articles from top pros.
- Resizable table windows (allows both shrinking and expanding)

Promotions
- Full Tilt Online Poker Series (FTOPS)
- Poker After Dark qualifiers
- Moscow Millions qualifiers
- Iron Man Challenge
- Tournament leader board prizes

Email
- support@FullTiltPoker.com

Overall, the traffic volume is in the very top segment of the industry. Real-money player statistics as of July 2008 show 10,500 ring-game players at peak hours and 70,000 tournament players at peak hours.

Doylesroom.com takes player loyalty very seriously and their Player Rewards program is based on the type of hospitality that Doyle has enjoyed and come to expect over the years. One of Doyle's closest friends, Jack Binion, the master of player loyalty programs, has set the standard that they embrace. According to Doyle Brunson, DoylesRoom. com is the only online room where he plays. It's lucky that it's named after him, then, huh?

Along with Brunson, the site sponsors his son Todd, Mike "The Mad Genius" Caro, Cyndy Violette, Hoyt Corkins, Dewey Tomko, and "Captain" Tom Franklin. DoylesRoom is big on flaunting its star power and is famous for giving away cash-prizes to players who eliminate the site's sponsored pros in its bounty tournaments and soon to be $250K Super Saturday Tournament.

DoylesRoom has attractive-looking software with good features. The tables themselves show a wealth of information, including individual bet sizes, active pot size (not including current bets), and current pot total. It also shows hand history where you can see your opponents cards if the betting goes to the river. The table setup is simple and the cards are very easy to read (especially your own hand, which shows up big and bright). DoylesRoom now offers themed or customizable tabletops with floor color and style. Other tweakable table options include four-color decks, game markers, hand descriptions, and a rabbit-hole camera. Each table's chat box is detachable, repositionable, and resizable (similar to that of Full Tilt, except DoylesRoom offers three preset sizes). When the chat box is downsized, the entire table becomes resizable, a nice feature for playing multiple games at once. In NL games, the software allows players to type in their bet, move a slider, chooses between raises (of the minimum, 3×, 4×, and max) or bets (of 1/4 of the pot, 1/2 of the pot, and all in) via buttons that calculate the amount.

The main lobby is innovative in that it gives players three completely different-looking formats to choose from. The first, the three-view lobby, is set up with collapsible and expandable lists of variants, limit-type, and stakes, much like searching for a file using Windows Explorer. This lobby organization is inherently filtered, and thus the software has no need for any further filters aside from hide full/empty tables (which it has). All in all, this makes for a very simple, easy to use lobby. The second option is called the advanced lobby, which uses a complex system of checkboxes and sliders to completely filter out the tables that you have no interest in seeing. This lobby is a breath of fresh air for those wishing to see only tables they'd be interested in playing at (which, I would imagine, is quite a few of us). The third option is for quick-play. It essentially asks you what kind of poker you want to play and then automatically matches you to a table. This option is meant for those wanting as few clicks as possible between them and poker.

Tournaments

DoylesRoom offers single and multi-table tournaments in Hold'em, Omaha, Omaha eight-or-better, Seven-card Stud, Five-card Stud and Five-card draw. The site offers numerous guaranteed-prize-pool tournaments (a minimum $4,000,000 guaranteed each month), which consistently reach beyond the posted prize pools. Most of tournaments range from a $.10 to a $215 buy-in and super satellites to the $250,000 guaranteed tournament for $5.55 or buy-in directly for $165. The buy-ins for most of the guaranteed tournaments are $20 or less.

Single-table sit-and-go tournaments are offered as 10-handed, six-handed, five-handed, or heads up, and come in normal-speed, turbo, super turbo, and extreme turbo variants. They are offered at buy-ins ranging from $0.10 to $1,000, although only those of $100 or less get much traffic. $10 sit-and-go's take only a minute to fill up after the first player has been seated while $20 sit-and-go's take about five minutes to start.

Cash Games

NL Hold'em is the name of the game at DoylesRoom, especially six-max games. You can easily find a game at even the highest limits. The pot-limit Omaha and Omaha eight-or-better cash games have very good traffic in all but the highest limits. (The fixed-limit Omaha tables are less frequented.) Stud usually has only a handful of populated tables, and only at the lowest limits. The site does offer half-pot-limit games, although these tables very rarely have players.

Stakes: $0.02-$0.04 up to $150-$300
Game Variety
- Hold'em (limit, no-limit, pot-limit, short-handed)
- Omaha (limit, pot-limit)
- Stud (seven-card high, seven-card eight-or-better, half-pot-limit, and five-card)
- Five-Card (draw and Stud)

Special Features
- Team Brunson poker pros
- Buddy list with sign-on alerts incorporated in software
- Weekly $175,000-guaranteed tournament
- The bounty tournaments with unique prizes ($500 for one bounty, $5,000 for two, $25,000 for three collected in the same tournament
- First-time bounty tournament players get free rebate after their first entry. (Those interested must pay the $27.50 buy-in and play in the tournament. Once the tournament is complete, a refund can be requested.)

PokerStars.com is the largest online poker site now that PartyPoker has doffed its crown. PokerStars sports the most players and the biggest guaranteed tournaments. The site also sponsors some huge WSOP main event winners, including Chris Moneymaker, Greg Raymer, and Joe Hachem. Until recently, poker personality Lee Jones also lent his delightful, competent poker room managerial skills to the site's big events (his permanent replacement is unknown, as of this writing). Nevertheless, a support member is always available in the chat box of the final tables at such events to answer any questions and resolve issues that may arise.

The PokerStars software is well conceived and implemented. The software covers most of its bases in terms of customizability, efficiency, ease of use, and usefulness. Users can import their own images to be used as their personal avatar and can customize tables with the large set of downloadable themes PokerStars offers. The software even allows users to designate which table theme is used for each table or type of game, enabling easier differentiation between limit and no-limit games or cash games and tournaments. The software also features resizable tables. It even allows users to enlarge tables, which most other sites with resizing don't. PokerStars' software is also unique in that it allows the resizing of its lobbies, both for its main lobby an for individual tournament lobbies. The table layout is attractive and all of the bet/pot-size numbers are prominently displayed.

Tournaments are well run at PokerStars. There is a wealth of information in the tournament lobby, including blind/payout structures, big/small/average stacks, running time, time until the next break, and total/current number of players. The entire blind/ break structure is easily accessible from the tournament lobby. (It even goes as far as to indicate every instance where hand-for-hand play will commence.) PokerStars also allows deal-making for its larger tournaments.

The software does not have checkboxes for "Wait for next blind and auto-post" when entering a normal table or "sit out at next blind" when preparing to leave a table (Those options do exist, but they are only present on speed tables). The table filtration system lacks a few organizational options like the ability to filter by a specific limit, opting instead to group limits into "micro," "low," "medium," and "high."

Tournaments
Sit-and-go tournaments fill up quickly but are always available. Single-table tournaments fill up within a few minutes and even larger multi-table tournaments have players registering at a rapid pace. PokerStars offers massive 180-person sit-and-go's and has the traffic to fill them up quickly. The guaranteed prize pool tournaments at PokerStars regularly go well beyond their guarantees and attract massive fields. PokerStars is also one of the few sites to have a good spread of non-Hold'em tournaments, including a $215 H.O.R.S.E. tournament every Sunday.

Cash Games
The multitude of cash games fill up quickly but it takes mere seconds to find active tables with available seats. PokerStars has the widest array of poker variants currently available online. Hosting the most players also translates to having the greatest mix of novice and professional players at its tables.

Stakes: $0.01-$0.02 up to $1,000-$2,000
Game Variety
- Hold'em (limit, no-limit, pot-limit, heads up, short-handed, speed)
- Omaha (high and eight-or-better)
- Seven-card Stud (high and eight-or-better)
- **H.O.R.S.E.** (including: Hold'em, Omaha, razz, stud, and stud eight-or-better)
- **H.O.S.E.** (including: Hold'em, Omaha, stud, and stud eight-or-better)
- Triple draw (deuce-to-seven)
- Five-card draw

Special Features
- Players can upload their own photos for their avatars.
- Support-assisted chops allowed at all final tables, although players must e-mail support to get them to the table.
- Annual World Championship of Online Poker (WCOOP) lets players join in on a relatively cheap, World Series of Poker-style tournament series with big prizes.
- VIP Loyalty Program
- One of the few sites to feature five-card draw, deuce-to-seven triple draw, **H.O.R.S.E.**, and **H.O.S.E.**

Promotions
- World Championship of Online Poker (WCOOP)
- Moneymaker Million
- PokerStars Caribbean Adventure

In general, the games at PokerStars vary between No-Limit, Pot-Limit, and Fixed-Limit. Full-table games, short-handed and heads-up tables are all available. Due to the size and geographical diversity of PokerStars, action can be found at pretty much any game at any hour. PokerStars offers plenty of tournaments and free rolls with great value and the traffic volume is the best in the industry. Real-money player statistics as of July 2008 show 22,500 ring-game players at peak hours and 155,000 tournament players at peak hours.

Overall, PokerStars is very professionally managed with a real "feel for poker." They offer massive player volume, game diversity and software quality plus generous promotions and bonuses for loyal players. The software is available for both MAC and PC users and is updated frequently to ensure safety and stability, with virtually no downtime as a result.

Email
- support@pokerstars.com

Note: The support staff specified that their system allows for prioritization depending on the subject line. E-mails requesting the presence of support staff at a final table for deal-making purposes, for instance, would receive a rapid response. Such e-mails should have subject lines like "URGENT - Deal in T#33801519" to be considered appropriately.

UltimateBet.com has huge sponsored poker personalities and sleek, unique interfaces are just two of the features for which UltimateBet is best known. Well-known poker pros Phil Hellmuth, Annie Duke, and Cliff "JohnnyBax" Josephy are among those who advocate for the site. As far as the software goes, Josephy has said (before he was sponsored by them), "I love their interface." Being one of the original legends of online poker, he should know.

The two key advantages the UltimateBet software has are the simplified "mini view" option and the speed at which chips are collected and cards are dealt. The mini view option minimizes superfluous graphics and displays all of the pertinent information for each hand in a long, skinny window. The combination of those two big features makes for a very efficient poker experience, especially for players who enjoy multi-tabling.

For those who prefer the full-table view, there are six options for background customization (the tabletop is always the same). The themes include Red Rock, Aruba, underwater, London, plain black, and, of course, Las Vegas. There are many useful, easy to manipulate checkboxes in the options menu, including behavior options ("confirm bet pot," "confirm fold," etc.) and display options (four color deck, "show whole dollars only," "full animation," etc.). The software allows users to have an animation- and information-heavy experience or an ultra-simple motif, whichever strikes their fancy.

The software is also unconventionally efficient in the way it deals with the chat box. Users are given a wealth of customizable options for chat in the options menu, including checkboxes for each type of chat (for instance, dealer, player, or observer).

The main lobby is separated into games, scheduled tournaments, and sit-and-go tournaments. The cash-games are grouped together by poker variant, but no filtration system is present therein to allow for the omission of certain stakes or full/empty tables from viewing. However, the entire list is sorted to make finding the right table a little easier. There is also a special tab that sorts by high, medium, low, no, and pot limit, but this tab mixes all of the poker variants together. The lobby displays average pot, percent of players who see the flop, and hands per hour.

Tournaments

UltimateBet has a rather unique, intuitive system for their sit-and-go. Players select the "table" offering the variant (NL Hold'em, Omaha, etc.), the style (shorthanded, turbo, etc.), and stakes they want and are taken to a waiting list. All players wishing to play in this kind of event go on the list and begins as soon as the table is full. This eliminates the annoyances of having to quickly click on and register for tournaments before they fill up or waiting for a new table to open up before you can register. The system also ensures that tables fill up at a consistent, rapid pace especially the lower-limit Hold'em tournaments.

The multi-table tournament schedule was formulated with the help of poker star Annie Duke herself. The new schedule includes Sniper (bounty) tournaments, a popular format wherein players are paid for each opponent they eliminate in addition to how well they place. UltimateBet offers a weekly $200,000 guaranteed tournament on Sundays that consistently requires an overlay for having too few entrants. This attendance deficiency is actually a boon for players looking to get more bang for their buck and play for dead money.

Cash Games

While there are plenty of games available for Hold'em, players will most likely have to join a short waiting list for any stakes over $0.10-$0.25. Games like royal Hold'em, deuce-to-seven triple draw, and pineapple usually have one to two small-stakes tables running at a time.

Stakes: $0.02-$0.04 up to $300-$600

Game Variety
- Hold'em (limit, NL, pot-limit, heads up)
- Omaha (high, eight-or-better, heads up)
- Seven-card Stud (high, eight-or-better, heads up)
- Razz
- **H.O.R.S.E.** (including: Hold'em, Omaha, razz, stud, and stud eight-or-better)
- H.O.S.E. (including: Hold'em, Omaha, stud, and stud eight-or-better)
- H.O. (including: Hold'em and Omaha eight-or-better)
- Triple draw (deuce-seven, ace-five)
- Royal Hold'em
- Elimination Blackjack tournaments

Special Features
- Mini view available for tables. View gives only the essential information and is an excellent option for players who multi-table
- Intuitive and efficient sit-and-go signup process
- Tournament schedule formulated with help of Annie Duke
- Choice of table background from a predetermined set of six
- Elimination Blackjack available within the same software

Promotions
- RAI$E loyalty program offers a cash-for-points option, point auctions for cool gadgets, merchandise, and experiences, and other innovating perks
- UltimateBet Online Championship (UBOC)
- UltimateBet.com Aruba Poker Classic satellites
- Sniper bounty tournaments
- Tournament leader board prizes

Email
- support@ultimatebet.com

 **Absolutepoker.com** is the home of the biggest bad-beat jackpot in online poker. It also hosts the Absolute Dream Package, wherein players can free roll their way to online poker's ultimate prize. Absolute Poker also offers a wide range of friendly and rewarding tournaments, alongside exciting and innovative promotions to suit players of all abilities. The Absolute Poker software was recently upgraded and now supports cutting edge graphics, faster dealing, table view options, resizable tables, and many other great new features. This site also allows players to upload personal graphics to create their own personalized avatar making Absolute Poker one of the most customizable poker sites out there. There is also a no-download version for Mac and PC users.

Other tweak-able options on the tables include: enable hot keys, four-color decks, display bet amount, and muting of sound effects. The tables include a standard set of pre-selected action checkboxes. The main lobby on Absolute Poker is easy to navigate. The cash games are separated into tabs by poker variant and then further still by limit-type (fixed, pot, and no-limit) or high/eight-or-better variants. Tournaments are split into sit-and-go and "tourneys" (meaning scheduled tournaments). The lobby also has a concise filter system, which can be selected by all games, limits, show, and buy-in.

The specific tournament lobbies at Absolute Poker are extremely helpful and easy to use. The lobbies list the current rank and chip count of every single player in the tournament a feature that even some of the largest poker sites don't have (many sites show simply the top 30 or 100 players' chip stacks and rankings).

The lobby displays a wealth of other information, including: blind structure, payout structure, big/small/average stack, time until next break, time until next blind level (and what it will be), and total/current number of players.

Tournaments
Absolute Poker has good sit-and-go traffic for buy-ins $100 and lower, plus the ever-popular turbo sit-and-go's. Multi-table sit-and-go's are often running for buy-ins $10 and lower.

- Single table tournaments from $.50+$.10 up to $200+$10
- Multi table tournaments from $.25 up to $150
- Private tournament capability to VIP members
- 40 Daily free rolls

Absolute Poker has a healthy schedule of tournaments with guaranteed prize pools that offer up to $75,000 (not including the weekly $150,000 guarantee). The guaranteed tournaments easily go beyond their posted prize pools with relative consistency. The big weekly $150,000-guaranteed tournament on Saturdays usually lures around 300 entrants (at $500 apiece for buy-in). Absolute also runs a $75,000-guaranteed tournament on Sunday.

Cash Games
There are not usually a lot of high-stakes Hold'em games running, but the mid- to low-limit games usually have plenty of tables to choose from (mainly six-handed tables: players at Absolute Poker seem to prefer shorthanded play). The number of populated cash games tables for the other offered variants (Omaha, stud, razz and H.O.R.S.E.) are relatively low (especially for razz), and virtually nonexistent in the higher-limits of these games.

Stakes: $0.02-$0.04 up to $150-$300
Game Variety
- Hold'em (limit, NL, pot-limit, six-handed, turbo)
- Omaha (high, eight-or-better)
- Stud (seven-card high, seven-card eight-or-better)
- Razz
- **H.O.R.S.E.**

Special Features
- Players can change the table felt via downloaded alternatives
- Absolute Buddy function allows players to track friends and chat with them within the software while playing
- Players can upload their own photo for their avatar
- Over 100 different tabletops and themes, many of which are user-generated
- Mouse-free play possible with keyboard shortcuts
- Instant Play, a download-free version of the software, is available and is compatible with Macs.

Promotions
- The Absolute Dream Package tournament, which awards online poker's richest prize package
- Bad Beat Jackpot; more than $10 million awarded since 2007 launch
- Absolute Assassins bounty tourneys
- Pro bounty tournaments
- $200K+ guaranteed in tournament prize pools each weekend
- Absolute Rewards loyalty program (points earned; can be used for free roll tournaments or merchandise)
- Tournament leader board prizes
- VIP program with various benefits, including exclusive bonuses, promotions, freerolls, and even VIP party invitations

Email
- support@AbsolutePoker.com

Known for fast and accurate replies for all email inquiries, Team Absolute also upholds the fastest cash out service online. They now are offering a deposit call center for fast and easy credit card transactions. Support e-mails are having trouble being blocked by some of the major portals such as AOL, MSN. So if you use one of these for email, make sure you add them to your list of safe emails.

Here are a couple of other Online Poker Rooms that I would like to mention also:

Stinky Fish Poker http://www.stinkyfishpoker.com
LockPoker   http://www.lockpoker.com
CarbonPoker http://www.carbonpoker.com
CakePoker http://cakepoker.com
PlayersOnly http://www.playersonly.com

Don't Play HEADS UP Cash Games....
I'm not opposed to playing heads up poker. It's actually my best game. But if you're playing heads up cash games, either online or in a casino, chances are the rake will eat you alive! I came to this conclusion today; when I set down at a $200 heads up HA game (Hold'Em / PLO mixed game) on full tilt.

My opponent had $50 and I had $200. After 30 minutes of back and forth action, I busted him. My profit was $10. Yeah, the other $40 was diminished by the rake. A much better option is playing heads up sit & go's. They play out like sit and go's. There's a bunch of different varieties, like turbo's, for faster action, or non escalating blinds, which play out more like a cash game. There's a fixed rake for heads up sit & go's that almost guarantees you'll pay less then in heads up cash games.

The only time when a heads up cash game would be beneficial is if you're playing $2,000 NL (or a limit equivalent) and higher. The rake is capped at a certain amount that should have little effect in comparison to the pot sizes.

Reviews Courtesy of CardPlayer.com

❝ It's hard work. Gambling. Playing poker. Don't let anyone tell you different. Think about what it's like sitting at a poker table with people whose only goal is to cut your throat, take your money, and leave you out back talking to yourself about what went wrong inside. That probably sounds harsh. But that's the way it is at the poker table. If you don't believe me, then you're the lamb that's going off to the slaughter. ❞

—*Stu Unger, three-time W.S.O.P. Champion, and without a doubt, the best player to ever play the game.*

CHAPTER TWENTY SEVEN:

BANKROLL MANAGEMENT

Some players say my bankroll is: "All the money in my wallet, my credit card, and all the money I can borrow, that is my bankroll…" Well, this may seem extreme, but the fact is that this holds true for most of the players out there.

In this Chapter, I want to give you some guidelines on how your bankroll should become. By starting out small and gradually moving up in stakes as you develop.

If you're completely new to poker, you probably shouldn't bring a lot of money with you on the way to the casino and play at the high stakes. It may be thrilling, and yes, you can win a lot more money, but you can also lose a lot more money a lot faster. As a beginner, it would be a shame for you to be turned off to poker right away from a few bad sessions. What you probably should do is start with a small amount of money and start playing the smallest games that your casino poker room offers. This will get you used to the way people play for real money and you can test out your new strategies and what you've learned without a huge financial risk. There are plenty of examples of players with discipline who start out with $50-$100, play nothing but $1/2 NL games, and end up $600 ahead in a few weeks. It happens.

❝ I think most people play way above where they should for their bankroll. ❞

—Kathy Liebert

Building a bankroll and choosing which tables is sort of climbing a pyramid. You'll usually notice that the most players play for the smallest stakes, and the fewest players play at the highest stakes. To climb each level, you need to first master the level you're at. Before you even start on a level, you need to have the sufficient amount of money to back the limits you're playing. Limit players can play for a while on 50x the big blind, and NL cash game players will need to start with more. You're going to run into streaks of bad luck and bad beats. Hopefully you'll always bounce back from it, but you need to have enough money in your wallet to ride out the storm.

❝ The hardest and most important part of bankroll management is moving down when you are on a losing streak. ❞

—Chris "Jesus" Ferguson

Stick to a small-stakes game at first. Keep playing it and be patient and disciplined. Over a few days, weeks, or even months, you may finally feel like you've completely mastered a certain level ($1/$2 for example) and can win consistently at those limits. At this point, you will probably have enough money to move up to the next level. Take a seat at a bigger game and try it out. Keep in mind, however, that as you play in larger games, the players' skill level will also increase on the average every time you move up. Keep playing well, master your limit, and keep moving up. Hopefully you'll be at the top of the ladder faster than you think.

❝ I have no bankroll management; I am stupid with my money. ❞

—Gavin Smith

One alternative to playing cash rings games is to try and test your skills by playing some low limit tournaments. You'll be up against a lot of crazy players who don't really care how well they do. Low-limit tournaments also typically have a good-size number of entrants. You'll need to play a tight game, especially early on in these tournaments, to avoid the early gamblers.

Knowing when to drop down into a lower level is a very tough decision. Determining a certain percentage or a certain amount of consecutive losing sessions should be some factors in making this worthwhile decision. Here are some reasons why you should drop down into a lower level:

- If your bankroll is too small for the level you are playing.
- You would end up making more money at a lower level.
- You want to drop down because playing a higher level scared is not the way to play a higher level.

Bankroll requirements are often argued among many players. But the general accepted formula should put you in a decent level for the amount of your bankroll. You can search any poker website and there are many books or forums to find the desired requirements for your particular game. I suggest having a bigger bankroll for the levels you decide to play. To do this you will have to be more patient with moving up. It's much better for your sanity, and therefore, your play.

" Never spend more than five percent of your bankroll on one tournament buy-in. "

—Jon Friedberg

As explained earlier, you really shouldn't trust yourself to gauge your own advantage in games. Ironically, that's just what you will have to do when deciding what stakes to play in. You can use all kinds of different reasons to justify what stake you should play, but in the end, you must be honest with yourself. Are you beating the players at the $3/$6 level? If you are would you make more money at the $1/$2 level?

Most poker players don't think about the reason "that they want to" as a legitimate reason to drop down in stakes. But, this should be the most legitimate reason for doing so. If you are having a difficult time, or are stressed, or unhappy and uncertain about playing higher stakes, then you should just move down until results tell you differently.

In conclusion, try to use your head when determining the correct level to play at in reference to your bankroll. Also when you do cash in a big tournament or a fortunate to place in the top three, I highly recommend that seventy percent of that money should be put in a bank or other investment. Don't let all your winning become lost on a losing streak. This has happened to so many of my poker friends and with a little common sense your bankroll management will seem easier than you thought.

The quotes are courtesy of Poker Pro Media.

❝ I used to play $16 nine-man turbo SNGs on PokerStars, and I would play 8 to 10 of them at a time... eventually my bankroll got big enough that I could afford to experiment a little and add on even more tables. I was adding 2 or 3 more tables each day as sort of a challenge to myself to see how many tables I could handle while still being able to play them optimally. **❞**

———

—Hevad Khan, he made the final table at the 2007 World Series of Poker Main Event, finishing in sixth place. His performance and exhilarating antics were completely hilarious and endearing.

CHAPTER TWENTY EIGHT:

ULTIMATE SIT & GO STRATEGY

The magnetism of Sit & Go tournaments (Single table tournaments) is that they offer the tournament experience in a compacted format. A multi-table tournament can take hours to play and still not pay off, if you go out before the money. Sit & Go's are usually over within an hour and offer loads of action from the start. They also present you with a stop loss. You know the maximum amount you can lose going in.

One of the ways to becoming a successful Sit & Go player is learning to master bubble play. The last thing anybody wants is to be the Bubble Boy, which means you need to get the most out of every hand you play during this critical stage. If you make solid moves from good positions and manage your chip stack wisely, you'll find yourself in the money before you know it.

Most Sit & Go's are single table tournaments also referred as a (STT); they consist of usually nine or ten players, and sometimes as low as six players.

Prizes are offered only to the players who finish 1st and 2nd, and sometimes 3rd. These tournaments don't care if you get an early lead or have a big chip stack. The only thing that matters in Sit & Go Tournament is not being eliminated before you're in the money (ITM).

Important facts I feel most players forget to realize when playing in these tournaments are as follows:

- When 6 or less players have been eliminated and for some odd reason you go all-in and lose, you win NO MONEY!
- When 7 players are eliminated and for some odd reason you go all-in and lose, you win 20% of the prize money!
- When 8 players are eliminated and for some odd reason you go all-in and lose, you win 30% of the prize money!
- When you're the last player remaining and have all the chips, you win 50% of the prize money!

Of course, nothing is more comforting than having the big stack when you're sitting on the bubble. As the chip leader, you can practice selective aggression and apply pressure to the smaller stacks. You especially want to focus on the players in second and third place, as they aren't going to want to put their chips at unnecessary risk. Because the shorter stacks are going to try to double up through you, you need to be careful about making loose calls just because you think you can afford them.

Let's say that you're short-stacked with just five or six big blinds. How you play your hand in this situation depends less on your cards and more on your position and the size of the other short stacks at the table. For example, you're in the small blind and the hand is folded around to you. If the big blind doesn't have you covered by very much, it's time to apply "medium ball" pressure. This play makes it really hard for him to call because he's risking his tournament in a very questionable spot. You put him in a position where he's the one who has to call you, and that's a big advantage.

Now let's change things up a little. Say you're sitting on about eight big bets on the button and the chip leader is in the big blind. If the action is folded to you in this situation, you can be much more selective about the hands you play. You still have plenty of chips to work with before the blinds come back around, which means you can afford to try to pick your spots. Personally, I'd fold hands worse than Q-10 here, but I'd probably play K-J, K-Q, any Ace, and all pocket pairs.

If you're sitting on just four or five big blinds in this same situation, you'll have to open up your game a little and play more hands. You've got to take some chances here and get your chips in, even if you may be no better than 50-50. Waiting isn't an option because the blinds will eat you alive if you allow it.

If you're playing a medium-size stack, you have more room to play, but still have to be careful about when, and from where you put your chips in the middle. Making a standard 3× or 4× raise with 15 or 16 blinds can still be risky because there's a good chance a bigger stack will re-raise and try to force you all-in before the flop. You really can't afford to make that call without a premium hand like Aces or Kings. You definitely don't want to call with something like A-K or A-Q because you're just a coin-flip against any pair and are dominated by pocket Aces or Kings. Folding here is a smarter move, especially if there's a short stack left to play behind you who is likely to call with a much wider range of hands and give you a better shot of making the money.

For example, let's say the small stack raises 5× the big blind from the button and the small blind folds. You're in the big blind and it's only four more bets for you to call, which means your odds are slightly less than 2-1. While calling here may in fact be the right decision, it's not automatic as far as I'm concerned.

I recommend taking a few seconds to really think through the situation, even if you're holding a pretty strong hand like A-8 or up, K-Q, K-J, or any pocket pair. Think about the other player and how he's been playing. If he raises every time he's in that spot, widen your calling range. But if he's a particularly good Sit & Go player or playing tight, he may not play many hands and you shouldn't call as frequently.

More often than not, when I'm the big stack in this situation, I'm not just flat calling here. Instead, I'm moving all-in. This is particularly effective because it puts all of the other players at the table to a tough decision. Again, the players in second and third aren't likely to get involved without huge hands, which lets me isolate the smaller stack.

In the end, winning a Sit & Go is about using whatever edge you've got. When you're down to the final four, take advantage of position and play your stack aggressively. Know when to back off and when to go for it. You'll still be at the table and in the money (ITM) when the bubble bursts.

The strategy I have for Sit & Go's isn't that much different from my "medium ball" philosophy. I know that "medium ball" has been preached throughout this book over and over; the fact is: I want this idea permanently ingrained into your thought process. You must play an "overly cautious" type of poker when starting out in a single table tournament, because any pot you get involved in puts you at risk of being eliminated.

Game Structure

Nearly all Sit & Go's consist of a table of six or a table of ten players. These games don't run at a certain time, they start when the table fills up. The Buy-in is started from as low as one dollar and go up to as much as several hundred. On tables of ten, prizes are usually divided between the top three finishers, with first place taking half the pot (so, $50 in a tournament with a $10 entry), second prize taking 30 per cent ($30), and third place taking 20 percent ($20). On tables of six players and referred as "six-packs" prizes are usually limited to the top two finishers, with the winnings split 75/25.

Chips and Blinds

As in a regular tournament, each player starts with the same number of chips, and blinds go up over time. If you're used to multi-table tournaments, it's important to note that Sit & Go tournaments usually start with fewer chips and the blinds go up more quickly. Usually players are given a stack of 1,000 chips (as opposed to 1,500 in most multi- table tourneys). Blinds go up according to one of two formats, either every ten minutes or every ten hands on a table of ten, and every twelve hands on a table of six.

Strategy

Sit-n-Go tournaments offer a lot more action than multi-table tournaments. Because players start with fewer chips and the blinds go up quickly, players need to at least keep pace or face being blinded out. Tables consisting of a lot of tight players tend to end up "playing the lottery" with large blinds forcing players to take big risks or face being blinded out.

Game Flow

Just like in multi-table tournaments, Sit-n-Go's move through a series of stages where the table will loosen or tighten up. Knowing how to change gears to take advantage of the flow of play is critical. Games will sometimes start with an outbreak of activity. Some players will try to double up, or establish a super-aggressive table image with huge bets before the flop. It's not unusual to see one or two players eliminated within the first few hands. Just like in a multi-table tournament, it's hard to read what these early big bets mean so it's dangerous to get involved without very strong cards. Play will eventually tighten up, with players eyeing each other up and getting accustomed to each other's styles. As the blinds go through the low to middle stage, play becomes even more aggressive.

Relative changes in stack sizes can create heavy betting situations with big stacks going after the little stacks, and the little stacks looking for opportunities to double up. Not all games are going to follow a script of course. The most important thing to remember about game flow is to watch for changing moods and capitalize, by going against the flow. Tight tables offer more opportunities for the aggressive player, and aggressive tables more opportunities for the tight player.

Observation

Observation pays off in Sit-n-Go's like in no other form of poker. You get to see all of the hands that all of your opponents are in for the duration of your stay. There are no moving tables like in a multi-table tournament, no players coming and going like in a cash game. That makes reading player styles and sending out the right messages even more critical.

Changing gears is also advantageous. Playing one style throughout a Sit-n-Go makes you far too predictable. If your game play has been staying "loose," then tightening up may induce bluffs and over-bets at your strong hands, while appearing too tight gives you more opportunities to steal chips and small pots later on. Observing the blinds is also more important in a Sit-n-Go. The blinds really start to hurt in the later stages, especially for the short stacks. Look for opportunities to turn that extra pressure to your advantage.

End Game

The final stages of a Sit-n-Go tournament are always exciting. It's virtually a game unto itself. The relative value of pocket cards go up as the table becomes short handed and players are forced to pay the (now quite expensive) big blind every third or fourth hand. Short stacks are under huge pressure to double up while big stacks are wary of giving them new hope. Hands need to be played aggressively at this stage and normally won't progress beyond the flop. Pre-flop raises come often as do all-ins after the flop. The slow play becomes a more attractive option here with a guarantee of fewer hands to beat you and marginal hole cards being played very aggressively. Betting also needs to become highly targeted, aimed less at the size of the pot and more at the size of an opponent's stack.

Players struggling in lower positions need to treat every bet as leading to a potential all-in situation. They also need to pay close attention to the blinds and calculate the number of hands they'll get to see before they're either blinded out, or their stack gets so low that a semi-bluff with an all-in would be easy to call. Remember, an all-in that's going to put your opponent below you if he loses is infinitely harder to call than one that isn't. As a rule of thumb, if you're short stacked and need to make a play. You're better off targeting a small or medium stack with a bluff, rather than the big stacks, which will be looser and more likely to call, with strong cards. Players with enormous chip stacks need to target the "short stacks" with aggressive play.

The first thing a big stack should do when a Sit & Go gets to the point where there is only one player left before the bubble, is add up all the chips on the table that aren't his. If there are a similar number or fewer chips out there than your own then you know right then that all you have to do is stay ahead of the blinds to be in a good position to win the tournament. Thinking that the table is going to be very loose, and throwing chips away by calling a lot of hands is throwing your advantage away.

That being said, the big stack shouldn't go into a shell and ignore opportunities to steal pots. Look for signs of fear at the table. Other players are bound to be worried about going out of the tourney before the money. Very short stacks "just hanging in" and surviving for an attempt at second or third place will fold easily to your raises and have the added bonus of making it harder for anyone at the table to call your strong bets. No one wants to go out of a tournament having been second in chips with nothing to show.

When you become low on chips and are hanging on for dear life. Generally speaking you are in the 'red zone' and short- stacked if your total number of chips adds up to less than six-6 times the existing big blind. Find a good hand and hope for the best. It's better to go out fighting that to be "blinded-out" with a terrible hand.

Here are Some General Rules for Sit-n-Go tournaments

1 - Don't drink ANY alcohol. Any impedance of your judgment can be deadly to your play. You must drink plenty of water or juices. Our body is much more refreshed when well hydrated and you will feel and play at your best.

2 - Be Patient, Be Patient, Be Patient. Wait for the best hands and fold the trash unless in an un-raised big blind. Professional poker players' DO NOT CHASE HANDS or waste chips especially when the flop puts them and their hand at a disadvantage and neither should you.

3 - Play Premium Hands = Premium Dividends. The top reason chip stacks drop putting you at a serious disadvantage is not the blinds. It's playing TOO MANY HANDS! When you become bored you are itching to play DO NOT LISTEN. JUST MUCK IT!

Wait for good hands worth firing bullets at the pot.

4 - Get Comfortable. You must find ways to stay at ease. If you are playing in a big tournament like WSOP or WPT events you may be playing more than 12 hours per day with a few breaks. You must find a way to stay in the comfort zone for both your backside & your state of mind. Many things can help. Keep pictures of the family, a lucky charm, an extra seat cushion or iPod nearby. By all means, you need to stay focused and relaxed.

5 - Never arrive late! It's said that some pros will sleep late and be blinded off until they make their grand entrance in the WSOP and WPT tournaments. Don't let this be you as every chip in front of you can help you build your stack & keep you alive when you do lose a hand. This is especially true online as you don't ever want to forget you entered a tourney only to find you have been blinded off, crippled, or even picked up from play. You just wasted your hard-earned cash.

6 - Nice Guys Never Truly Finish Last. Be courteous to your fellow players. There are many players that are just plain nasty to be around and play with. They are always trying to put you on TILT. You have to be the bigger person and ignore all of that. Keep your composure and always be polite. Soon other players remember how you react and how you play. They will soon learn if you can be "put on TILT" and you would be pleasantly surprised to learn what kinds of advantages you gain by being "Mr. Nice guy."

7 - No Distractions! If you're playing on-line it simply means what it says. Play when you WILL NOT become distracted AT ALL. Distractions keep you from your "A" game. If you are playing "live" poker it works the same way.

8 - Fight The All-In Itch Pre-Flop. I know seeing A-A pop into your hands gets your blood pumping and your nerves jumping but try to refrain from ALL-IN JUMPING. I know its tempting to do so, but here is why. YOU ARE HERE TO MAKE THE MONEY, FIRST AND FOREMOST. Do not risk your tournament life on a blind ALL-IN call no matter what. Go ahead and raise up the blinds, as you wish to get the drawing hands out but also pay close attention to the flop. A-A is a great starting hand but a bad flop can still kill your hand.

9 - Luck. You can't script luck, but if you can keep #1 thru #10 true to form then you just need to have faith that a little luck will come your way. Just take advantage when you do and hopefully you will make the money and maybe even the final table. Most of the time, I will find ways to manufacture my own luck, by reading the players.

Conclusion

By applying these simple rules to your Sit & Go game, they will generate success in the long run. I cannot express enough that being patient and letting the "bad" players weed themselves out by their inexperience.

Concentrating on placing third, second, and first is the key to making Sit & Go profitable to your bankroll.

CHAPTER TWENTY NINE:

MOVING FROM ONLINE TO PLAYING LIVE

Moving from online, to traditional or land-based card rooms ones can be a tough transition.

While all of the games are basically played the same, there are subtle differences that can be difficult to adjust to if you're used to playing online. It limits certain factors (most notably "tells") that affect how you play the game.

While playing online, we have much less to go on than when playing in a live game. Online, all you have is any memory of this player from previous hands and sometimes, you can sense when they pause before acting or if they act immediately; occasionally, this info can be useful. Was the pause on purpose to throw us off? Was it because the player caught something useful? Was it just an internet connection burp?

There are many online tells that you will have to adjust to when making the change to playing live instead of online. Let's review some common online tells:

Speed

For online players, the key to tells is often in the speed, how quickly the other player acted either individually or in response to another's action can speak volumes about their hand. Why? Because online poker rooms like to make things simple for their customers and so put action boxes below the tables. When a player is dealt a hand, they have many options to select their next action, (fold, check, call, raise, raise any bet, etc.). Depending on the type of player and which option they selected, you can often gauge the power of their hand.

The quick call. When a player calls your hand quickly, they're typically trying to shake you up and pretend that their hand is stronger than it really is. It's usually a weak draw, and they want to keep you from betting again.

Instant bet/raise (early). Players who bet quickly, but not too much, early in the hand typically have strong cards, and had reached their decision to play before it was even their turn to act.

Instant bet/raise (river). Be wary of the instant bet or raise on the river. This typically translates to a strong hand, but they want you to think that they're bluffing. Watch out.

Instant check. A player in early position who checks automatically may be slow-playing a strong hand to see what kind of action they can get from others at the table. If the same player was in late position and did this, it typically means that their hand is weak.

Slow check. Players who take their time before checking are usually holding a weak hand, and are most likely on a draw. They want you to think they're considering raising to prevent you from betting so they can see another card.

Other Online Tells

The complainer. Arguments can get pretty heated with a bad beat, even online. Note which players are "chatting" and how angry they are. If a player is irritable through several hands (I've seen it go on for over an hour) consider them to be aggravated or frustrated to the point where their actions will often become illogical and counterproductive. This basically means they are, "on tilt."

Debating team. When a poor player is taking a while before acting, they may be debating whether or not to call with a weak/moderate hand. If the player is strong, they typically have strong hand but want you to think they're weak. Be sure to note any player that uses this maneuver for future reference.

Raise…OK, I'm out. Frequently raising pre-flop and then folding either at the flop or if someone re-raises is typically the sign of a player on tilt.

Betting the Turn. In Hold 'em, if a player has checked and called on the flop, but bets on the turn, it's typically a signal that they missed their draw and are bluffing. Re-raise them.

In some case where players take a long time to make a decision, such delay is not necessarily a valuable tell. Many players are active on several tables simultaneously, making their attention at your table minimal. They could simply be involved in a serious hand at one of their other tables, and weren't able to get back to act quickly enough. And even if they're not at another table (which you can usually check) they may be having connection problem that has slowed their play.

Also, the anonymity of the environment makes people more comfortable playing a wider range of hands, betting foolishly, and otherwise doing things that they normally would never try with a table full of faces staring back at them.

All of these things are possible, so that early on during a session of hands or first few rounds of a tourney, we have only the tiniest info on the other player to tip us off. After several hands or a few rounds, you might notice a pattern that will help you beat the other players. Sites that have a note taking feature are helpful and if used to your full advantage, can accentuate your game against this person in the future. Do note however, that table and button position online is just as important, if not more so, than live play. With little information about the other player to rely on, being able to act after someone is especially important.

In many cases, such poor play as is often found online is a huge advantage of playing at home. Since a solid player will triumph numerous times for every bad beat and "suck out" they suffer. But as any online poker player with experience will tell you, it can be a very frustrating experience.

In on-line play, it's important that the other players NOT get a read on you. Vary your style and change the size of your bets often to confuse them. Try your best to act in the same length of time every hand unless you're bluffing or representing a good hand.

First and foremost, you're not squaring off "face-to-face" with the other players; they're just images on a screen. When you get to the casino it is a whole new ball game.

Do NOT be predictable to other players but still PLAY YOUR GAME. If you have a maniac constantly raising you, wait for a good hand to make him pay. Do not just call to see the flop, or you will get murdered and will have tossed away valuable chips much more often than you will hit your flop.

PART EIGHT

Essential Information for Poker

CHAPTER THIRTY:

FINEST POKER ROOMS IN THE UNITED STATES

Bay 101
1801 Bering Dr San Jose, CA 95112
Phone (408) 451-8888

Bay 101 is one of the largest card-rooms in northern California, with about 40 tables. The poker side of the room is completely separate from the other games. It is a few miles from the San Jose airport, right in the heart of Silicon Valley. It has been at its present location, San Jose, California, for twelve years. It remains Northern California's premiere example of how a card room should be designed to accommodate the players.

You would be amazed by how blessed the Bay 101 is, the players are exceptional and there is action in the poker room no matter what time of day it is. The staff at the Bay 101 will exceed your expectations. It makes for such a great time when the poker staff takes care of you in such a way that the Bay 101 does. You do not even have to get your chips; they will bring them to you.

San Jose's premier card club has a rich history. Sutter's Club was founded in 1929 by Joseph Sutter, Sr. at Old Aviso Road and Highway 237 in Alviso, California. Through those early years the club was a very popular entertainment spot in the South Bay Area. When Mr. Sutter died in 1947, Joseph Sutter, Jr. took over the business and added 5 poker tables in 1961.

When the State of California began widening Highway 237 in 1992, the Alviso location closed and a new site was selected on Bering Drive, just off East Brokaw Road at U. S. Highway 101. Bay 101 opened in September of 1994, and quickly earned recognition throughout the gaming community as one of the finest clubs on the west coast.

Bay 101 Casino is home of the World Famous the Bay 101 Open. They offer you an exciting environment for casino card playing, delicious American and Asian cuisine in their restaurant and deli, as well as a sports bar, banquet facilities, and hair salon. Their game experience is distinct from other casinos. They serve you from a delicious menu at your game table while you play.

Players love it, and Bay 101 staff love to be at your service. Bay 101, in San Jose, may be one of the most unique card rooms in California. The card rooms are not casinos; there are no slot machines and very few "other" casino games are allowed except for those that are considered "card" games, which generally means Pai-Gow and several multi-player variations. On the poker side of the action, the games are generally more standard.

There is plenty of room around the tables. Good restaurants with table side service and a very knowledgeable, attentive staff make Bay 101 a very pleasant room to play. Because this is a free standing building, there is also lots of available parking in a private, well lit and secure lot.

If there was a drawback to the Bay 101 experience, it is that the local government controls the gaming codes. All California card rooms are subject to Local as well as State regulation and the City of San Jose have some strange, understanding of how to regulate poker. NL poker is not allowed at Bay 101 because of these local regulations. If you are going to play here take some time to acquaint yourself with the fairly bizarre forms of spread limit games that do fall within the gaming guidelines. Their $5/$200 spread limit is pretty much the same as NL Texas Hold'em. The amazing thing about the Bay 101 was how many players were at the tables any time of the day. They take their poker very seriously in San Jose, CA, and the Bay 101 has been blessed with many great players. Antonio Esfandiari and Phil Laak started here playing the $3/$6 before they made it big.

Limit Hold'em is dealt at:
Min Buy-in is $30.00
$3/$6, $6/$12, $8/$16, $12/$24, $20/$40, $40/$80, $80/$160

Spread Limit Hold'em is dealt at:
Min Buy-in is $50.00	Min Buy-in is $400.00
$5/$200	$10/$200

These are not just advertised games; they occur every weekend and many weekday nights. $40/$80 limit games are up and running as are most of the lower limits. Don't ask for any other limits, these are the only ones the law allows. The only Seven Card Stud game on the board is $4/$8. The same goes for the $4/$8 and $10/$20 Omaha games.

The smaller $60 tournaments are re-buy events with 500 starting chips and 500 more for each re-buy. Played with the same structure as the 3,000 chip events, these actually play like a NL Texas Hold'em tournament unless you are the chip leader.

The highlight of the Bay 101 calendar is the annual WPT Shooting Star tournament in March. This is the only NL Texas Hold'em event allowed at Bay 101. The unique aspect of the Shooting Star is the "Star Bounty." Each of the starting 50 tables has a designated "Shooting Star" with a $5,000 cash bounty that is paid at the table when the Star falls. This also means that if you enter the event you are guaranteed to play your first table with one of the big name professionals. Of course, as the tables break down there is a good chance that tables will have more than one Shooting Star bounty up for grabs.

Weekly satellites are available for the Shooting Star; Super Satellites begin in late February and Mega Satellites begin March 8th. If you would like to see the "Shooting Stars" up close and personal, there are two Day Ones on March 12th and 13th. Bay 101 is a very good venue to watch and play poker.

Courtesy of Four Winds Casino Resort

Four Winds Casino Resort
11111 Wilson Rd New Buffalo, MI 49117
Phone: (866) 494-6371
The state of Michigan's newest casino, Four Winds Casino Resort in New Buffalo, opened August 2, 2007 and is home to the Midwest's only World Poker Tour® Poker Room. Players can participate in promotions and win seats on the World Poker Tour. The World Poker Tour consists of 17 high stakes poker tournaments and draws the leading pros and accomplished amateurs for an $8-12 million prize pool. At Four Winds, their poker room has no dealers and all the tables are fully electronic.

The World Poker Tour Poker Room offers Texas Hold'em and Omaha in-limit and no limit style play at stakes that accommodate all level of players. The Poker Room holds

14 PokerPro® tables with seating for up to 124 people at a time. This includes 12 tables seating 10 people per game and two head's-up tables featuring one-on-one action…

Please check the Four Winds Casino Resort Web site at www.fourwindscasino.com for the dates of upcoming tournaments.

Sit & Go Tournaments: Buy-ins range from $25 – $500 and the players finishing in the top three spots are guaranteed payouts. Blinds increase every 15 minutes. These tournaments are held 24 hours a day.

Texas Hold'em Tournaments: Texas Hold'em Tournaments are held several times daily, with buy-ins ranging from between $50 – $250.

Chicago Charitable Games
Phone (888) 715-4837

Chicago Charitable Games and ChicagoPokerLive.com is a weekend poker tour dedicated to raising money for charity, while hosting the best events in town that are geared towards the poker players needs. We offer games and tournaments to fulfill every poker player's dreams, from the serious experts out there, to the newbie are getting ready to cut their teeth! (This means new players who have only played online or in small home games, which are looking to get their feet wet in the world of live poker CCG is the place to do this).

Chicago Charitable Games (CCG) and ChicagoPokerLive.com helps local and national charities host successful charitable poker nights. CCG is dedicated to helping charitable organizations with their fund raising needs without sacrificing the needs of poker players.

We here at CCG know that the poker players are what drive these charitable events, and we will do everything in our power to host the best events, with the most tournaments and cash games to ensure that the poker players are enjoying themselves, as well as helping charity. CCG understands that one does not need to take an unfair amount of rake or charitable cost in order for the charity to have the most profitable night possible. CCG will make sure that the charities it works with will understand the importance of happy players and will do all it can to promote the fairness of the game, host enjoyable poker nights, and work with its players to "continually have the best games in town", says Mike P. from Chicago.

Chicago Charitable Games is a family owned business that is dedicated to helping raise money for charities with great causes. Chicago Charitable Games Inc. is owned and operated by Ken and Bert Kaulen, and their father Ken Kaulen Sr., a family that is working hard to improve the game of poker while helping small to medium sized charities to raise money. Chicago Charitable Games works exclusively with several locations and suppliers in and around Chicago in order to bring our patrons the best poker possible in the Midwest. We offer more tournaments, better structures and larger payouts than any other poker room you will find in the state of Illinois. Chicago Charitable Games prides itself on helping poker players find the best games with the most prize money, all the while helping to raise money for worthy causes.

Chicago Charitable Games is owned and operated with its patrons and charities in mind first. Nothing is more important to Chicago Charitable Games than the best events and raising the most money for charity. We thank you for taking the time to visit our website and would love if you contacted us with any suggestions or questions that you may have about the website, the events, or just to learn more about poker in the Chicago land area.

LIVE CASH GAMES and SIT & GO TOURNAMENTS
WILL START AT 2:00PM and RUN ALL DAY LONG

Cash Games Offered:
$2/$4 & $5/$10 Limit Hold'em
$1-$2, $1/$2, $2/$5, $5/$10 NL Hold 'em
$1/$2 & $2/$5 Pot Limit Omaha H/L and High
Plus several other ring games spread on demand!

Sit and Go Tournaments Offered:
$25, $50 and $115 Sit & Go Single Table Tournaments
$50 and $100 Head's up Tournaments
$30 Pot Limit Omaha Sit & Go with $20 Re-buys
$80 Heartland and WSOP Single Table Satellites...
(1st pays $450, 2nd pays $240)
Plenty of Multi-Table Tournaments running all day long as well.

There is lots of action here; I highly recommend playing here whenever you get the chance.

Courtesy of Harrah's Tunica

Harrah's Casino-Tunica
13615 Old Highway 61 North
Robinsonville, MS 38664
Phone (800) 946-4946
The Harrah's Casino offers one of Tunica's premier poker rooms. They host 2 WSOP circuit events, and have an array of daily tournaments. Like most Tunica poker rooms, they have great room rates. You'll find a wide game selection on one of their 14 cash tables.

Courtesy of Cornell & Company / Mike Wilson

Buffalo Thunder Resort & Casino
30 Buffalo Thunder Trail
Santa Fe, NM 87506
Phone (505) 455-5555
The Hilton Santa Fe Buffalo Thunder is located on 500 acres of high desert land in Santa Fe, New Mexico. With architecture inspired by pueblos, the resort features 61,000 square feet of casino gaming space, including a 10-table poker room. There are two lounges with nightclub atmospheres, live music and comedy shows. The hotel boasts two bars and six restaurants, one of which is headlined by celebrity chef Mark Miller. Also featured are two outdoor pools and spa tubs that share a poolside grille. The hotel's Towa Golf Course was designed by Hale Irwin and Bill Phillips. All 390 guestrooms incorporate authentic American Indian design elements and décor. Lose yourself and relax as you roam the countryside.

Courtesy of Palms Casino Resort

Palms Casino Resort
4321 West Flamingo Road
Las Vegas, NV 89103
Phone (702) 942-6961
The Palms Poker Room gives you the best chance to have a celebrity playing at your table. Their 10 table poker room is conveniently located, close to everything including self-parking which couldn't be easier and valet that's always available. The poker room is divided into two rooms with six tables in the main room offering limit games and four tables on the high limit side where no-limit is played. The Palms provides a comfortable poker room with a knowledgeable staff, located in one of the most exciting casinos in the world and throws in the convenience of modern technology.

Courtesy of Hustler Casino

Hustler Casino
**1000 West Redondo Beach Blvd.
Gardena, CA 90247
Phone (877) 968-9800**

Publishing has been the trump card always played by Larry Flynt. As a diverse businessman, Mr. Flynt not only has the very successful Hustler Magazine (started in 1974), but also has an aviation company and a chain of retail stores. Filling out his royal flush, Mr. Flynt tapped the gaming market and built a beautiful new Casino in Gardena, a suburb of Los Angeles. The bankrupt El Dorado was purchased by Mr. Flynt in 1998, razed and re-constructed into the 55,000-square foot Hustler Casino.

After pouring over 50 million dollars into the establishment, the grand opening took place June 22, 2000. Mr. Flynt took personal pride in overseeing the design and decoration of the card room, dressing it out in first class luxury. He made certain the casino maintained an elegant architecture and unsurpassed furnishings. Beautiful reproductions of Gustav Klimt paintings adorn the walls, huge plasma-screen televisions are strategically placed throughout the casino to appeal to all clients, and it is truly a sight to behold.

Hustler Casino offers a variety of amenities, including the most robust Player Reward Card program in Los Angeles. Players use reward points for complimentary meals, gift and apparel items from the casino's gift shop or the flagship Hustler Hollywood retail store in Hollywood, Blackjack Match-play coupons, valet parking and even tournament entry fees.

Other amenities available include table-side massage, Larry Flynt's Bar & Grill, sushi and sashimi, and a beautiful gift boutique featuring Hustler logo apparel and gift items and Hustler's trademarked magazines.

Since 1997, Larry Flynt has hosted "the biggest seven-card stud game in the world." The game started in Larry Flynt's home but moved to his casino when it opened. As of April 2007, the buy-in is $200,000, with $1000 antes and stakes of $2,000-$4,000. Unlike most high-stakes ring games, Flynt's game is held in a corner of the casino's main poker room. Regulars at the table include Phil Ivey, Barry Greenstein, and Ted Forrest. Tracy Edwards the Casino Manager, creates an atmosphere for all types of players. Although Texas Hold'em is by far the most popular poker game, he provides varied games and limits to give each player a choice for their poker preferences.

"The Hustler Casino is turning out to be quite a force in L.A. gaming," says Marketing Director Al Underwood. He also stated, "Poker players have a unique way of conveying information through word of mouth, so when the word gets around that the game is on, it spreads like wildfire." Hustler Casino is unique in that it hosts the largest continuous $1,500-$3,000 stud game in the world. It also claims the highest blackjack limit in California, up to $6,000 per hand.

Although Hustler Casino only entered the gaming market this millennium, it offers the perfect atmosphere for high rollers, movie stars, California visitors, and especially, the beginning player. Pleasure and comfort abound. The Hustler Casino staff eagerly prepare for you one of the best all-round gambling experiences in the state of California.

This casino has lots of very soft and passive players, even among the regulars. The Hustler Casino has a friendly, casual atmosphere with a local card room feel. Larry Flynt and celebrities can often be seen playing, as an added bonus

Number of Tables: 55 Poker- 30 Cal Games

NL Ring Stakes:
$1/$2 blinds (Buy-in: $50 to $100)
$2/$5 blinds (Buy-in: $100 to $300)
$5/$10 blinds (Buy-in: $500 to No Maximum)

Limit Ring Stakes:
$2/$4 up to $4000/$8000

Tournament Stakes:
$100 up to $1,500
Player Card:

Free to players. Points are redeemable for food, gift shop merchandise, tournament entry fees, Blackjack Match-play coupons and more.

Courtesy of Harrah's Horseshoe Tunica

Horseshoe Casino-Tunica
1021 Casino Center Drive
Robinsonville, MS. 38664
Phone (662) 357-5608
The Horseshoe is a Harrah's property and hosts some medium sized limit Hold'em games, and also offers a good NL Hold'em and PL Omaha mix in their 16 table room. Lisa Cromption is the manager at the Horseshoe Poker Room. Brooks Bradley is the day shift manager and perhaps one of the best dealers on the planet. The new room at the Horseshoe is very nicely appointed and doesn't seem an afterthought like the old Horseshoe room. There's plenty of action here and the biggest limit, NL and PL Omaha games and the free food is very good here. If you are ever in the room and seated near the $10/$20 Hold'em table, listening for the table talk, it's worth the rake just for the entertainment.

Courtesy of Golden Nugget

Golden Nugget
129 East Fremont Street
Las Vegas, NV 89101
Phone (702) 386-8383
The New Golden Nugget Poker Room is one of the most beautiful rooms in Las Vegas. This is the third incarnation of the Poker Room at the Nugget in the past two years. The casino is undergoing major renovations under the new ownership of Landry's restaurant chain and the poker room is by far and away the best of the renovations to date. The Golden Nugget Poker Room has been relocated to the right side of the main cashier cage.

The Golden Nugget has brought in all new 10-handed Texas Hold'em tables. The tables are dressed in a beautiful light golden colored felt, a tan leather rail with cup holders, and commitment lines. The table designs fit perfectly with the Golden Nugget Poker Room decor. The chairs are light brown in color, very comfortable, have wheels, and a curved back that provide the utmost in support for the poker player spending several hours in the Golden Nugget's Poker Room.

Overall, the brand new Poker Room at The Golden Nugget Casino is one of the most beautiful and classy low roller poker rooms in Las Vegas. Players won't find the high limits games here, but this is a great place for some low limit action and action it is!

Courtesy of MGM Mirage

Bellagio
3600 S. Las Vegas Blvd.
Las Vegas, NV 89109
Phone (888) 987-6667
Be exhilarated with hand after hand of world class poker action at the Bellagio. Their Las Vegas poker room is one of the stops on the famed World Poker Tour. Within its 7,000 square feet are 40 tables and two high-limit areas, the most prominent of which is Bobby's Room, an exclusive two-table enclave named in honor of 1978 World Series of Poker Champion Bobby Baldwin.

For your ultimate enjoyment, this smoke-free Vegas hot spot includes 24-hour table-side dining, complimentary beverage service, safe deposit boxes, a full-service cashier cage, an overhead state-of-the-art music system, eight 32 inch television monitors, and eleven

42 inch plasma screens. The Bellagio is the epitome of all poker rooms. The quality of the dealers, floor men, cocktail drinks and even the chairs are all superb. The non-smoking room holds 30 tables and is open 24/7.

As always, lavishness comes with a price, and the lowest limits you'll find here are $4/$8 limit and $2/$5 NL Hold'em. There are plenty of higher limit games from $20/$40 and an elevated area where the stakes go from $300/$600 to $4,000/$8,000. There is also a separate section in a glass-windowed room, where the real poker is played.

To further inspire your game, the walls are adorned with artwork depicting past Bellagio tournaments and World Poker Tour events, as well as a LeRoy Neiman-commissioned painting of high-stakes poker greats. If you're in the mood to meddle with the best, I suggest only playing here. The vast majority of tables at the Bellagio are Texas Hold'em, NL and limit, tables. There is also some seven-card stud and Omaha at higher limits.

There are two different areas to sign up, a high limit board and a lower limit board. The main desk at the front of the room is for signing up for $4/$8 and $8/$16 Limit Texas Hold'em, and $2/$5 and $5/$10 NL Texas Hold'em. If you want to play higher limits, ask where to go and they will point you to the right man for the job. If you are willing to play more than one type of a limit game, I recommend that you sign up for two lists, since some lists move faster than others, depending on which day of the week you're playing.

The Bellagio also hosts World Poker Tour events, but these are held in another area of the casino. However, the Bellagio does hold daily NL Hold'em poker tournaments. The buy-in is $500 Sunday through Thursday and $1000 on Friday and Saturdays. Each day these tournaments start at 2 pm, and there are satellites starting at 9 am.

On any given night, in a glass-windowed room in the back, (usually a $200,000 minimum buy- in) you can see professional poker players such as Doyle Brunson, Erick Lindgren, Daniel Negreanu, Phil Laak, and Jennifer Harman, playing poker. The stakes of the game have different limits, but are often $4000/$8000 limit Hold'em. It's not a closed game, but I recommend having $75,000 to $100,000; they would love to play with you. The Bellagio always has been my favorite and first place to play in Vegas, right off the plane ride from Chicago. There is always such a diverse crowd of players at a table. Plus, the mix of people from all over and of all skill levels, combined with a slew of top-shelf cocktails, ensures some of the funniest tables I've ever played.

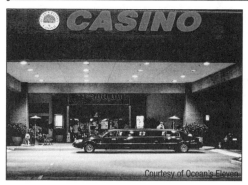

Courtesy of Ocean's Eleven

Ocean's Eleven Casino
121 Brooks Street
Oceanside, California 92054
Phone (760) 439-6988
Ocean's Eleven Casino, (Est. 1997) is one of the premier poker rooms, and one of the friendliest in Southern California. It is located about 40 miles north of San Diego, or 80 miles south of Los Angeles. They attribute their success to their dedicated employees, who treat everyone like they are part of the family. "Our employees are as friendly and professional as it gets," says Bob Moyer, General Manager and Partner. Ocean's Eleven has been a pioneer of the "no abuse" policy since day one.

This is another reason why poker players enjoy playing here is its non-intimidating, nonsmoking, friendly atmosphere. Ocean's Eleven boasts as many as 45 tables, with choices of Texas Hold'em and Omaha. This casino has no slot machines. Ocean's Eleven is a card room, pitting player against player rather than the house, and is not a part of any Indian tribe gaming.

Horseshoe Casino-Southern Indiana
11999 Avenue of the Emperors
Elizabeth, IN 47117
Phone (866) 676-7463
The Horseshoe Casino Southern Indiana has a great feature that you don't find at many casinos, The World Series of Poker Room.* It is a state-of-the-art venue featuring 30 tournament-caliber tables, where highly skilled dealers and seasoned casino hosts well-versed in the Binion style of poker keep the action going.

There, you'll discover poker the way it's meant to be: from Texas Hold'em to Omaha and Stud, nobody knows poker better than Horseshoe.

Along with the finest in poker playing action, Horseshoe also offers a truly luxurious atmosphere featuring exceptional service and the best cash and comps in the business. From the moment you step into the casino, your every need is attended to. The courteous hotel staff, knowledgeable casino hosts, friendly dealers, and fast wait staff are all committed to giving you the very best of everything, and then some.

Included are generous rewards that are easy to get. In fact, there's only one rule when it comes to comps: if you're gambling, you will be taken care of. It doesn't get any simpler than that. Nothing complements amazing action quite like an incredible meal. Poker players in the mood for huge steaks and fresh lobster will certainly find it at the famous Jack Binion's Steak House. Praised in reviews and recognized by the Distinguished

Restaurants of North America, it's quite simply one of the best steakhouses in the country. Their buffet has to be one of the best buffets that I have ever been to.

Big Time Poker!

Now it's time you got in on the poker craze that's sweeping the nation. Enter the World Series of Poker Room and try your hand at a variety of poker games.

Their comfortable Poker Room is consistently voted the best in the market, and with over $1 million in recent renovations they plan to keep it that way. They're sure to have something for everyone from beginners to experts, from NL Texas Hold'em to Seven-card Stud.

*WORLD SERIES OF POKER are trademarks of Harrah's License Company, LLC ("Harrah's"). Harrah's does not sponsor or endorse, and is not associated or affiliated with Eat Professional Poker Players Alive! or its products, services, or promotions

Seminole Hard Rock Hotel & Casino - Hollywood

1 Seminole Way, Hollywood, FL 33314
Phone (954) 583-3250
The Hard Rock Casino in Hollywood, Florida is a poker player's dream. The Hard Rock casinos are the latest jewels in the gambling crown of the Seminole tribe of Florida. The best adjective I can think of to describe the Hard Rock's poker room is "flamboyant." There are 50 new

tables, tastefully laid out in a beautiful, softly lit, nicely carpeted room. The ceilings are enormously high, giving the room almost an open-air feel. The chairs are well padded and very comfortable. The chips are new, as are the cards. The games are great, too. Florida law does not permit limits higher than $5, nor NL games with higher than a $100 cap on the buy-in. Nevertheless, within those confines, the games are dynamic.

They have NL Texas Hold'em with blinds of $1/$2, $2/$5, and even $5/$10 (yes, with only a $100 buy-in). In addition to the NL games, the room spreads $1/2 and $2/$4 Limit Hold'em and Omaha eight or better. They offer Seven-card Stud when there are enough players. They rake 10% up to a maximum of $5.

Their poker room runs terrific and has fairly big tournaments. There's a daily bounty tournament with a $100 - $350 buy-in, depending on the day of the week. On Saturday there's a $500 tournament with one $500 re-buy. This is poker at its best..

Courtesy of Seminole Hard Rock Hotel & Casino - Tampa

Seminole Hard Rock Hotel & Casino - Tampa
5223 N. Orient Road Tampa, FL 33610
Phone (813) 627-7625

The Hard Rock Casino in Tampa, run by the Seminole tribe of Florida, is a 150,000-square foot casino, the largest in the state. They have 50 tables, spread $1/$2 and $2/$5 NL Hold'em with a $100 capped buy-in. They spread $2/$4 limit Hold'em and $1-$5 limit Stud. There are regular tournaments as well. This is the action room in the Tampa area. There are many younger players, most with iPods, sunglasses, or baseball caps, just as you see on television.

The poker room takes the standard-for-Florida 10-percent, $5-maximum rake and a $1 jackpot drop. The jackpot goes for a bad beat jackpot and a high hand bonus. The latest bad beat jackpot was colossal at $125,000. You needed to have your quads beaten. A royal flush in spades paid the player $500. The other royal flushes of different suits paid $100.

The Hard Rock Casino in Tampa is a great place for playing cash games. You can simply feed off of the tourists. Otherwise you can enjoy yourself playing in the well-organized tournaments.

Obviously I can't list every Poker room out there. Here is a small list of other Casinos that I recommend you play at if you are in the area:

- **Agua Caliente Casino** – Rancho Mirage, CA
- **Akwesasne Mohawk Casino** – Hogansburg, NY
- **Aliente Station Casino** – North Las Vegas, NV
- **Ameristar Casino** – Black Hawk, CO
- **Ameristar Casino** – Council Bluffs, IA
- **Ameristar Casino** – East Chicago, IN
- **Ameristar Casino** – Encino, CA
- **Ameristar Casino** – Kansas City, MO
- **Ameristar Casino** – St Charles, MO
- **Ameristar Casino** – Vicksburg, MS
- **Argosy Casino** – Lawrenceburg, IN
- **Argosy Casino** – Riverside, MO
- **Argosy Casino** – Sioux City, IA
- **Arizona Charlie's Casino** – Las Vegas, NV
- **Artichoke Joe's Casino** – San Bruno, CA
- **Atlantis Casino Resort** – Reno, NV
- **Aquarius Casino Resort** – Laughlin, NV
- **Bally's Atlantic City Hotel & Casino** – Atlantic City-NJ
- **Bally's Las Vegas Hotel & Casino** – Las Vegas, NV
- **Barona Valley Ranch Resort & Casino** – San Diego, CA
- **Beau Rivage Resort & Casino** – Biloxi, MS
- **Belterra Resort & Spa** – Florence, IN
- **Binions Horseshoe Casino** – Las Vegas, NV
- **Bicycle Casino, The** – Bell Gardens, CA
- **Black Oak Casino** – Tuolumne, CA
- **Blue Lake Casino** – Blue Lake, CA
- **BlueWater Resort & Casino** – Parker, AZ
- **Boomtown Casino** – Biloxi, MS
- **Boomtown Casino & Hotel** – Verdi, NV
- **Borgata Hotel Casino & Spa** – Atlantic City, NJ
- **Boulder Station Hotel & Casino** – Las Vegas, NV
- **Buffalo Run Casino** – Miami, OK
- **Cache Creek Casino** – Brooks, CA
- **Cactus Pete's Casino** – Jackpot, NV
- **Cadillac Ranch Casino** – Longview, WA
- **Caesars - Atlantic City** – Atlantic City, NJ
- **Caesars Palace** – Las Vegas, NV
- **California Grand Casino** – Pacheco, CA
- **Cameo Club Casino** – Stockton, CA
- **Cannery Hotel & Casino** – Las Vegas, NV
- **Canterbury Park Racetrack & Card Room** – Shakopee, MN
- **Capitol Casino** – Sacramento, CA
- **Capitol Club** – Sacramento, CA

- **Carson Nugget** – Carson City, NV
- **Casino Arizona** – Scottsdale, AZ
- **Casino Aztar** – Evansville, IN
- **Casino Aztar** – Caruthersville, MO
- **Casino Del Sol** – Tucson, AZ
- **Casino Fandango** – Carson, NV
- **Casino Morongo** – Cabazon, CA
- **Casino Pauma** – Pauma Valley, CA
- **Casino Real** – Santa Clara, CA
- **Casino Royale** – Modesto, CA
- **Catfish Bend Casino** – Burlington, IA
- **Cher-Ae Heights Casino** – Trinidad, CA
- **Chukchansi Gold Resort & Casino** – Coarsegold, CA
- **Chumash Casino Resort** – Santa Ynez, CA
- **Circus Circus Casino** – Las Vegas, NV
- **Cities of Gold Casino** – Sante Fe, NM
- **Cliff Castle Casino** – Camp Verde, AZ
- **Club Cal Neva** – Reno, NV
- **Club Caribe Casino** – Cudahy, CA
- **Club One Casino** – Fresno, CA
- **Colorado Belle Hotel Casino** – Laughlin, NV
- **Colorado Central Station Casino** – Black Hawk, CO
- **Colusa Casino Resort** – Colusa, CA
- **Commerce Casino** – Los Angeles, CA
- **Coushatta Casino Resort** – Kinder, LA
- **Creek Nation Casino** – Tulsa, OK
- **Crystal Casino & Hotel** – Compton, CA
- **Daytona Beach Kennel Club** – Daytona Beach, FL
- **Delta Club Card Room** – Stockton, CA
- **Derby Lane** – Saint Petersburg, FL.
- **Desert Diamond Casino** – Sahuarita, AZ
- **Desert Diamond Hotel & Casino** – Tucson, AZ
- **Deuces Wild Casino and Lounge** – Auburn, CA
- **Diamond Jack's** – Bossier City, LA
- **Diamond Jim's Casino** – Rosamond, CA
- **Diamond Jo Casino** – Northwood, IA
- **Diamond Lil's Cardroom** – Renton, WA
- **Don Laughlin's Riverside Resort & Casino** – Laughlin, NV
- **Downstream Casino & Resort** – Quapaw, OK
- **Dubuque Greyhound Park** – Dubuque, IA
- **Eagle Mountain Casino** – Porterville, CA
- **Eastside Cannery Casino & Resort** – Las Vegas, NV
- **Ebro Greyhound Park** – Ebro, FL
- **El Cortez Hotel & Casino** – Las Vegas, NV
- **Eldorado Hotel & Casino** – Reno, NV
- **Eureka Casino** – Mesquite, NV

- **Excalibur Casino** – Las Vegas, NV
- **Fantasy Springs Resort & Casino** – Indio, CA
- **Feather Falls Casino& Lodge** – Oroville, CA
- **Fiesta Henderson Hotel & Casino** – Henderson, NV
- **Fiesta Rancho Hotel & Casino** – North Las Vegas, NV
- **Firelake Grand Casino**– Shawnee, OK
- **Fitzgerald's Casino & Hotel** – Las Vegas, NV
- **Flamingo Casino** – Las Vegas, NV
- **Flagler Greyhound Track** – Ft. Lauderdale, FL
- **Flamingo Casino** – Las Vegas, NV
- **Fort McDowell Casino** – Shea, AZ
- **Fortune Bay Resort & Casino** – Tower, MN
- **Foxwoods Resort Casino** – Ledyard, CT
- **Garden City Casino** – San Jose, CA
- **Gilpin Casino, The** – Golden, CO
- **Gold Coast Hotel & Casino** – Las Vegas, NV
- **Gold Country Casino & Hotel** – Oroville, CA
- **Gold Rush Gaming Emporium** – Grass Valley, CA
- **Gold Sombrero Cardroom** – Merced, CA
- **Gold Strike Casino Resort** – Tunica, MS
- **Golden Acorn Casino** – Campo, CA
- **Golden Gates Casino: Poker Parlour** – Blackhawk, CO
- **Golden Moon Hotel & Casino** – Choctaw, MS
- **Golden West Casino** – Bakersfield, CA
- **Grand Casino Biloxi** – Biloxi, MS
- **Grand Casino Coushatta** – Kinder, LA
- **Grand Casino Hinckley** – Hinckley, MN
- **Grand Casino Mille Lacs** – Onamia, MN
- **Grand Sierra Casino & Resort** – Reno, NV
- **Greektown Casino** – Detroit, MI
- **Green Valley Ranch Resort** – Henderson, NV
- **Gulfstream Park Racing & Casino** – Hallandale, FL
- **Hard Rock Casino & Hotel** – Catoosa, OK
- **Hard Rock Casino & Hotel** – Las Vegas, NV
- **Hard Rock Casino & Hotel** – Biloxi, MS
- **Harrah's - Atlantic City** – Atlantic City, NJ
- **Harrah's - Harvey's Lake Tahoe Casino** – Stateline, NV
- **Harrah's - Las Vegas** – Las Vegas, NV
- **Harrah's - New Orleans** – New Orleans, LA
- **Harrah's - North Kansas City Casino & Hotel** – Kansas City, MO
- **Harrah's - Reno** – Reno, NV
- **Harrah's - Rincon Casino & Resort** – San Diego, CA
- **Harrah's - St. Louis** – St. Louis, MO
- **Hawaiian Gardens Casino** – Hawaiian Gardens, CA
- **Hinsdale Greyhound Park** – Hinsdale, NH
- **Hollywood Casino** – Aurora, IL

- **Hollywood Casino** – Tunica, MS
- **Hollywood Park Casino** – Inglewood, CA
- **Hooters Casino Hotel** – Las Vegas, NV
- **Horizon Casino & Hotel – Biloxi, MS**
- **Horseshoe Casino & Hotel** – Bossier City, LA
- **Horseshoe Casino** – Council Bluffs, IA
- **Horseshoe Casino** – Hammond, IN
- **Imperial Palace Hotel & Casino** – Las Vegas, NV
- **I.P.** – Biloxi, MS
- **Island Resort & Casino** – Harris, MI
- **Isle of Capri** – Bettendorf, IA
- **Isle of Capri** – Biloxi, MS
- **Isleta Casino & Resort** – Albuquerque, NM
- **Jackpot Junction Casino** – Morton, MN
- **Jackson Rancheria Casino & Hotel** – Jackson, CA
- **Jai-Alai - Dania** – Dania, FL
- **Jai-Alai - Miami** – Miami, FL
- **John Ascuaga's Nugget** – Reno, NV
- **Jumer's Casino & Hotel** – Rock Island, IL
- **Kewadin Casino** – St. Ignace, MI
- **Klondike Casino** – Eureka, CA
- **Lac Courte Oreilles Casino Lodge & Convention Center** – Hayward, WI
- **Lake Elsinore Hotel & Casino** – Lake Elsinore, CA
- **Leelanau Sands Casino** – Peshawbestown, MI
- **Lucky Buck Card Club** – Livermore, CA
- **Lucky Chances Casino** – Colma, CA
- **Lucky Derby Casino** – Citrus Heights, CA
- **Lucky Lady Card Room** – San Diego, CA
- **Lucky Nugget Card Club** – Deadwood, SD
- **Lumiere Place** – St. Louis, MO
- **Luxor Casino** – Las Vegas, NV
- **Majestic Star Casino & Hotel** – Gary, IN
- **Mandalay Bay** – Las Vegas, NV
- **Mardi Gras Racetrack & Gaming Center** – Hollywood, FL
- **Marina Club Casino** – Marina, CA
- **Menominee Casino-Bingo-Hotel** – Keshena, WI
- **Meskwaki Bingo & Casino** – Tama, IA
- **MGM Grand Hotel & Casino** – Las Vegas, NV
- **Miccosukee Resort & Gaming Center** – Miami, FL
- **Midnight Rose Casino** – Cripple Creek, CO
- **Mike's Card Casino** – Oakdale, CA
- **Mirage** – Las Vegas, NV
- **Mohegan Sun** – Uncasville, CT
- **Monte Carlo Resort & Casino** – Las Vegas, NV
- **MontBleu Resort Casino & Spa** – Lake Tahoe, NV
- **Motorcity Casino** – Detroit, MI

- **Mountaineer Racetrack & Gaming Resort** –Chester, WV
- **Muckleshoot Casino** – Auburn, WA
- **Napa Valley Casino** – American Canyon, CA
- **Naples-Ft.Myers Greyhound Track** – Bonita Springs, FL
- **New York-New York Hotel & Casino** – Las Vegas, NV
- **Normandie Casino** – Gardena, CA
- **Northern Lights Casino** – Walker, MN
- **O'Sheas** – Las Vegas, NV
- **Oaks Card Club** – Emeryville, CA
- **Ocean View Cardroom** – Santa Cruz, CA
- **One-Eyed Jacks Card Room** – Sarasota, FL
- **Oneida Casino** – Green Bay, WI
- **Orleans, The** – Las Vegas, NV
- **Nugget Hotel & Casino** – Pahrump, NV
- **Palace Club** – Hayward, CA
- **Palace Station Hotel & Casino** – Las Vegas, NV
- **Palm Beach Kennel Club** – West Palm Beach, FL
- **Palomar Card Club** – San Diego, CA
- **Paradise Casino** – Yuma, AZ
- **Paragon Casino & Resort** – Marksville, LA
- **Paris** – Las Vegas, NV
- **Pechanga Resort & Casino** – Temecula, CA
- **Peppermill Casino** – Reno, NV
- **Pete's 881 Club** – San Rafael, CA
- **Planet Hollywood Resort & Casino** – Las Vegas, NV
- **Players' Poker Club** – Ventura, CA
- **Plaza Hotel and Casino** – Las Vegas, NV
- **Poker Flats Casino** – Merced, CA
- **Poker Palace** – North Las Vegas, NV
- **Potawatomi Bingo Casino** – Milwaukee, WI
- **Prairie's Edge Casino Resort** – Granite Falls, MN
- **President Casino-St. Louis Riverfront** – St. Louis, MO
- **Red Rock Casino Resort Spa** – Las Vegas, NV
- **Reno Hilton Casino** – Reno, NV
- **Rio Casino** – Las Vegas, NV
- **Riviera** – Las Vegas, NV
- **Royal River Casino** – Flandreau, SD
- **Running Aces Card Room** – Columbus, MN
- **Sam's Town Casino** – Tunica, MS
- **Sam's Town Casino** – Las Vegas, NV
- **Sahara** – Las Vegas, NV
- **San Manuel Indian Bingo & Casino** – Highland, CA
- **Sandia Resort & Casino** – Albuquerque, NM
- **Sands Regency Casino & Hotel** – Reno, NV
- **Santa Ana Star Casino** – Santa Ana Pueblo, NM
- **Santa Fe Station Hotel & Casino** – Las Vegas, NV

- **Seneca Niagara Casino** – Niagara Falls, NY
- **Seven Clans Casino** – Thief River Falls, MN
- **Seven Feathers Hotel & Casino Resort** – Canyonville, OR
- **Shooting Star Casino and Hotel** – Madnomen, MN
- **Showboat Casino - Atlantic City** – Atlantic City, NJ
- **Soaring Eagle Casino** – Mount Pleasant, MI
- **South Point Hotel and Casino** – Las Vegas, NV
- **Spirit Mountain Casino** – Grand Ronde, Oregon
- **St.Croix Casino** – Turtle Lake, WI
- **Stratosphere** – Las Vegas, NV
- **Suncoast Hotel & Casino** – Las Vegas, NV
- **Sunset Station Hotel & Casino** – Henderson, NV
- **Sycuan Casino** – El Cajon, CA
- **Tampa Bay Downs** – Tampa, FL
- **Texas Station Casino** – North Las Vegas, NV
- **Treasure Island** – Las Vegas, NV
- **Treasure Island Resort Casino** – Red Wing, MN
- **Tropicana Hotel Casino** – Las Vegas, NV
- **Trump Taj Mahal Casino** – Atlantic City, NJ
- **Turlock Poker Room** – Turlock, CA
- **Turning Stone Resort & Casino** – Verona, NY
- **Tuscany Suites & Casino** – Las Vegas, NV
- **Ute Mountain Casino** – Towaoc, CO
- **Valley View Casino** – Valley Center, CA
- **Vee Quiva Casino** – Laveen, AZ
- **Venetian, The** – Las Vegas, NV
- **Viejas Casino** – Alpine, CA
- **Village Club Card Room** – Chula Vista, CA
- **Wheeling Island Racetrack & Gaming Center** – Wheeling, WV
- **White Oak Casino** – Deer River, MN
- **Wild Horse Pass Casino** – Chandler, AZ
- **Wild Wild West Gambling Hall & Hotel** – Las Vegas, NV
- **Wildhorse Resort & Casino** – Pendleton, OR
- **Win-River Casino** – Redding, CA
- **Winstar** – Thackerville, OK
- **Wynn** – Las Vegas, NV

❝ Poker may be a branch of psychological warfare, an art form or indeed a way of life – but it is also merely a game, in which money is simply the means of keeping score. ❞

—Anthony Holden, is a poker player, and spent a year playing professionally while researching his 1990 book "Big Deal: A Year as a Professional Poker Player.

CHAPTER THIRTY ONE:

POKER MAGAZINES

Bluff Magazine

Bluff Magazine reaches more poker players per month than any other poker magazine. "The Thrill of Poker" is more than just a slogan. *BLUFF Magazine* truly captures all of the excitement that has made poker the phenomenon it is today. Currently, over 100 million Americans play poker regularly and *Bluff* targets not only the serious player, but also the new generation that has been attracted to poker by the ever-present TV and online presence.

From advice on how to play, to what it's like to spend a day with the hottest poker players in the world, *Bluff* covers all aspects of poker, on and offline. Equally informative and entertaining, *Bluff* engages long-time players, and today's new generation of poker pro alike.

Bluff has been the foremost innovator in poker media since their inception:

- They are the largest poker magazine in the world.
- They exclusively broadcast the World Series of Poker via radio.
- They invented the first Fantasy Poker League.
- They held the first Online Poker Tour, the Bluff Poker Tour.

- They are the only publication to provide poker content to ESPN.com and Askmen. com

Eric Morris, Co-President & Publisher Prior to Bluff Media, Eric spent 10 years launching and managing a myriad of successful publications for various publishers including Gambling Online Magazine, European Homes and Garden and Women's Health and Fitness. Prior to entering the publishing industry, Eric was the morning show producer and personality at KBGG radio (Big 98.1 FM) in San Francisco, CA.

Matthew Parvis, Editor-in-Chief, Bluff Magazine Matthew was first introduced to Bluff Media in June of 2005, when he won a seat to the WSOP Main event through the inaugural Bluff Poker Tour. A few months later, after learning of his background as a successful producer in New York City, Parvis was hired by Bluff to help manage the quickly growing publications editorial department. Since October of 2005, Parvis has helped grow and maintain relationships with the industries top professional players, and writers helping establish Bluff as one of the top poker entities in the industry.

BLUFF reaches the largest targeted audience of poker players of any publication in the U.S. With a circulation of 225,000 copies, BLUFF can be found at local poker events, card rooms, and on newsstands nationwide.

Poker Pro Magazine

Poker Pro Magazine is unique in the world of publishing. Launched four years ago by a few regular guys who just love the game, the small firm's goal was to create a glossy, informative, high-end, fun publication at a time when poker magazines were little more than free, cheaply produced publications that you found littering the floors of casino card rooms. The guys wanted something different, a professional-quality monthly devoted to both professional and recreational players.

It is this love of the game that shines through on every page of *Poker Pro*. It is this passion for poker, knowledge of its history and hope for its future that has garnered a reputation for *Poker Pro*, as the magazine that is not afraid to "tell it like it is" when it comes to the poker world. Because it is not "corporate" like the big boys in poker publishing, Poker Pro will take a stand when forces within or outside of the poker world threaten the game. The game comes first. Making a buck comes second.

Poker Pro Magazine reaches a targeted audience of poker players with a circulation of over 150,000 copies per issue. You can find *Poker Pro Magazine* at card rooms in over 25 states, major poker events, and at newsstands in the U.S. and Canada.

Young entrepreneur Dan Jacobs and marketing guru Will Jordan, an ex-Marine, wanted a magazine that reflected their passion for competition around the felt. Both are accomplished players (Jordan, for example, cashed three times in the 2008 WSOP), and they wanted Poker Pro to capture both the fun and profitability of poker. That is what you will find on every page – how to have fun and improve your game – all in a slick package with a glossy cover, quality paper, insightful writing, pro strategy tips and good photography.

To help make that package slick, they hired Editor-in-Chief John "Johnny Quads" Wenzel, who for more than fifteen years has been one of the most successful high stakes cash-game players in the State of Florida – and a magazine professional who has worked as reporter, editor, photographer and designer at newspapers, magazines and tabloids in three states. Wenzel has a journalism and mass communications degree from the hotbed of college and online poker – the University of Wisconsin in Madison – home to such players as Phil Hellmuth, Phil "OMGClayAiken" Galfond, Mark "P0ker H0" Kroon and many others.

"Johnny Quads" – the 2006 Oklahoma State Pot-Limit Hold'em champion – is somewhat unique in poker publishing. Most editors are either poker players who want to be editors, or editors who don't know anything about poker, but Johnny is one of the few who knows both poker AND publishing. Wenzel is so devoted to poker that he once took a part-time job as a poker dealer just to see if it would improve his game. He is the author of three published books on poker, including "Everything Hold'em."

The Unlawful Internet Gambling Enforcement Act and a shaky economy have put a dent in the company's revenue stream, but while many poker publications have gone under recently, Poker Pro Media is bullish on poker and has launched four new poker-related titles: Poker Pro Europe, Online Poker Pro, Online Poker Pro Scandinavia and a French language edition of Poker Pro. Poker Pro Europe regularly gets kudos as one of Europe's best poker magazines, and Online Poker Pro – which as of this writing mainly circulates in the UK – is the largest publication devoted to Internet poker.

And, oh yeah, remember that publication that started out in a cutthroat business just a few years ago – Poker Pro? Today it's one of the top three poker magazines in the world in terms of circulation, and many say that for overall quality, it's Number One. Whether that is true or not is a matter of opinion, but there is one thing everyone agrees on: It pushed the other guys to get better

---

Australian Poker Weekly

An independent publication, *Australian Poker Weekly* provides the most complete, authoritative, and interesting source of news and information from the world of poker.

Australian Poker Weekly readers enjoy regular, exclusive columns by leading poker identities, profiles of star poker players, special behind the scenes gossip and photographs as well as all the latest poker tournament news and results, updates on internet poker and poker travel reports.

It all adds up to the best coverage of the mighty poker phenomenon that is sweeping the world.

The only weekly poker publication in the world, *Australian Poker Weekly* is distributed FREE-OF-CHARGE directly into the hands of those who want to read it.

Australian Poker Weekly boasts a circulation of 20,000 and a readership in excess of 30,000 and is available FREE throughout Australia and New Zealand wherever the game of poker is played...hotels, clubs, and casinos.

Publisher and Editor of the *Australian Poker Weekly*, Alfred Markarian has been working in sports publishing since 1980 and is an avid poker player.

Ante Up, Florida's Poker Magazine

Ante Up, Florida's Poker Magazine, got its start as an audio show at the St. Petersburg Times, Florida's largest newspaper.

For more than three years, Scott Long and Christopher Cosenza hosted the award-winning weekly Ante Up Pokercast at The Times, building a loyal, worldwide audience known as the "Ante Up Nation." that spanned more than 30 countries.

Long and Cosenza decided to leave *The Times* and devote their lives full-time to the game they love in the summer of 2008. They created Ante Up Publishing LLC, and while they continue the pokercast, their flagship product quickly became *Ante Up, Florida's Poker Magazine*, a monthly, full-color glossy that quickly became the authority on everything poker in the state of Florida.

Each month, thousands of rounders from Pensacola to Key West keeps up to date on news, results, and happenings from Florida's more than 55 casinos, poker rooms and free poker leagues. Each month also brings regular features like Cosenza's Poker Vision TV column, Long's Holdout column on games other than Texas Hold'em, Dr. Frank Toscano's Healthy Bet health column, John Lanier's Nothin' But Net Internet column, and strategy columns from pro Lee Childs and ex-FBI agent Joe Navarro.

Ante Up Publishing also has grown into a poker media company, with the magazine, pokercast, Web site, e-newsletters and live events.

Poker Player

Not a monthly or bi-monthly magazine, *Poker Player is a newspaper* that's been bringing news to players, poker fans, card room employees and casino managers since it was first published more than 25 years ago.

Poker Player Newspaper lives up to its motto as "The Player's Voice," bringing news about events, promotions, tournament results, and political happenings that affect the world of casino poker and online poker too. And they bring them to you immediately, along with insights from poker experts, tournament directors, card room managers, leading gaming attorneys, and others who are in a unique position to shed light on today's fast-moving events and place them in a perspective that is easily understood by readers.

News comes first. The most important aspect of a poker periodical is to bring the news to poker players. And NEWS dominates their front pages, not expert opinions. If it's newsworthy in the world of poker, you'll read about it first in *Poker Player Newspaper.*.

Major Tournaments of concern to all players are listed in our Tournament Schedule. Daily Tournaments are listed in their own schedule.

Expert columnists; The top experts in the poker world bring our readers how-to information on playing games, anecdotes from the past, clever stories of enduring interest, and the wisdom from a life of playing for high stakes. These include: Mike Caro, Lou Krieger, Ashley Adams, Tony Guererra, Richard Burke, Jennifer Newell, Barbara Connors, Wendeen Eolis, Phil Hevener, I. Nelson Rose, and many more.

Card room related entertainment. Card rooms and casinos featuring entertainment on their property will find those listings in our entertainment schedule, along with reviews and items of interest from Entertainment Editor, Len Butcher.

Connect to their web site. A copy of each issue can be found on our web site:

http://www.pokerplayernewspaper.com

This bring additional readership to players without access to public card rooms. Details that cannot get into the paper because of space limitations are also found on their web site.

Poker Player Newspaper is edited by well-known poker player and prolific writer Lou Krieger, who's authored more than 400 columns and articles on poker strategy, and penned 11 top-selling poker books.

Card Player

Card Player is the premier poker magazine, established in 1988. *Card Player* is published biweekly, for a total of 26 issues per year. It is the only ABC-audited poker publication, with an established circulation of 102,000 including more than 21,000 paid subscribers. It is distributed to most of the poker rooms across the country, and to various amateur poker leagues, championship poker tournament events, and charity poker events, and also is available through subscription. Every issue provides expert strategy and analysis, covers the tournament circuit, and addresses important issues within the poker industry.

Card Player is dedicated to poker players of all skill levels, ranging from beginner to professional. Whether speaking to our audience through *Card Player* magazine or the CardPlayer.com website, the content is fresh and focused on those like us who love the game of poker. Their readers are serious about poker, and so are they.

CardPlayer.com

CardPlayer.com was established as a full-service interactive website in 2002. Some of the information on the site includes: industry news, tournament coverage, player profiles, tips/tools, and much more. The website also has language-specific versions from Europe, Brazil, Italy, France, Finland, Spain and Germany. CardPlayer.com's traffic has increased substantially since 2004, when it averaged 22,000 daily unique visitors and more than 4 million page views per month. The average number of unique visitors is currently more than 50,000 per day, with an average of more than 19 million page views per month. In addition, CardPlayer.com has more than 309,000 opt-in subscribers to its e-newsletter, which is sent out twice a month. Card Player.com recently launched a new in-depth online poker section and Card Player TV.

Inside each issue of *Card Player*, you will find:

Strategies & Analysis

Poker's top players provide detailed discussions and opinions on various aspects of the game, making Card Player the most informative learning tool in the poker industry. In-depth articles help readers improve their game and become winning players.

Commentaries & Personalities

The greatest names in the game offer different viewpoints and perspectives on the important issues affecting the poker industry.

Updates from the Tournament Circuit

With a virtual army of reporters at every major poker event, and a host of celebrity writers, such as Daniel Negreanu and Phil Hellmuth, *Card Player* is the only publication dedicated to keeping the poker world abreast of all happenings on the poker tournament circuit.

Product Reviews, News, and Feature Content on the Poker Lifestyle
Every issue provides all the important headline stories in the poker world and features articles about the hottest players in the game today, capturing the poker lifestyle like no other publication. Considered the industry standard, *Card Player* tabulates standings for poker's most prestigious award in every issue, the Player of the Year.

Card Player TV
Card Player Media publishes more than just magazines. With advances in technology and communication constantly evolving, *Card Player* focuses on meeting these changes head-on with its multimedia division. By taking advantage of other venues of the media, *Card Player* continues to move with the times giving players and poker fans across the globe the latest happenings in the poker world through the latest innovations in media coverage. Card Player provides several types of poker multimedia for poker fans at its leading industry web site: CardPlayer.com. Highlighting the biggest faces in the industry, Card Player TV provides insightful and informative poker news and entertainment shorts for viewers at CardPlayer. com. Card Player TV features a weekly poker news show as well as a Cribs-style show exploring the homes of professional poker players. Card Player TV also features channels such as Lifestyle, Strategy, and Tournament.

Streaming video, one of *Card Player's* most popular features, generates a large audience for the downloadable poker content. Featured segments have included poker superstars like 2006 World Series of Poker main-event winner Joseph Hachem, poker's "Robin Hood" Barry Greenstein, the legendary Doyle Brunson, recent NBC National Heads-Up Poker Championship winner Paul Wasicka, and the "Poker Brat" Phil Hellmuth. Sponsorship opportunities through Card Player TV include: 10-second commercials with clickable links, channel sponsorship, marquee sponsorship, and five-minute infomercials.

Card Player POKER & SPORT
Card Player Poker & Sport covers all aspects of poker from an international perspective. It is distributed monthly to more than 30 countries and has a circulation of more than 12,900 copies. The magazine can be found in leading European poker rooms, clubs, and pubs, and on newsstands in the UK, Ireland, and Sweden. It also has a growing number of subscribers throughout the European region. The features of *Card Player Poker & Sport* are similar to those of its United States counterpart, but localized for the European market — covering all aspects of the poker industry, including tournament listings, product reviews, strategies, interviews, sports betting, and much more. Card Player Media also publishes localized versions of *Card Player* magazine in Brazil, Italy, France, Poland, Finland, Sweden, Spain, Estonia, Slovenia, Bulgaria, Romania, and Germany (web).

Rounder Magazine

Rounder Magazine, which launched in December 2006, is a gaming lifestyle magazine published monthly. The magazine is distributed to casinos throughout the United States. It is also sold on magazine shelves, including Books a Million stores located throughout the country.

The fashionably hip magazine, which features the sport of poker, also includes insightful articles and schedules relating to the NFL, College football, the PGA, Nascar and MLB. This editorial variety, mixed with stunning photography, showcasing trendy fashions, and the popular Rounder models. This makes *Rounder Magazine* the most anticipated gaming magazine to hit the stands each month.

The beautiful 'Rounder Girls' are selected to appear in the magazine and attend promotional events throughout the country. From time to time, the cover girl may be a celebrity model and actress such as March 2008 cover model April Scott (Deal or No Deal/Dukes of Hazard 2) or a poker beauty such as Vanessa Rousso. Rounder Girl Search contests are organized at various casinos and nightclubs, giving the 'girl next door' a shot at celebrity status. The attention the Rounder Girls receive at promotional events rivals that of celebrities.

If you think you have what it takes to be the next Rounder Girl,

Contact: casting@rounderlife.com

Rounder Magazine is producing a new network television series featuring Poker Pros, Celebrities and their entourage of beautiful girls traveling the nation on the Rounder Tour Bus in a fun reality TV setting.

Rounder Life TV will travel the U.S. with Poker Pros, Celebrities and their incomparable Rounder Girls. "Livin' it up" in style at the hottest Casino Resorts in the country, showcasing all the entertainment and amenities they have to offer. Get a peek into the life of a rounder, (exclusive parties, the hottest night clubs, top restaurants, "High Roller' suites) and go behind the scenes of *Rounder Magazine* model photo shoots set in exotic locations. Rounder Life is an exciting TV series for poker enthusiasts to see how the Pros "ROLL."

CHAPTER THIRTY TWO:

POKER FORUMS & PODCASTS

Here are some of the Poker Forum & Podcast websites that I felt my readers would like to be a part of:

DrCheckRaise.com

DrCheckRaise.com is a great strategy based poker forum. Ken Callis started up the website and in a short time has amassed a significant number of members. The key to the quick growth of this poker forum was the concept itself. Simple. Many Poker Forums are difficult to navigate and dry to read. DrCheckRaise.com has a little something for everyone from the beginner to the professional. He has also made it light hearted and fun in several ways, and often hosts free poker clinics in his chat room moderated at times by special guests.

Often Ken comes up with concepts and challenges that keep some fun in the game as well as inspire a learning experience.

The atmosphere of this forum always seems cordial. You really don't find players talking down to one another, but respecting each others opinions and ideas which help to breed a free flow of poker concepts.

You are doing well if you can find a group of people like this to discuss poker hands and poker concepts to facilitate your growth as a poker player.

DrCheckRaise.com has been instrumental in helping players in disputes with online gaming sites. The combined talents at DrCheckRaise.com resulted in the collection of monies owed to the players by poker sites that have gone out of business. In his spare time DrCheckRaise also writes a weekly column for Australian Poker Weekly called "Poker Clinic by DrCheckRaise."

DrCheckRaise.com is free to join yet provides it's members with several financial benefits such as free rolls and discounts on poker related products as well as deposit bonuses at major poker sites.

"It's not a game...it's a lifestyle"

ThePlayr.com

ThePlayr.com began as the fan site for Gus Hansen and has transformed itself into a wildly popular poker forum, poker news portal and poker strategy site. The Playr.com forum is an internationally recognized, friendly forum with great strategy advice. It caters for all levels of players, from beginners, high and medium rollers to even some of the best professional poker players in the world. Their motto is "The Playr.com, where players become winners!" and they mean it!

At The Playr.com you can ensure every question will get an answer; big or small. There are various sections of the forum to cater for all your forum needs.

At The Playr.com you will find a main forum section containing:

- **"Poker Lounge"** which is for general discussion about poker. You can post your wins, losses and bad beats or discuss your favorite poker sites and pros. They even have a special thread for the ladies and hot poker topics and challenges. A great place for you to unwind.

- **"Poker Strategy"** for discussion of poker strategy for all types of poker. Here you will get what ever advice you need, or can give advice to other players based on knowledge and experience. No play advice ever goes without being discussed in this thread. From playing pocket aces to folding and coin flips. Everyone has their say.

- **"News and Gossip"** containing all the latest poker gossip, news and rumors on all the major events, casinos and juicy gossip on pros and winnings.

- **"Off Topic"** for discussing and posting non poker related subjects. Here you can join in our playr.com trivia, forum games or post your favorite music or jokes as some fine examples.

- **"The Playr League Discussion"** which is where we discuss and post results from our famous Playr.com poker league which members are free to participate in and greatly encouraged to on a weekly basis.

If you are of Danish, German or Italian culture you may find the International forums a further asset of theplayr.com.. The International Forums are specifically for Danish, German and Italian players and cater for their every need in their own language. The international forums have a great community atmosphere for each individual country. All members are warmly welcomed into their origin community with open arms.

Theplayr.com is much more then a forum, there is nothing that you will not find to satisfy your poker needs. As mentioned above theplayr.com forum has an international poker league which runs weekly. All forum members are encouraged to join. To cater for everyone they hold 2 tournaments each week, one for the more beginner level players and one for the more advanced.

Most of the playr.com forum members participate in both as a points tally runs to determine "The Playr.com champion" at the end of the year. All tournaments include prize money payouts and points for our leader board. In addition they participate in both because the tournaments are a cut above the rest. After playing in the tournament you are sure to get feedback on your performance, good or bad, they are fun, exciting and very; very friendly. The tournaments are the best weekly player gathering money could buy.

If the tournaments are not what you are after you may find theplayr wiki is right down your alley.

The playr wiki is a collaborative website that anybody can edit or add to. I'm sure everybody has heard of and seen Wikipedia. Fortunately for the playrs at the playr.com its poker strategy content is not great, leaving the door open for forum members to create their very own playr. Wiki!

The goal of ThePlayr Wiki is to create excellent poker strategy content. Basically members are writing, reading and using the ultimate poker strategy guide. Only relatively new the playr.com members are yet to create poker room reviews, poker player profiles and of course lots and lots of content relevant to ThePlayr.com. This is where they will house the results for ThePlayr League tournaments and the tournament standings.

The playr.com urges all members to use this new feature to its full potential by adding, editing or simply just reading. Again, anyone can add content to it and is encouraged to do so. You are also free to add anything non poker related.

As theplayr.com is very friendly and community based forum they have also added a live chat feature where you can sit and talk to friends about anything you like. At any stage you could find, the site owners, moderators or some of the worlds best poker pros at your disposal. Of course it is also a great place for you to chat to all the new found friends which you will develop quickly in the forum.

There is a beginner's guide where you can read up on all aspects of poker to start you on your way. On this page we've gathered all the information you need, if you are just starting your adventure in the world of poker or simply need to freshen up on some of the basic elements of this amazing game. Here you'll find answers to the most frequently asked questions on how to get started. You'll get a thorough introduction to the rules of Texas Hold'em and Omaha – the two most popular games of poker – and you'll be able to pick up all necessary information on how to play the game. In addition you'll get loads of great advice certain to get you started winning at the tables right away. You can also choose to take our guided tour by clicking "Beginners' Tour" just below. The tour will take you step-by-step into the world of online poker and equip you with the knowledge and tools needed to take on this fascinating game.

At ThePlayr.com they compiled the biggest archive of poker knowledge available online. Here you'll find everything you ever wanted to know about online poker – from the most basic guidelines for beginners to advanced tables and calculations showing key probabilities vital to perfecting your game.

Thorough walkthroughs of the rules of the different games of poker, guides to the different limits, analyses of the styles of play, tables of probabilities and statistics, reviews of poker books, the experts' take on how to choose your starting hands and the ultimate poker dictionaries are just some of the things you'll find in the submenus here in "All About Poker". These submenus have the following content for your interest:

Rules: Everything worth knowing about the rules of the game – from Texas Hold'em to Seven Card Stud and from Cash Games to Heads-Up Tournaments.

Poker Strategy: This is where you'll find guides to the different styles of play as well as elaborate material on winning chance and the crucial calculation of pot odds. Also in Poker Strategy we've compiled a variety of useful tools to improve and sharpen your game.

Poker Theory: In the submenu Poker Theory you can read poker experts' advise on how to choose and play your starting hands in poker. You'll also find easy-to-understand statistics and tables of probability fundamental to mastering the math behind the game.

The Toolbox: The game of poker is best learned at the tables, because nothing beats actual experience. But don't cheat yourself out of getting the upper hand by learning from the experiences of others as well. In The Toolbox you'll find our reviews of the most important literature written and software designed to give you that extra little edge at the tables.

The Language of Poker: The biggest and most elaborate poker dictionaries of the language of poker are found right here at ThePlayr.com. The Ultimate Poker Dictionary is by far the most extensive poker dictionary available anywhere, and in the Chat Dictionary you'll discover, what your opponents are actually saying in the chat, when they comment on another of your winning hands. This is also the submenu where you'll find our huge list of the nicknames of all the starting hands in poker.

Live Poker

They also have a section dedicated to live poker only. Playing poker live is completely different from playing online. It's just so much more intense when you're actually holding the cards and moving the chips around yourself.

When you can physically look into the eyes of your opponents, hear your own heart pumping faster and feel the sweat in your palms when you pick up the Aces or push in on a huge bluff – that's when poker really comes alive.

Here in the Live Poker section you'll find complete calendars of these major tournaments as well as a few other big ones. Also, you'll find money lists and historical results — all accessible from the left menu. In the menu on the left, you'll also find a live calendar, where we're constantly updating current and upcoming tournaments. By clicking each tournament, you'll be linked directly to the tournament's Web site if one exists.

Poker Cinema

Poker Cinema is the last and most colorful part of this section, and there you'll be able to watch – directly in your browser – the best, funniest, wildest and most amazing clips the web has to offer.

In our Poker Cinema, we've uploaded and categorized an insane number of clips, and we are constantly adding new ones. There are literally hundreds of hours of incredible poker footage ready to be enjoyed on your screen. If it's on tape, we've seen it and uploaded the best of it for you to watch.

Theplayr.com forum runs continual promotions, competitions and events for their members where you can win theplayr.com merchandise and stand out in the crowd as a proud forum member and many other cool prizes. They offer great sign up bonuses for various poker sites and even go as far as getting you started in online poker and their league by at times providing you with FREE cash with no need to deposit.

Visit www.theplayr.com register FREE of charge, the members of theplayr.com are delighted at every new playr that joins.

See You at the Playr.Com, Where Playrs Become Winners!

CardMafia.com

CardMafia.com is one of the hottest growing sites in the poker world today. Conceptualized by Joseph "JoeFRek" Johnson in December 2003, he revitalized the site in June 2007.

Joe is a hands-on Administrator along with MJ "little mb2" and they have 5 Super Moderators that are in different parts of the world. Joe is a family man with 4 children and a sailor in the US Navy. He has dedicated himself to making CardMafia one of the premier poker forums on the internet today.

The CardMafia site itself is a very clean and organized forum. There is something for everyone that joins. From a weekly league that runs 4 different days, to help with understanding all facets of different poker games, such as, NL Texas Hold'em, Omaha, Omaha 8, and H.O.R.S.E. This is the place to learn and share knowledge in all different areas of card play. The members not only grow in card play but also with support and encouragement become a family. There is a Syndicate Poker Series league that is team play for the site members. Also members enjoy many freerolls.

Being an active member of Cardmafia is like going home. People are friendly with a little of a competitive edge. Yet, they are extremely supportive of other members of the site, offering encouragement and railing each other during card games. There is staking for members that have shown active membership to the site. Personal BAP's are another way members work with each other to build bankrolls. Blogs on bankroll management and helpful hints are also available to all who seek the knowledge.

Today, Cardmafia is at 1400+ members and growing steadily. If you want a forum to be active in, to enjoy, grow with, then come join our family, we welcome you and will be waiting...

CardMafia: "Life on the Felt Mobster Style...We Make Poker the Family Business"

Poker Pod Radio

http://pokerpodradio.com

Poker Pod Radio is the new standard for all poker podcasting. New, but growing. We not only cover all topics about poker, but we add a little sports and news for your pleasure. Join host Jack McAdoo and other guests as they talk poker, politics, and sports. Please listen to us at www.pokerpodradio.com and on ITunes. Ask questions and give them comments on how they are doing, good or bad. And please, tell your friends!

Poker Pod Radio 1686 N Belcher Rd Clearwater, FL. 33765

E-mail: poker@pokerpodradio.com

Pokerroad

http://www.pokerroad.com

As poker participants and fans are being uncovered in record numbers, media within the poker industry has followed suit and intensified. Several traditional media outlets have emerged to inform the masses. However, PokerRoad aims to turn the corner with fresh, innovative and irreverent content.

The brainchild of established poker professionals Barry Greenstein and Joe Sebok, PokerRoad redefines the way poker fans look at the game. Barry Greenstein is heralded as one of the top players in the game, and his knowledge and expertise are treated as gospel on the tournament circuit. Sebok has branded himself as one of the new faces of poker and his established media presence is unparalleled.

PokerRoad reaches out and provides industry news as only poker insiders can. As well, PokerRoad is reinventing the concept of poker radio, one show at a time. PokerRoad has your ears covered for everything from strategy to gossip to just general poker tomfoolery. PokerRoad is a one-stop radio network. Along with the addition of video content in the pipe line, it is obvious that PokerRoad is a must for any serious poker fan.

Ante Up Pokercast

http://www.anteupmagazine.com

For more than three years, Scott Long and Christopher Cosenza hosted the award-winning weekly Ante Up Pokercast at The Times, building a loyal, worldwide audience known as the "Ante Up Nation." that spanned more than 30 countries.

"Pass the SUGAR!"

—*Joe Hachem, chiropractor turned professional poker player who won the 2005 W.S.O.P. championship and holds a WPT title.*

GLOSSARY OF POKER TERMS

Absolute Nuts- The best possible hand, based on the board cards. Sometimes simply called 'the nuts'.

Ace-High- A five card hand that contains one Ace, with no straight or flush or a hand with no pair in it.

Ace Magnets- A pair of kings as hole cards (K, K).

Aces Full- A full house with three aces and any pair.

Aces Up- A hand that contains two pairs, one of which is Aces.

Action- Checking/Betting/Raising. A game in which players are playing a lot of pots is considered an "action" game.

Active Player- A player who is still in the pot.

Add-on- A purchase of more chips (optional) at the end of the re-buy period in a tournament.

Aggressive Player- A player who bets, raises, and re-raises a lot, this is a commonly used poker term in tournament events.

All-in- That moment when all your chips are in the middle and your fate is resting with the poker gods.

American Airlines- Having a pair of Aces as your hole cards.

Angling- Taking action or talking when it is not your turn in order to mislead your opponent. Some consider this to be cheating; others consider these tactics to be part of the game.

Animal- Nickname for a player that is loose-aggressive. Animals are involved in too many hands and will almost always bet and raise when given the opportunity, often with garbage hands. Also referred as a manic.

Ante- A term used in poker to refer to the first money wagered on a hand, or the minimum that each player id required to put into the pot before a new hand can begin.

Baby- A low-ranked card (usually 2 through 5)

Back Door- A draw that requires two cards to complete a straight, flush, or full house. For example, to complete a flush the correct suit must hit on the turn and the river.

Backdoor Flush- A hand with three cards that would support a flush, but needs the remaining turn and river cards to make it happen.

Back-door Straight- A hand with three cards that would support a straight, but needs the remaining turn and river cards for the straight.

Bad Beat- this refers to losing a hand when you were the strong odds favorite to win. An example of a bad beat would be holding pocket Aces against a player holding pocket 9's, and your opponent ends up beating you by hitting another 9 on the last card.

Ballerina- A starting hand of a pair of twos (2, 2).

Bankroll- The amount of money you have available with which to play poker over a particular period of time.

Barn- A hand with a full house.

Behind- A player at the poker table, who acts after you. "I had three players acting behind me."

Belly-Buster- This is a old-school term for an inside straight draw or gut shot draw.

Best of It- To be a favorite to win.

Bet- Any money wagered during the play of a hand.

Bet the Pot- When a player bets the amount of the pot.

Bicycle- A straight that is A-2-3-4-5.

Big Blind- The position two to the left of the button, who is forced to pay a full small, bet prior to the hole cards being dealt in Texas Hold'em.

Big Slick- In Texas Hold'em, an Ace and a King (suited or unsuited) as your hole cards.

Big Sister- Refers to holding an Ace and Queen as your two pocket cards. This hand is also known as "Big Slick's slutty sister."

Blank- A card that appears useless. Also known as a rag.

Blinds- Texas Hold'em Poker uses what's called a "blind" structure, meaning that two people on the table must post a bet prior to seeing their cards. Since they are forced to bet without seeing their cards, they are playing "blind", thus the name of those bets are called "blinds". There are two blinds, the big blind and the small blind. The small blind position must post half the minimum bet and sits immediately to the left of the dealer. The big blind must post the full minimum bet, and sits immediately to the left of the small blind, two seats to the left of the dealer. As the deal rotates around the table, each player takes turns posting the small blind and the big blind bets. This blind structure forces the action on the table since there will always be a pot to win. So, for example, if you are seated at a $5-10 limit Hold'em table, the small blind must post $5 and the big blind must post $10 bet. As play rotates around the table, each player may choose to call that $10 bet, raise, or fold. When it's the small blind's turn, that player only needs to call $5 to play the hand.

Blind-off- When a player is playing in a tournament but is absent from the table he is "blinded off". This means his blinds are posted when it is his turn to post even though he is not there.

Blind Raise- When a player raises without looking at his hand.

Bluff- To bet with an inferior hand in the hope that your opponents will fold.

Board- The board refers to the community cards that are dealt face up on the table. In Texas Hold'em, there will ultimately be five community cards on the "board". The board does NOT include the two private card dealt to each player. So, if someone were to say, "the board plays", the player means that the five community cards make his best poker hand and he is not using any of the two private cards dealt to the player

Boat- A nickname for a full house.

Bottom Pair- Making a pair containing the lowest cards on the board.

Bounty- A special cash prize for knocking a particular player out of a tournament - usually a famous player.

Bracelet- A bracelet is given to any player who wins an event at the World Series of Poker. Bracelets are sometimes used to measure how much success a player has in tournaments (Phil Hellmuth has 11 bracelets).

Break- To discard a card from a pat hand, or a card that would ordinarily be kept.

Brick & Mortar (B & M)- Land-based casinos (not online).

Broadway- An Ace-high straight. A-K-Q-J-10

Bubble- Placing high in a tournament but not winning any money.

Bullets- A pair of Aces.

Bump- To raise.

Burn Card- Any card placed in the discard rack without being entered into play. After the deck is shuffled and cut, one card is "burned."

Bust a player- To eliminate a player by taking all of his or her chips.

Bust Out- To lose all of your chips.

Button- Also called the "Dealer Button", this is a white puck (usually with the word "Dealer" on it), that signifies the dealer's position on the table. The dealer's position is significant because he is the last player to act for that hand. The Dealer Button rotates around the table, so each player takes turns being "on the button".

Buy-in- The minimum amount of money required to enter a game.

Call- To place an amount of money equal to a previous opponent's bet.

Calling Station- A player who only calls bets and does not take advantage of their good hands by raising. They also will not fold very often so you should not bluff them but need to show down the best hand.

Cap- To take the last of the maximum amount of raises allowed per round of betting.

Card room- The room or area in a casino, where poker is held.

Case- Chips, A player's last chips.

Case Card-The fourth card of any rank that makes Four of a Kind.

Cash Game- A game whereby players can buy-in and cash out when they please.

Cash Out- To leave a game and convert your chips to cash.

Check- To decline to bet or to pass, when it is your turn to act.

Check-raise- the act of checking a hand, in hopes of luring your opponent to bet, so that you may then raise over him and build a bigger pot to win.

Chips- tokens used at gaming tables instead of using cash.

Chop- To return the blinds to the players who posted them and move on to the next hand if no other players call. It also means to "split the pot".

Cold- a player on a losing streak

Cold Call- Is to call two or more bets at the same time. For example, if one player calls and another player raises you are forced to call two bets.

Collusion- When two or more players conspire to cheat in a poker game.

Community Cards- Cards placed in the middle of the table and shared by all players.

Connectors- A starting hand of two cards in sequence, such as Q-J, 7-6, or 9-10.

Continuation Bet- A bet made after the Flop by the Pre-flop aggressor as a continuation of the original raise. Used to win the pot right there or figure out how strong the hand is after the Flop.

Cowboys- The name for two wired kings in the hole.

Cripple the Deck- Your hand contains most or all of the beneficial cards that could be used in conjunction with the cards on the board.

Crying Call- To make a call with a bad hand and there are no helpful cards to come out, while surely you're expecting to lose.

Cut off- One seat to the right of the button/dealer position.

Dark- Taking action, such as checking or betting, without seeing your hole cards. When someone mentions that they call in the "dark," they are doing this without even looking at there cards.

Dead Button- When the seat where the dealer button is located is not occupied, due to a player busting out or leaving.

Dead Man's Hand- Two pair - Aces and Eights (Wild Bill Hickock was shot in the back while playing this hand).

Dealer- A casino employee who deals out the cards to players in various games at a poker table.

Deuces- A starting hand containing a pair of Twos.

Domination- When two players hold the same card rank and one player has a better kicker. For example, A-K dominates AJ because they both share an Ace. The only way A-J can win is by hitting a Jack. The A-K is always dominating the hand because if an Ace hits the board the A-K is still winning. Therefore, the A-J has only two outs while the A-K has five outs (excluding any Straight or Flush Draws).

Donkey- Someone who is very bad at poker.

Double Belly Buster- Is the name for an inside-straight with two ways to win. Say you have 7-4 in the hole and the board cards are 2-5-8. You need a 3 or a 6 to catch one of your two inside-straight draws.

Double Up- In NL, winning a head's-up pot when you have gone all-in and doubling up your chip stack.

Doyle Brunson- It's a Hold'em hand consisting of a 10-2 (Brunson won the world championship two years in a row on the final hand with these cards).

Drawing Dead- Drawing to a hand that, even if it hits, will lose to a hand that is already better.

Drop- Fold.

Drop Box- On a gaming table, the box serves as a repository for cash, markers, tips and chips. On a further note, once money goes in there you never see it again.

Ducks- A starting hand containing a pair of Twos.

Dump- To fold a hand.

Edge- The casino's advantage over the player in any game, this is also referred to as the house edge.

Equity- Your mathematical share of the pot and your chances of winning it. Say you have pocket Aces against two people, your pot equity is over 70 percent of the pot.

Expected Value (EV) Expectation- Is the amount of profit or loss you would expect to make if there were no variance in poker. If you are dealt A-Ks three times, you are expected to win a certain amount of times with that hand. Therefore, a raise with A-Ks is playing the positive expectation of your cards. In the end, your A-Ks will show a profit due to probability.

Face Cards- The King, Queen or Jack of each suit.

Family Pot- When everyone at the table has entered the pot.

Fast- Used to describe playing a hand very aggressively.

Favorite- To be the favorite, you have the best chance to win the current hand at play.

Fifth Street- Also known as the "river" card. In flop games, this represents the fifth community card on the table and the final round of betting.

Fill Up- To make a Full House from trips or a set.

Final Table-This is the last table of a large multi-table tournament. Ahhh.... The Promise Land!

Fish- A loose player who loses his or her money regularly.

Fixed Limit– The betting is predetermined for each round.

Flash- To show one or more of your cards, usually when it is not required to do so.

Flat Call- To call one or more bets without raising, when you are quite sure that you have the best hand, this is also very similar to making a "smooth call."

Floor man- An employee of the card room who makes rulings and decisions.

Flop- In Texas Hold'em, each player has two cards dealt to them, and then shares five community cards. These five community cards, however, do not all get dealt at the same time? There are rounds of betting at certain intervals during the deal. After the first two cards are dealt to each player, there is a round of betting. Then, three of the five community cards are dealt at one time on the board. This is what's known as the "flop" - the first three cards being dealt on the board. The fourth card is called the "turn", and the final, fifth card is known as the "river".

Flop Games- Poker games (Hold 'em and Omaha) that are played using community cards that are dealt face up in the center of the table.

Flush- Any hand consisting of five cards that are the same suit.

Flush Draw- A hand where you have 4 of the 5 cards needed to make a flush. For example, if you are holding two clubs, and the board flops two more clubs, you would be holding a flush draw. You would need to draw an additional club to complete the flush.

Flush- Five cards with the same suit, not in a sequence.

Fold- To decline a bet and throw your hand away, when it's your turn to act.

Forced Bet- A required bet that starts the action on the first round of a poker hand.

Four of a Kind- Four cards of the same number or face value ("quads").

Four-Flushed- Having the four cards of a flush in your hand or on the board against you. When you have two of the four cards in your hand, you're in great shape to make your flush.

Fourth Street- In flop games, it is the fourth community card dealt (also known as "the turn") and represents the third round of betting.

Free Card- When you get to see another card without needing to call a bet.

Free Card Play- Betting or raising in late position on the flop in the hopes that the other players will check to you on the turn, giving you the option of seeing the river card for free.

Free Ride- A round in which no one bets.

Freeroll- A tournament with no entry fee.

Freeze Out- A tournament that only ends when one person has won all of the tournament chips.

Full House- Any three cards of the same number or face value, plus any other two cards of the same number or face value.

Grinder- One who bets smaller then usual.

Gut Shot- a hand where you have 4 of the 5 cards needed to make a straight, but your 4 cards are not "connected" or in sequential order, so you need a single card

in the middle of your straight to complete the straight. You're holding 5 6, and the board shows 7, 9, 10. At that moment, you have a gut shot; only the 8 will make your straight. This type of hand is also known as an "inside straight draw" or a "belly-buster straight draw".

Hand- The cards in a player's hand or one game of poker in which a pot is won. When you hear or read this term, understand it in its context so you won't be confused.

Head's up- One on one play, usually the final two at the end of a tournament

High-Card- To decide the first dealer in the flop tournaments each user is dealt a single card and the player with the highest card (based on the card and the suit order - of spades, hearts, diamonds & clubs) becomes the theoretical dealer.

High-Low- Split pot games.

Hit- When the flop cards are helpful to your hand.

Hold'em- This is also known as Texas Hold'em, where the players get two down cards and five community cards.

Hold up- When a hand that is leading manages to win the pot at the showdown.

Hockey sticks- Two sevens as hole cards (7-7).

Hole Cards- The first cards dealt to you that your opponents can't see.

Hooks- A pair of jacks.

House- The casino or card room that is hosting the poker game.

Image- The perception that the other players at the table have of your playing style.

Implied Odds- Bets that you can reasonably expect to collect in addition to the bets already in the pot if you hit your hand.

In Position- To have position on your opponent; is being able to act last post flop. UTG raises and you call on the button and will be in position for the rest of the hand.

Inside Straight- Four cards which require another between the top and the bottom card to complete a straight. Players who catch this card make an Inside Straight.

Inside Straight Draw- Also known as a belly-buster straight draw gut shot straight draw.

Jackpot Poker- A form of poker in which the card room or casino offers a jackpot to a player who has lost with a really big hand (usually Aces full or better).

Jacks-or- Better- A form of poker in which a player needs to have at least a pair of jacks to open the betting.

Jam- To move all-in in a no-limit or pot-limit game.

Kansas City Lowball- Form of lowball poker in which the worst poker hand (2, 3, 4, 5, 7 of different suits) is the best hand. It's also known as Deuce to Seven.

Keep Them Honest- To call at the end of a hand to prevent someone from bluffing.

Key Card- A card that gives you a big draw or makes your hand.

Key Hand- In a session or tournament, the one hand that ends up being a turning point for the player, either for better or worse.

Kick It- Raise.

Kicker- The kicker refers to your tie-breaking card. For example, if I am holding an Ace and King, and the board shows Ace, 5, 7, 2, J - I would have a pair of Aces with a King kicker. My opponent may have an Ace also, but with a weaker kicker, in which case I will win the showdown.

Kill Pot- A method to stimulate action. It is a forced bet by someone who has just won a pot(s).

Knock- Check.

Knuckle- To check (as in knocking on the poker table).

Kojak- A hand that contains a K-J.

Ladies- Two Queens.

Late Position- Position on a round of betting where the player must act after most of the other players have acted (usually considered to be the two positions next to the button).

Lay Down- When a player folds.

Lead- The first player to bet into a pot.

Limit- The set amount or amounts that may be bet, often expressed as 5/10 ($5 bets on the first two rounds and $10 bets thereafter).

Limp-In- To enter a hand with a call before the flop.

Limper- The first player who calls a bet.

Live Blind- An instance where the player puts in a dark bet and is allowed to raise, even if no other player raises. It's also known as an "option".

Live Card(s)- In Stud Games, cards that have not yet been seen and are presumed to still be in play.

Live Hand- A hand that could still win the pot.

Live One- A not so knowledgeable player who plays a lot of hands.

Look- When a player calls the final bet before the showdown.

Loose- To play more hands than should be played.

Lowball- Is a form of draw poker in which the lowest hand wins the pot.

Make- To make the deck is to shuffle the deck.

Main Pot- The center pot. Any other bets are placed in a side pot(s) and are contested among the remaining players. This occurs when a player(s) goes all-in.

Maniac- A very aggressive player who plays a lot of hands.

Marry- To become too attached to a hand, usually seeing a showdown when it was very clear that you should have folded earlier.

Maverick- starting hand of Q-J

Middle Pair- To have a pair containing the second highest card on the board.

Middle Position-Somewhere between the early and late positions on a round of betting (the fifth, sixth and seventh seats to the left of the button).

Minimum Buy-In- The least amount you can start a game with.

Monster- A very big hand. In a tournament, a player who begins to accumulate chips after having a small stack is considered to be a monster.

Muck-To discard a hand.

No Limit- NL , a game where players can bet as much as they like (as long as they have it in front of them) on any round of betting.

Nut flush draw- A hand that needs one more card for the best possible flush.

Nut- the best possible hand, such as "nut straight" or "nut flush;" this can sometime become the second best hand depending on the river card of course.

Nuts- The best possible hand, based on the board card. Sometimes called the absolute nuts.

Odds- The probability of making a hand vs. the probability of not making a hand.

Off suit- Cards of a different suit.

Omaha- A game in which each player is dealt four down cards with five community cards. To make your hand, you must play two cards from your hand and three from the board.

On Tilt- Playing recklessly, usually due to losing the previous hand.

Online Poker- Poker that is played on the internet, for either real or play money.

Open-To make the first bet.

Open Card- A card that is dealt face-up.

Open Pair- A pair that has been dealt face-up.

Open-ended Straight- Four consecutive cards whereby one additional (consecutive) card is needed at either end to make a straight.

Open Ended Straight Draw- When you can hit either end of your draw essentially having eight outs if there are no Flush Draws out. Therefore, your hand is J-T and the board cards are 9-Q-2 rainbow. You need a King or an 8 to complete your Straight.

Option- When it is the Big Blind's turn to act and he has the option of checking or raising.

Outs- Cards that can come that will improve your hand.

Over card- A card that is higher than other cards, usually in reference to the community cards.

Over the Top- One player raised $50, and then another player re-raises to go over the top for more.

Paints- Face cards, Jack, Queen, or King.

Pair- Two cards that are the same rank (such as two kings).

Passive-A style of play where someone is reluctant to bet or raise.

Pat or Standing Pat- Drawing zero cards.

Playing the Board- When your best 5 card hand equals the 5 cards on the board. This usually occurs in 2 situations. The first is when there is a very high hand on the board. An example would be if the board was A-A-K-K-A. Assuming you didn't have 4-of-a-kind then you would.

Pocket Rockets- Pair of Aces.

Position- Your place in the order of betting action. If you act first, you are in first position.

Post- To post a blind so you can enter the hand.

Pot- All the money that has been placed in the middle including all bets, blinds and antes.

Pot Equity- The amount of money your hand should win. For instance, pocket Aces against one opponent with K-J suited has 83.15% pot equity. Therefore, 83.15% percent of every dollar belongs to the Pocket Pair pre-flop.

Pot Limit- A game where you are allowed to bet up to the amount in the pot.

Pot Odds- The odds offered to you by the money in the pot. If the pot is $400 and you must call a $100 bet, you pot odds are 4 to 1. You must include other players' bets and calls as part of the pot.

Probe Bet- A small bet meant to gain information about the strength of you hand by noticing the reaction of other players to your bet. Made by a player who was not the pre-flop aggressor.

Prop- Someone who gets paid by a poker room to play in their games, usually to start games or play in shorthanded games.

Protect- When you have the winning hand after the flop you want to protect that hand from drawing hands by betting an amount that makes it unprofitable to chase. In limit poker, it is much more difficult to protect a hand in a large pot.

Quads- Four of a kind (such as four aces).

Rags- Bad cards, usually low cards.

Railbird- Someone who is watching a game.

Rainbow- When three cards of all different suites flop or when there are all four suites on the board out of the four cards being shown.

is a rainbow board with no possible Flush Draws.

Raise- To place a higher bet than an opponent has already placed.

Rake- The amount a card room takes from each pot, usually a percentage that has a set upper limit.

Read- An assumption of what cards a player has. ("I had a good read on him and still lost.")

Redraw- A further way to better your hand. For example, you have AQ and the board is 8-9-T-J, a King on the river will improve your hand to the Nut Straight.

Re-raise- To raise after an opponent has raised.

Ring Game- Any non-tournament game.

River- The last remaining community card. There is one final round of betting.

Rivered- To get beat by a hand that is made on the river - usually a bad beat.

Rock- This is an extremely tight player at the table.

Rough- A low-ranking hand or a hand that is worse than most others of the same class. An 8-7-6-5-3 is a "rough 8" and a player who does not draw to a T-9-6-3-2 is "standing pat rough."

Round- When the button has moved completely around the table and everyone has had a chance to deal.

Rounders- A popular poker movie: starring Matt Damon. A "Must Watch" if you're reading this book.

Route 66- A pair of sixes as hole cards (6-6).

Royal Flush- The best possible hand, a royal flush is a straight flush involving the Ten, Jack, Queen, King and Ace.

Runner-Runner- To hit both the turn, and the river to make your hand. ("I went all-in with a straight, but he hit runner-runner spades and got a flush.")

Running Bad- A player on a losing streak.

Running Good- A player on a winning streak.

Sailboats- A pair of fours as hole cards (4-4).

Sandbag- Concealing the strength of your hand for inducing bets or bluffs from your opponents.

Satellite- A tournament that lets you enter another tournament if you win.

Scare Card- A card that may complete your opponents draw or better your opponent's hand. When you have the Top Pair of Kings and an Ace slips off the deck this is a scare card.

Seat Charge- The amount of money some card rooms charge per hour to play in addition to, or in place of, a rake.

See- To call.

Semi bluff- To bet with a hand that may not be the best but has a good chance to improve to the best hand.

Set- Three of a kind (such as three jacks).

Shark- A common poker term: a good player that wins often.

Short Stacked- To have the smallest stack of chips at the table.

Showdown- At the end of the final betting round, it's when all active players turn their cards face up to see who has won the pot.

Side Pot- An additional pot made when one player is all in and 2 or more other players are still betting.

Sign-Up Bonus- A cash bonus for new online, real money players.

Sit and Go- Also known as a single-table tournament, it starts when all the seats are filled (usually two, six, or nine seats).

Six-Perfect- The second best possible hand in Razz: A-2-3-4-6.

Slow Roll- Stalling your opponent by waiting to show a winning hand.

Small Blind- The amount put in the pot by the person immediately to the left of the dealer "button" prior to the cards being dealt.

Smooth Call- To call a bet with a hand that actually warrants a raise.

Solid- A fairly tight player (and reasonably good).

Smooth- A high-ranking hand or a hand that is better than most others of the same class. A draw to 7-4-3-2 is "smooth" and a T-6-4-3-2 is a "smooth ten."

SNG- An abbreviation for a sit and go tournament.

Snow- To stand pat with a hand that is unlikely to win at showdown. A bluff is a betting decision, while a snow is a drawing decision. Usually a player who snows must bluff to win, although a "semi-snow" is possible as well.

Snowmen- A pair of eights as hole cards (8-8).

Speed Limit- A pair of fives.

Stack- The player's amount of chips.

Stay- When a player remains in the game by calling, rather than raising.

Steal- To force an opponent to fold when you don't have the best hand.